THE
CITY OF MAN

Prophecies
of a World Civilization
in Twentieth-Century Thought

by W. Warren Wagar

1963

HOUGHTON MIFFLIN COMPANY BOSTON

The Riverside Press Cambridge

To Hudson

Preface

THIS book was originally written in 1956, during the author's first year of graduate work in history at Yale University. Only a few lines of that ancient draft survive here. But in spirit it remains the same book: it discusses with as little caviling as possible the visions of world order of a generation of modern prophets. As in 1956, the author makes no effort to conceal his solidarity with these prophets, and he believes that the idea of an organic world civilization can become the great directive Myth of the century which lies before us. History is a creative process. Either man moves on to this next creative task, or he dies.

I wish to single out three people for special thanks. First, Mr. Hudson Cattell of Lancaster, Pennsylvania, who collaborated with me in the early stages of the Yale project; without him, it would never have been written. Then, Professor Franklin Le Van Baumer of Yale, whose counsel and criticism have been unfailingly inspiring. Finally, Mr. Craig Wylie, Managing Editor of Houghton Mifflin Company, who encouraged me to transform the Yale manuscript, which I was too fainthearted even to let him read, into a book. His confidence may have been misplaced, but it persuaded me to go to work. I am also in his debt for much invaluable editorial help in the past two years.

Wellesley, Massachusetts   W. WARREN WAGAR
August, 1962

Contents

INTRODUCTION: The Search for Synthesis   1

CHAPTER ONE: The Biography of a Vision   11

Utopia and Cosmopolis   13
Eastern Approaches   18
The Classical Heritage   26
Respublica Christiana and Dar al-Islam   33
Modern Prophets, 1600–1900   43
Crisis and Renewal: The Twentieth Century   53

CHAPTER TWO: History as Prophecy   67

The Vogue of Clio   69
The Biological Key   72
Cycles and Millennia   83
Lines and Spirals   98
The Doctrinaires   112

CHAPTER THREE: The Concert of Cultures   127

The Organic Society   129
World Philosophical Synthesis   134
Religion and the World Order   155
The Integration of Knowledge   173
The Arts in Cosmopolis   189

CHAPTER FOUR: The World Commonwealth   195

      Culture, Community, Commonwealth   197
      World Economic Integration   208
      World Government   221

CHAPTER FIVE: Who Will Integrate the Integrators?   237

EPILOGUE: The Deep End   259

Notes   273

A Basic Library of Recent Books on World Order   291

Index   303

Introduction

The Search for Synthesis

The Search for Synthesis

"ALONG the great highroads of the world," Carl Gustav Jung wrote in 1931, "everything seems desolate and outworn." Seized by an exhausting anxiety, twentieth-century man has lost his sense of direction. Scaling the heights of power has only made him dizzy. "Everything," says Erich Kahler, "is in flux, everything is open to question, everything is involved in perpetual change and dissolution." Paul Tillich compares the anxiety now universal in Western civilization with the mental climate of Europe during the decline and fall of Rome and the waning of the Middle Ages.[1]

But the twentieth century confronts humanity with the most radical crisis in history; and the responsibility is man's alone. Since a certain summer day in Sarajevo in 1914, he has blundered into a fantastic career of assassination and violence. He has slaughtered millions in mechanized total war, fed his children to genocidal furnaces, prostituted his flesh and spirit to the service of leviathan states, and crowned his work with the invention of nuclear nightmares capable of killing all life on earth. The final folly is to be consummated, without frenzy or passion, in a pair of superbly logical strategic blows.

Before this destiny the individual man stands somehow helpless. "We . . . have the feeling," writes a distinguished Spanish philosopher, "that the direction of history has slipped

from our hands and that the world — the entire planet, no
longer only a part of it — is being borne on by a great wave."
For an American colleague, "August 1914 is the axial date in
modern Western history. . . . The sense of power over the
material universe with which modern man emerged . . .
changed on that date into its opposite: a sense of weakness
and dereliction before the whirlwind that man is able to
unleash but not to control." [2] The serious literature of most
Western countries is now drenched with apocalyptic imagery.
The "cyclical" historians, Spengler, Toynbee, Sorokin, and
their disciples, predict the imminent going-under of modern
civilization. A whole generation of men of faith, exponents
of a neo-orthodox "theology of crisis," have rediscovered the
doctrine of ineradicable original sin. The most characteristic new departure in Continental philosophy, existentialism,
finds anxiety the normal condition of the self as it trembles
precariously on the brink of death and meaninglessness. We
are the "hollow men" of T. S. Eliot, the "stick-men" of
George Grosz; we are the engineer Prokop in Karel Capek's
Krakatit, turning everything we touch into high explosives
by a kind of helpless inner compulsion, mangling our hands
and hearts in the act.

At the same time, man is still as capable of health and joy
as ever, which adds a grotesque dimension to the world crisis.
Children still play and lovers still pair, even in the ruins of
gutted cities; there are carnivals and parades even now in a
world that may be sentenced to annihilation; no presenti-
ments of disaster spoil most of everyday life. The spectacle
of happiness in the climate of crisis should leave the sensitive
historian breathless with horror — except that he, too, is a
stockholder in the corporation of humanity. He cannot always tune his human feelings to the stern pitch of his per-
ceptions.

But there is no evasion of the essential issue. The sudden
change in the mood of Western art and thought during the

past fifty years reflects with reasonable accuracy the plight of
modern man. It may not always present a balanced view of
human nature. Anxiety is only one possible response to life.
But the anxiety of the twentieth century is more than the
creaturely anxiety of finite, fallible man disclosed by existentialist analysis. Humanity has survived the ordinary hazards
of creatureliness for thousands of years, and has the resources
to go on surviving them forever. What is unique, and intolerable, is the moral collapse of all the great world civilizations, which threatens to drain life dry of meaning and
wrenches every people loose from its historical moorings.
The civilizations of man are tearing themselves to pieces. At
the heart of the spiritual sickness in modern art and thought
lies the endlessly repeated experience of social breakdown in
our time. World wars, revolutions, dehumanizing totalitarian regimes, racial violence, and business depressions have
rolled over mankind like titanic shock waves, just when the
Western world had imagined it stood in sight of eternal
peace. In the nineteenth century, Kierkegaard and Nietzsche,
the spiritual fathers of modern existentialism, could be written off as psychopathic curiosities: today, Jean-Paul Sartre,
the author of *Nausea* and *No Exit,* speaks almost as much for
his generation as Erasmus or Voltaire spoke for theirs. The
change is not inside the self, but outside, in the objective
world of people, places, and things. It rushes on irresistibly.
Everything a man has, is threatened. Turning away from
anguish to the consolations of work or family, love or leisure,
will not do. There is no peace at any price.

Many thinking people have responded to the challenge of
calamity by clinging all the more desperately to the still surviving fragments of old dogmas. In the West, a dedicated
remnant insists, like the hero of Ionesco's play, on the preser-
vation of the dignity of the self in a world of stampeding
rhinoceroses. If the solitary human person were the only
human reality, the existentialists, the bearded new romantics,

and the rugged individualists would be entirely right: but they ignore man's civility. For other thinking people, the only refuge is the faith of their fathers, a return to the spiritual sources of ways of life now in process of disintegration, which can no more be put back together again than Humpty-Dumpty. In the Marxist-Leninist superstates, all the world's ills are somehow miraculously identified with the maladies of the nineteenth-century Western European working classes. In much of Asia and Africa, salvation is sought through the old Western tribal gods of nationalism.

Other thinking people, principally in the West, have chosen to meet the challenge to man's survival by a simple rejection of the instruments of terror. A dismayingly large fraction of liberal opinion in mid-century has succumbed to the lure of fetchingly packaged panaceas. For tens of thousands of otherwise sane human beings, the nations will be persuaded to surrender their means of self-defense through negotiated "disarmament." Or they will simply strip themselves of their sovereignty in favor of a "world constitution." Or world peace will be won by sheer "pacifism."

But in all the thousands of books provoked by the twentieth-century world crisis, these partial views and these cheerful fantasies are transcended time and again by flashes of authentic prophetic insight. The present study is an effort to assemble in one place the widely scattered elements of still another approach to the future, which looks on the crisis of our time as the birth pangs of a new world civilization. This is not yet a distinct school of thought, much less an "ideology." But the realization steadily grows that we are in the midst of an immensely complex world revolution. On the one hand, the binding forces and structures of the traditional civilizations have been shattered; on the other hand, all civilizations have been flung willy-nilly into a precarious and premature geophysical unity. And the realization steadily grows of the inevitability, if we survive at all, of an organic world civilization built to the new planetary scale of human life: not simply or even necessarily a world government, or a world economy, or a world religion, but a completely viable world civilization.

For all its overtones of old-fashioned Utopianism, this may be the most vital vision in the thinking of our time. It cuts through the blinkered imagination of bigotry to inspire Marxists and Catholics and religious leaders of every faith. It grips some of the century's leading philosophers. It pervades our speculations on the patterns of history. It demands what may be an impossibly vast transfiguration of human life, and it leaves nothing untouched or unquestioned; but its devotees argue, with conviction, that nothing less radical is any match for the world crisis.

Recent anticipations of world order not surprisingly take almost as many forms as there are books and prophets. Independent scholars as various as Arnold Toynbee in history; Karl Jaspers, Sir Sarvepalli Radhakrishnan, William Ernest Hocking, and F. S. C. Northrop in philosophy; Pitirim Sorokin in sociology; Erich Kahler and Lewis Mumford in the humanities; and Sir Julian Huxley and Father Pierre Teilhard de Chardin in biology, have each in the past quarter century produced prophecies of a world community of man based on the insights of their fields of special competence. The Roman Catholic Church, the world communist movement, Islam, the Bahai Faith, and many other groups wedded to a particular creedal orthodoxy have all, according to their peculiar and always lopsided genius, contributed prophets of a coming planetary society. Many movements and individual thinkers have tried to envisage at least some one or two salient features of a possible new world order: its sciences, its religion, its economy, its political life, its social structure, its obligation to human personality. What brings together the prophets explored in the present study

is not their consciousness of any common cause, since they
often come from hostile camps, hold dissimilar world-views,
and work with different basic concepts, but rather their
awareness of the disintegration of the existing order of
human life and their attempt to find formulas of constructive
response.

This, then, is a study of the search for a philosophy of
world order in recent thought. If the search is ultimately
successful, it will supply coming generations with a life-
orienting and life-fulfilling objective in an age staggered by
confusion. And before time runs out for mankind, men may
succeed in passing from the sphere of thought to the sphere
of concrete practical action.

But the project of an organic world civilization is not really
new. All through history, men have responded to the collapse of old social orders by creating new social orders extensive enough to secure civil peace and humane values
within the geographical limits of the society. In the present
crisis, since here on earth geographical limits no longer exist,
the only possible response true to man's nature as a social
animal, is the building of a world civilization. If the response has succeeded before, on a continental scale, it can
succeed again, on a planetary scale. Nothing at least absolutely vetoes it. The remedy must be as efficacious as ever.

A word of explanation. An organic world civilization is
not a Utopia, nor do any of the prophets surveyed in this
book so regard it. It will be a world of finite men and
women, no less corruptible than the men and women of imperial Rome, the Han and Gupta empires, or medieval Latin
Christendom. It will draw deeply on the durable wisdom of
the traditional civilizations, and it will share in their human
shortcomings. But it must be a flourishing concern, a business in full operation, able to minister to the needs of all
men, able to respond flexibly to new crises, able to grow and
thrive in growing. It is the best form of life possible for man-

kind in an age of unlimited technics and a world community
of peril. Its contours can only be guessed at, and yet it will
not arrive by accident. In some never exactly foreseeable
measure, to anticipate the future is to bring it under control.

But we have long since passed the time when manly faith
and simple courage in any quantity however great could
guarantee us success. Because civilization-building takes centuries, and we may have only a few years left, it would be
absurd to promise ourselves a happy ending in the tradition
of fairy tales and celluloid melodramas. The wolves are
not howling outside the ramparts of civilization: they have
broken in. Their breath is hot on our cheeks. The human
race has abruptly reached that unexpectedly dangerous stage
in its evolution when it must live, and go on living for all
time, with material means ready at hand to accomplish
quickly and easily its total destruction. These material means
will continue to increase in potency with each passing year.
But the human beings who inherit this arsenal of ultimate
weapons — biological, chemical, thermonuclear, radiological
— will be in substance the same irritable apes who first overran the planet only a few thousand years ago. They may
grow in knowledge and strength, but they cannot entirely
escape their instincts. Can men, remaining men, always
through bluff or diplomacy or good sense somehow manage
to avoid Armageddon? Karl Jaspers suggests that perhaps
no extraterrestrial species has made contact with ours for
the precise reason that no race can survive anywhere in the
cosmos which has reached man's present level of technology.
They all annihilate themselves in thermonuclear holocausts.
And Jaspers, though hopeful, admits that our survival is intellectually "improbable." [3] In brief, we are guilty and
doomed to die unless we can escape to the sanity of a new
civilization built to the world scale of human intercourse.

Finally, this is also a century that makes all life before
it seem nearly insipid. No sober assessment of our chances,

not even the soul-sickness endemic in our times, can rob us
of the Nietzschean joy of confronting with courage a world
in disintegration. We live dangerously. Wrestling on the
precipice makes for profound dizziness, but also for a quick-
ening of every sense. "Joy is deeper still than heart's grief,"
says Zarathustra; and Albert Camus tells us to imagine even
Sisyphus happy. "The struggle itself toward the heights is
enough to fill a man's heart." [4]

Whoever enlists in the cause of man in this age will find
no time for tears. We are the vital link between the traditional civilizations of a well remembered past and the emergent world civilization. We stand between. If we break
under the strain, there will be no future. All posterity is in
our keeping. Such a task against such towering odds joins
man to man and weaves meaning into the vast fabric of confusion. It can be the difference between the life and death
of the soul.

One

The Biography of a Vision

Utopia and Cosmopolis

THE DREAM of an integrated world order is one of the oldest rational visions of civilized man. In a sense, it created civilization. Yet the dream has never been fully translated into reality, even in the largest empires. Premodern men lacked the physical means, and would-be integrators time and again suppressed ways of life and habits of thought unlike their own, preferring the whips of compulsion to the arts of integration, when they were put to the test. In theory and practice both, man has never been one psychospiritually organic species. He has wanted to be, and his human finitude has defeated him. Every quest for one God, one ultimate Reality, one brotherhood of man, one true faith, and one true commonwealth is a search, against the grain of man's egoism, for world order; but he captures an authentic vision of his goal only rarely, like a mountain peak glimpsed for a moment through heavy clouds.

Still, this is an epic quest. Before trying to study the form it takes in the twentieth century, it may be useful to recall a few important landmarks in the history of the vision of world order — more cautionary, perhaps, than inspirational; and yet, measured against the whole range of twentieth-century thought, most earlier centuries and civilizations experienced the will for world harmony far more spontaneously than our own. To many of them, it was all but instinctive,

even if they failed for lack of means or impetus to build a true
world order. For us, it is something to be learned painfully,
almost against our instincts. We who have made the sovereign
nation-state a thing to be worshiped, and who have also paradoxically purged our souls of all gods, truths, and faiths, and
stand naked in our impudence before what we call "nothing-
ness," will have to come to believe in the possibility of an integrated world civilization by hard and bitter discipline. And
we can begin to recapture that sadly attenuated sense of unity
and wholeness only by learning something of the history of
the idea of world order. In so doing, we find ourselves in a
meaningful struggle; we encounter an illuminating purpose.

There are, really, two symbols of the best state of man on
earth, which compete with one another throughout history.
H. G. Wells liked to interpret all the drama of world history
as the tension between man's animal affection for the narrow
comforts of tribe and village and his self-surpassing search
for the widest possible community of thought, wealth, and
work. In the history of thought, this can be translated into
the often unrecognized antithesis between the Utopia and
the Cosmopolis.

The utopia is the perfect town, a community of friends
and neighbors, an uncomplicated warm nest from which all
the noise of the real world is excluded. The half-mythical
Chinese sage Lao-tzu preached such a utopia six centuries
before Christ. "Let there be," he wrote, "a small country
with a small population." The people would see the nearest settlement just across their frontiers, but "right down
to old age and the day of their death, they will not trouble
to go there." [1] Plato idealized the classical Greek city-
state in *The Republic,* the first great Western utopia, and
his eloquent ghost haunts the pages of most utopian books
since, from More, Rousseau, and Proudhon to B. F. Skinner's
Walden Two today. Earnest admirers of what, since the
nineteenth century, has been called "culture" also like to

point with awe to the cultural achievements of classical Athens and Renaissance Florence. Here Western civilization allegedly lived its finest hours: the triumph of the superb few over the teeming world states of Babylon and Rome.

But over against this attractive picture of quality gloriously trouncing quantity is the evidence of a long-lived tradition of cosmopolitanism in every great civilization. Cosmopolis means simply, from the Greek, "world-city." The world-city is the inevitably large spiritual and intellectual and administrative capital of a civilization, of the whole known civilized world. Or, more broadly, it is the quintessence of a civilization, the gathering of all its vital human resources into a living organic unity. A cosmopolis is not a utopia; it is not the best of all possible worlds, but the boundless community of the best in the world-that-is. A world of utopias would be a world of isolated saints. Cosmopolis is simply the world in a state of optimal integration.

The cosmopolitan ideal appears whenever a people reaches out and discovers and comes into intimate communion with other peoples. Most primitive societies begin with an unshakable conviction of their own centrality in the cosmos. Westermarck found much the same naïve ethnic egoism even among the Eskimos, the Hottentots, and the Australian aborigines.[2]

But trade, travel, war, and the exchange of ideas have almost always worked wonders with ethnocentrism. Out of the travail of empire-building, especially, comes revelation. The world opens out. Gods, morals, styles, world-views agglomerate and, under the best conditions, fuse to produce a richer, fuller way of life. Even when reaction sets in, for any number of reasons, and a people cleaves unto itself again, as Jews, Germans, and Irishmen have often tried to do, there is no return to the purity of the past. Civilizations cohere stubbornly; the cosmopolitan spirit survives in the most intractably provincial societies.

"Civilization," writes Lewis Mumford, "is the never-ending process of creating one world and one humanity," [3] and even the briefest tour through history will bear him out. Seen in its broadest perspective, the idea of a world community, a cosmopolis, is one of the great civilizing forces in the evolution of man, whether the final purpose of existence be located in the world of here and now, or extended to some transcendental sphere out of space and time. The Confucian civilization of the Far East illustrates perfectly what orthodox Christians would have to label a society founded on a "secular" cosmopolitanism. The Indian subcontinent has produced less than its share, perhaps, of cosmopolitan social philosophy, but its characteristic world-views proclaim the unity of all being and a spiritual cosmopolitanism more philosophically cogent than any other traditional civilization has contrived. In the West, the doctrine of the world-city first found significant expression in the Hellenistic world after the conquests of Alexander the Great; it developed along radically different and yet equally powerful lines in the law and thought of Imperial Rome and in early Christianity; the two joined forces in the world-view of medieval Christendom. The cosmopolitanism of the Christian Middle Ages had its Islamic counterpart in medieval Northern Africa, Moorish Spain, and the Near East.

In modern times, the history of thought can be interpreted, without much exaggeration, as a desperate search, either for some parochial *ersatz* religion to fill the void left by the crumbling of the traditional faiths, or for a new cosmopolitanism, a new vision of the brotherhood of man and the metaphysical unity of being, to supersede without wholly rejecting the organic world-view of the Middle Ages. Most of the great seventeenth-century philosophers invented ingenious systems which had at least the merit of attempting a total explanation or systematization of reality. Their fusion of medieval values with the methods and learning of the new science of Galileo and Newton fathered the Enlightenment of the eighteenth century, an age of cosmopolitanism *par excellence*. "I am a man before I am a Frenchman," said Montesquieu, and even Napoleon justified his greed for glory by dreaming of the reintegration of Christendom. In the ninteenth century, the idea of the world-city lost ground; but Saint-Simon and Comte almost made a religion of it in France and Britain, and there were other major prophets less familiar to English-speaking readers, from Krause in Germany to Fedorov in Russia and K'ang Yu-wei in China.

This first chapter studies the perennial vision of cosmopolis in its historical perspective, but not merely for the pleasure of exploring the past. Unlike utopia, cosmopolis has been the animating ideal of real civilizations. It has inspired genuine conquests, both military and moral. It has shaped religions, created philosophies, and moved men of action. Time and again, mankind has achieved at least a partial realization of cosmopolis within the geographical limits of a whole civilization. If today the idea of a cosmopolis literally worldwide in proportions can snatch a disintegrating humanity from the jaws of chaos and give form and purpose to life, it will draw much of its strength from the consciousness in its true-believers of its deep roots in history. This is no johnny-come-lately among ideas. It was already thousands of years old when modern European man began shoveling his sons into the Molochs of nationalism, racism, and class warfare, and it will still be here, God or Reason willing, long after they have crumbled to powder.

Eastern Approaches

THE VISION of a world in perfect integration appeared first, perhaps, in ancient China. If Lao-tzu was the first utopian, Confucius — or his posthumous disciples — were among the first cosmopolitans.

Historians are always at pains to point out that the Far Eastern peoples evolved along quite different lines from the peoples of the Western world. The most convincing explanation relies on the simple facts of Oriental geography. Southeast Asia and the East Indies are equatorial tropics, unsuited by climate and flora for the development of highly advanced indigenous civilizations. Japan is a rugged volcanic archipelago, isolated by oceans from all but the vast Chinese land mass, and destined from the start to learn the arts of civilization from China, much as prehistoric Britain depended for her progress on contact with the Continent. The only possible cradles of Oriental civilization were the fertile river valleys of northeastern China.

But unlike the river valleys of the ancient Near East, those of China bounded nearly all the land best fitted by soil, latitude, and climate for the flourishing of a complex urban civilization. Once established there, the center of civilization could not shift to other areas, as it moved from Mesopotamia and Egypt to Greece, Rome, and all Europe in Western history. Although many natural barriers crisscross the face of China, dividing her into several distinct regions with distinct ways of life, civilized China in the first millennium before Christ enjoyed a relatively high degree of geographical unity. Surrounded on all sides by barbarian tribes, immense deserts, the highest mountain ranges in the world, tropical forests, and the Pacific Ocean, ancient China was a world in herself, quite sealed off from the other main centers of civilization. In the third century B.C., she even achieved political integration at the rough hands of the first Ch'in emperor, which has lasted, with interruptions, down to the present time. For thousands of years China has been not so much a single country, and certainly not a nation in the Western sense, as the center and chief component of a highly sophisticated civilization.

It follows, then, that until recent centuries Chinese thought could not develop an idea of universal brotherhood on the scope of the Stoic, Christian, or Muslim movements in Western history. The Chinese always put China in the center of the universe and called the peoples on their borders barbarians, since, within the broad limits of their knowledge and experience, nearly all other peoples *were* barbarians. At the same time, because of the earliness of their development of a great unified civilization of continental proportions, joining one third of humanity under the rule of a single government, the Chinese were among the first peoples to expound the idea of the world-city in all its dimensions.

From the beginning, the Chinese mind has displayed a passion not matched even in medieval Europe for a sense of the harmonious connectedness of things. The leading schools of thought have looked for, and found, order in the world. There is a cosmic order, reflected in the regular motions of the heavens and the regular sequence of the seasons. Human society, at its best, follows the cosmic example. Each man and woman and child has his appointed place and duty:

the highest task in life is to obey scrupulously the dictates of nature, disclosed to man by human wisdom. It is not strange that most Chinese, Lao-tzu's subtle primitivism notwithstanding, have idealized the universal state, not only because of the actual unification of China in the third century B.C., but also because the universal state best corresponds to the unity of the cosmos.

In point of fact the cosmopolitan ideal in Chinese thought may antedate the Ch'in Dynasty. Although scholars are divided on the question of the authorship of the writings traditionally ascribed to Confucius — suggesting Western difficulties with Homer and the Old Testament — much Confucian literature clearly goes back to original sources in remotest antiquity, and Confucius himself was a contemporary of Pythagoras, born some three hundred years before Shih Huang-ti, the Ch'in emperor who forged the first Chinese empire. In these oldest writings, the doctrine of the harmony of the cosmic and earthly order is already well developed. Annalists look back on a golden age when all Chinese acknowledged one emperor. Confucius is represented in *The Book of Rites* as distinguishing between the "lesser peace" possible in his own time and the "great unity," or *ta t'ung*, the world commonwealth in which all men once worked, and should ideally always work, for the general welfare, holding goods in common and never locking their gates.

Although the idea of a *ta t'ung* appears only in material composed after Confucius' death, most of the great philosophers of the feudal era before Shih Huang-ti shared a passionate desire for a unified world. They bowed to the inevitability of feudal lords, but they clung, somewhat like the Hapsburgs, to the dream of a world state under an emperor who would faithfully execute the law of nature. Motzu, a contemporary of Socrates, is best remembered for his doctrine of universal love. Only if all men loved their

fellows without distinction, he argued, would world peace
be possible. But accepting the will of heaven as the standard
of righteousness, they would also obey their superiors unques-
tioningly. Clan patriarchs would fashion their laws after the
laws of rulers of states; rulers of states would follow the
emperor; and the emperor would follow heaven, acting as
"the final arbiter of all teachings and ideas."[4] Meng-tzu,
or Mencius, the most prominent of Confucius' posthumous
followers, described an ideal state in which the emperor
would be a sage, succeeded on his death by a younger sage
chosen by him and approved by heaven, which is to say, the
natural world order. Finally, just a few years before China's
unification in the third century B.C., the Legalist philosopher
Han Fei-tzu rejected the tender-minded moralism of both
the disciples of Mo-tzu and the Confucianists to insist on the
practical necessity of a universal empire, consisting entirely
of soldiers and workers, ruled despotically by an absolute
monarch.

The Ch'in emperors followed more closely the advice of
Han Fei-tzu than of the Confucian schools, but under the
Han Dynasty which followed, China enjoyed a long period
of peaceful unity and good government. The Confucian approach prevailed. While the Stoics were teaching the brotherhood of man in the Mediterranean world in the second
century before Christ, Tung Chung-shu, the most influential
of the Han Confucianists, was adapting Confucian ideals to
the ripe realities of the Han world state.

Some of his cosmological speculations only amuse the
modern reader, but they express vividly the ageless human
longing for a meaningful universe. Reasoning like a medieval
schoolman, Tung found that the five elements — wood, fire,
earth, metal, and water — correspond exactly to the five
viscera of the human body; and the four seasons to the
four limbs. A man's head is round, like heaven, and his nos-
trils blow like the winds. What is written in heaven, is

written in the bodies and lives of men. Above all the universal state must mirror the will of heaven. The emperor is vested by heaven with the task of regulating all things on earth in harmony with the celestial order. The laws are eternal, and must be kept. Each man has his proper place, and must remain there. To disobey constituted authority, violate laws, betray the emperor, or fail to observe prescribed rules of behavior is to defy heaven. Misfortune among men stems from disobedience; if the whole empire totters, the emperor himself is to blame. For Tung, the ruler in his person had the supreme task of unifying heaven, earth, and man. Hence the character for "king": 王 The three horizontal strokes symbolized heaven, earth, and man, and the line connecting them represented the king's role as the harmonizer of all three. That this was a totally erroneous etymology is all the more significant.[5]

From Tung, the Confucianist philosophy of world order passed on to future generations, and became the official doctrine of imperial China. Through all the later vicissitudes of Chinese history, the Confucian vision, as amplified by Tung, persisted almost without opposition down to recent times. The last great philosopher of imperial China, K'ang Yu-wei, whose idea of world order is examined below,* was at bottom a devout Confucian, although he borrowed extensively from Western sources. The doctrine of one world, one state, and one civilization was taught and lived in China for over two thousand years.

At first glance, that other largely self-contained continental Eastern civilization, the Indian, generated a world-view wholly alien to the Chinese. Most Chinese thinkers have taken for granted the unity of nature and mankind, and focused their energies on illuminating the good life available on earth. The Indian emphasis runs all the other way, to-

* See pp. 51–52.

ward the transcendence of mortal life and the absorption of
the self into the undifferentiated absolute reality which lies
beyond the veil of visible objects.

But it is worth noting that Chinese and Indian thought
essentially furnish the same answer to the problem of the
unity of the cosmic order, of which men are part. They are
not dualists, in the usual Western sense. The world is metaphysically one, for Indians and Chinese alike, and this belief has profoundly influenced the thinking of twentieth-
century Indians confronted with the spectacle of a divided
world on the road to suicide.

Before modern times, however, India had much less experience than China of unified rule. Indian history is a long
tale of woe. The perennial tension between higher and lower
castes, originating in the subjection of the indigenous Dravid-
ian population by the Indo-Iranian invaders of the second
millennium B.C.; the wide cultural gulf between North and
South; the ravages of the repeated waves of Muslim conquerors after A.D. 1001, and the subsequent fission of the
North Indians into Muslims and Hindus and Sikhs; and
the persistence, through everything, of strong traditions
of local and regional independence, all have conspired to
make the idea of world order on earth implausible. Climate
may also have influenced the peculiar twist of the Indian
mind. The Aryan invaders who first created Indian civilization poured down into the valley of the Indus from the
bracing uplands of the Iranian plateau, but most of the land
they overran is tropical or semi-tropical. They came into
India with much the same world-view as Homer's Greeks,
but under the influence, perhaps, of the enervating Indian
sun, they lost their primitive exuberance and devoted their
brains to devising ways out of the world, instead of ways
of making life on earth more harmonious.

In any event, the best known Indian political philosophers
of antiquity, like Aristotle's contemporary Kautilya, were

content to preach a ruthless realism more Machiavellian than Machiavelli. Among rival states, the law of the fishes, *matsya-nyaya,* always prevailed: the big fish ate the little fish. Strong states gobbled up weak. It was hopeless to try to transfer the ethics of individual conduct within the state to the realm of international politics.

And yet, as Heinrich Zimmer points out in his *Philosophies of India,* there was also "an ancient mythical ideal — an idyllic compensatory dream, born of the longing for stability and peace — which represents a universal, world-wide empire of enduring tranquillity under a just and virtuous world-monarch, the *cakravartin* . . . who should put an end to the perpetual struggle of the contending states." [6] Scholars have traced the myth of the *cakravartin* back to pre-Aryan legend, but it first appears prominently in Indian political thought in the Pali canons of early Buddhism. For the devout Buddhist the *cakravartin* was no less than the secular counterpart of the Buddha. The "superior man" of Buddhist doctrine could become either a world-teacher, the Buddha, or a world-ruler, the *cakravartin,* manifesting on a secular plane the same universal principles of benevolence and righteousness manifested by the Buddha on a spirtual plane. Buddhist literature prophesies with apocalyptic vividness the coming of the *cakravartin* in some future age, attended by a perfect white elephant, a milk-white horse, a magic wishing stone, a perfect queen, a perfect finance minister, and a perfect general-in-chief. He would march into each of the four quarters of the earth in turn, subjecting all kings to his rule not by force, but by the awesome power of his righteousness. Utopia and cosmopolis merge in a single splendid image. In the rare example of the great Buddhist emperor Asoka, in the third century B.C., the image was almost brought down to earth. Asoka's extraordinary success as a unifier of his usually invertebrate India and his enlightened philosophy of government undoubtedly owe something to the pervasive influence of this cosomopolitan vision of early Buddhism.

But it was essentially a vision, even a dream, remote from the realities of ordinary political life in India. Meanwhile: the law of fishes, and the pursuit of *moksa*, spiritual release from fleshly illusion.

Although the ancient Indians were not conspicuously successful in achieving either a world state or a rational philosophy of world order, their passion for unity on the spiritual plane has made many Indian thinkers of Gandhi's generation, and Nehru's, powerful spokesmen for the cause of world integration in our time. The thinking of Aurobindo Ghose, Radhakrishnan, and others, will be sampled in later chapters.

The Classical Heritage

ADVANCED civilizations existed along the banks of the Nile and in the river valleys of Mesopotamia some two thousand years or more before anything of comparable complexity emerged in the Orient. But the Western mind was definitively shaped in classical Greece, as many generations of devout Hellenophils have labored long to prove. The distinctive Western outlook — its art, philosophy, literature, and even much of its theology — stems from the approach to life and thought taken by the Greeks from 600 to 200 B.C.

Ignorance and pride of race led at first to the same ethnocentrism that typified most other Mediterranean peoples in ancient history. The Greeks began by dividing the world into Greeks and barbarians, men who spoke Greek and men who spoke non-Hellenic languages, all of which sounded to the good Hellene like "bar . . . bar . . . bar," hence the word *barbaros* in Greek, and *barbara* in Sanskrit. Since the Greeks themselves, even in 600 B.C., had only recently emerged from pure barbarism, and they confronted across the sea civilizations of prodigious antiquity and sophistication, it was inevitable that their real attitude to the "barbarian" world should take a different course from the Chinese attitude.

The Greek mind moved from revolution to revolution in a span of just over three hundred years, discovering in an entirely unique way, unduplicated by Eastern thinkers, the unity and rationality of the cosmos. The early cosmologists, from Thales to Democritus, suggested penetrating metaphysical explanations for the composition and motion of the sensed world. Socrates, Plato, and Aristotle probed into the inner cosmos of man, establishing the sciences of epistemology and logic. Finally, in the third century B.C., the Stoics connected the external universe and the universe of man with the concept of a world state.

Although the Stoic vision of world order, which dominated the serious thinking of classical pagan civilization until the fall of Rome, is inconceivable without the earlier Hellenic background, it is astonishing to recall how very great that final leap was. For all their wisdom, Plato and Aristotle preached a narrow and aggressive patriotism. Plato's utopian Republic was an idealized Greek *polis*, or city-state, independent, armed, and aloof. Aristotle saw no further than a world of sovereign city-states each entitled to make war on the other, and non-Greeks, he thought, should be treated and thought of as slaves. The paradox of philosophers preaching the universal laws of reason and nature applicable to all men, on the one hand, and advocating a political philosophy of ethnic imperialism and plural sovereignties, on the other hand, suggests that the Greek intellectual revolution was moving too rapidly even for the Greeks.

But signs of a new turning appeared even before Plato and Aristotle. Trade, colonization, and war over the centuries brought the Greeks into intimate contact with the whole ancient world. The first important intellectual reaction came in the fifth century B.C. among the traveling professional teachers who called themselves Sophists. They advertised courses in almost everything, but as thinkers some of them soared higher than historians — prejudiced by Socrates, who hated Sophists — have usually reported. Their travels put them in touch with scores of different ethical codes, explanations of the universe, theologies, and canons of beauty. Some shrugged and adopted a fatalistic relativism. Others, like Antiphon, fragments of whose work were recovered for the first time early in this century, insisted that although customs vary, men everywhere are men. Since they share the same *physis,* or nature, there must be a universal law, superior to the ephemeral laws of men, everywhere the same, which made nonsense of the distinction between Greeks and barbarians cultivated by the Greek philosophers. Plato and Aristotle expended no little effort to prove the Sophists wrong. The laws of nature, they said, could not be applied so literally. Greeks were Greeks, slaves were slaves, and barbarians were barbarians, by their own particular natures.

All through the first half of the fourth century, the Greek world was in process of disintegration, struck a fatal blow by the fratricidal struggles of Athens and Sparta. Schools of philosophy emerged, contemporary with those great chauvinists Plato and Aristotle, which took a sour view of civilized values. Some hailed physical pleasure as the highest good; others — like the Cynics — preached a kind of Taoist or Rousseauian return to nature. The same Diogenes who slept in a tub and went prowling the streets with a lantern in search of an honest man gave the Cynic school a certain notoriety in the ancient world which it still enjoys in the modern. It was the Cynics, in fact, who coined the word *kosmopolis,* meaning by it that a man should have no city, or *polis,* of his own, since cities were worthless heaps of corruption, but should take the whole world for his home, and live like the dog.

What ultimately gave the Cynic doctrine of the world-city a constructive and humanizing turn, sparking its transformation from a bitter primitivism into the most exalted social philosophy of classical civilization, was the remarkable career of Alexander of Macedon. Like Shih Huang-ti a century later in China, Alexander forcibly united under one

government most of the known civilized world. Although
his state did not survive him, it was soon re-created on an
even grander scale by the Romans. Alexander's best modern
biographer, W. W. Tarn, attributes to him personally the
dream of a world commonwealth, forged by conquest but to
the end that *homonoia,* human concord, should be established among the nations.[7] From strictly contemporary documents Tarn's thesis is unprovable, but Alexander did at
least clearly try to integrate the hitherto hostile cultures of
Greece and Persia, and his empire did pry the Greek mind
loose from its ingrained provincialism. From the late
fourth century on, Greek, Near Eastern, and Egyptian artists
and thinkers mingled freely, and this so-called Hellenistic
culture quickly captured Rome. One of its first fruits was the
Stoic philosophy.

The first Stoic writings follow the conquests of Alexander,
but the first Stoic, Zeno — not the earlier Zeno who proposed the famous paradoxes — was a student of the Cynic
philosopher Crates. A gaunt, shy man, he came to Athens
in or after 317 B.C., from the island of Cyprus, and began
teaching in 302. With the Cynics, he agreed that the city-
state was not enough. Man owed his allegiance to something higher than his city, but it is not merely the world at
large, men and animals indiscriminately lumped together,
as the Cynics had taught. The world, according to Zeno,
was under the rule of a single universal divine law, pro-
mulgated by divine reason; and men, through their unique
gift of reason, could learn and obey the cosmic will. With
the gods, they constituted a spiritual world-city, in which
differences of blood and birth mattered not at all. As the
Stoic philosophy evolved in the third century, it insisted
on the ultimate unity of God, viewing Zeus as the one supreme power in the universe, a thoroughly rational law-
giver commanding men to love one another and live in
peace. But in spite of Alexander's conquests, or perhaps

because of their impermanence, Hellenistic Stoicism never
formulated a theory or program of world political unification. Only the wise man could ever fully participate in the
world community, and it was more an affair of the mind and
the spirit, than of the flesh. Still, Stoic cosmopolitanism
is the first major step in Western intellectual history from
the idealization of the city-state to the gospel of the universal community. G. H. Sabine even describes the death
of Aristotle and the rise of Stoicism as the most decisive
breaking point in the history of political thought.[8]

Stoic philosophy reached Rome in the second century
B.C. Like many another transplanted world-view, it flowered
in new forms in its new surroundings. Romanized Greeks
and native Romans in the more pragmatic mental climate
of the rapidly rising Roman state, already an empire in fact
if not in name, gave to Stoicism a more worldly interpretation. The cosmopolitan spiritual community of men of reason broadened into a more genuinely universal community
of all God's creatures, and it took on a concrete political dimension. The political instability of the Hellenistic world
immediately after Alexander's death had discouraged thinking men from too deep an involvement in politics. The
Stoic wise man would seldom soil his hands. But Rome was
another matter. Little by little, most of the known world
was crushed, with or without its consent, to the mailed bosom
of Rome, and enjoyed henceforth the mixed blessings of the
Pax Romana, the Roman peace. With Augustus Caesar in 31
B.C., even the forms of the old patrician city-state government
began to yield to frankly imperial institutions. At its peak,
the Roman empire united sixty million people in a single
state extending over more than one million square miles,
nearly the size of China under the Han Dynasty. Confronted
with the reality of the Roman world state, Stoic thinkers
could not help but see Rome, in at least a limited sense, as a

political embodiment of their world-city. It became the duty of the reasonable man to serve the state, to protect it from wrongdoers, and to devise for it a code of law in harmony with divine reason.

Roman political and legal thought is eclectic, but the Stoic elements in it held the ascendancy for many centuries. Cicero was more a Stoic than anything else. The playwright and philosopher Seneca and the ex-slave Epictetus were highly articulate Stoics. And the last of the "Good Emperors" of the second century A.D., Marcus Aurelius, left to posterity in the form of his *Meditations* perhaps the most resplendent single collection of Stoic wisdom. Roman law developed a *jus gentium,* or law of nations, comprehensive enough in scope and imagination to provide standards of justice for the whole various population of the empire; and it, too, was basically Stoic in inspiration. Stoic legal philosophers insisted on bringing Roman law as near as possible to the laws of nature herself. Whether they succeeded or not, their fundamental belief in the existence of a divinely ordained natural law overriding all human positive law clearly influenced Roman jurists searching for universally valid standards of right and wrong.

Rome almost succeeded in justifying Pliny's description of her as the "mother of all nations," and if, in the end, the Roman experiment in world government failed, it was perhaps because Rome never quite lived up to the stratospheric idealism of the Stoics. The Stoics, for their part, never quite gave their whole minds and souls to the task of transforming the Roman empire into the authentic world state of their philosophy. No Stoic ever was so dazzled by Rome as to equate literally the Pax Romana with the universal community. Imperial Rome retained, in her institutions and habits of thought, much of the narrower patriotism of republican Rome. Roman civic pride interfered with Roman world responsibilities. The subject states of the empire,

despite the gradual extension of Roman citizenship to nearly
all free men, were never firmly welded into a dynamic political entity; an imperial senate composed of representatives
chosen by the several provinces meeting in Rome to advise
the emperor might, for example, have created the necessary
esprit de corps, but nothing of the sort developed. No theorist, to say nothing of practical men, succeeded in shaking off
once and for all the lingering notion that the Roman empire
was still, fundamentally, a city-state that had just happened
to conquer the world. The transformation from *polis* to
kosmopolis never completely took place. As emperor, wrote
Marcus Aurelius, "my city and fatherland . . . is Rome, as
a human being it is the universe." He could not reconcile
the two roles.

At heart the Stoic philosophy remained to the end a
product of Hellenistic world-weariness and discouragement.
It lacked ebullience. It taught resignation to fate, contempt
for foolishness, and indifference to pain. The Stoic wise
man, even in his Roman metamorphosis, found it impossible to live fully in the world of sensed reality while at the
same time acknowledging allegiance to a higher order of
reality. He believed in the unity of all things, but he
preferred, like the early Christian saints and martyrs, to save
his deepest feelings for the contemplation of the Absolute.

Respublica Christiana and Dar al-Islam

THE FALL of Rome did not by any means end the search for world order in Western civilization. Roman law continued to thrive and rule in the Eastern Roman empire centered in Constantinople throughout the Middle Ages. In Western Europe a new civilization gradually emerged, politically almost a chaos, but spiritually and culturally more completely integrated than the Roman empire had ever been, and in the most important respects more than Europe today.

Historians serve up scores of explanations for the success of the "medieval synthesis." Perhaps the main point is that medieval man, in molding a new civilization, conserved most of the highest achievements of the old. He found himself the heir of what seemed at first an unsurpassable past; and he built modestly on the ruins of massive foundations. To take the most decisive example, his world-view grew out of classical philosophy and the Christian faith. Of these potent ingredients he made a subtle synthesis without adding much of his own, although his success after centuries of Roman failure is worth careful notice. In all likelihood, what saved medieval man from a hopeless eclecticism, apart from the natural death in the Roman debacle of a numerous clutter of second-rate cults and philosophies, was his almost fanatical sense of cosmic and human unity. "Wherever we turn," says Maurice de Wulf in his classic survey of medieval civilization, "we find . . . everyone dreaming of universal harmony." [9] As often as not, the dream informed the deed.

It is ironic that so otherworldly a faith as Christianity should have proved more successful than the classical philosophies in bringing the idea of world order down to earth, but the job could not have been done without classical philosophy, especially Stoicism. Nor would it have been done, probably, without the irresistible challenge to the Christian clergy of a whole continent restored to barbarism by Rome's collapse and eager for regeneration. In the twilight years of imperial Rome, radical otherworldliness was as natural for Stoics and Christians alike as for the holy men of India. But later, after barbarism had done its worst, men of good will saw in the classical doctrines of natural law, cosmic harmony, and cosmopolis, and in the now legendary unity of the Roman empire, ideas indispensable to the building of a new social order. Many Christian writers, and among them St. Augustine, had attempted a synthesis of the classical and Christian traditions even while Rome still stood. By the thirteenth century, this work found its ultimate fulfillment in the thought of Aquinas and Dante.

The synthesis of classical philosophy and Christianity was more than a simple marriage of convenience to save civilization from the barbarian's axe. They found one another's company congenial. But it had not always been so. At the outset, Christianity had been preoccupied with eschatology, the study of "final things." The faith of Jesus of Nazareth and his disciples was grounded in the conviction that the world could not last much longer. In the face of approaching doom, earliest Christianity warned humanity to repent and seek the favor of its omnipotent Father in heaven.

But as the world remained intact, as Christ failed to return to judge between the quick and the dead, and as

Christian thought evolved beyond its first perfervid proc-
lamations, bridges were built, or discovered, between faith
and philosophy. From prophetic Judaism, Christianity inherited its belief that the cosmos was the creation and care of a
single God, easily identifiable with such pagan concepts as
the Stoic Zeus. Isaiah had even bequeathed to Christianity
the prophecy of a world state, worshiping the one true God
and ruled from Israel, this last point, if taken literally, a not
too charming relic of Hebrew ethnocentrism. But whereas
Judaism has always remained a religion for a select people,
the principal early Christian sects fully universalized the
Hebrew God, spreading the gospel to Gentiles as well as Jews,
and insisting not only on the fatherhood of God but also
on its corollary, the brotherhood of man. Unlike Judaism,
Christianity became a missionary faith, and like all missionary faiths, it did not discriminate. As it grew, it acquired
along the way an immense assortment of ideas from those
whom it touched or converted. In good time, Christianity
captured the whole Roman empire. By the early fourth
century, it was the state religion. It is surely not flippant
to add that the responsibilities of such high office made the
Church, and Christianity with it, deeply concerned for man's
secular, as well as spiritual, welfare. With the help of pagan
philosophy, the main stream of Christian thought began to
turn decisively from eschatological fantasies to the synthesis
of a world-view that ministered to the whole range of human
need.

In particular, Christian thinkers had to see God's will in
the Roman state itself. In his oration in 335 on the reign
of Constantine, Eusebius celebrated the passing of "the era
of multiple principalities and tyrannies, the product of diversity in worship, and the coming of world unity under
one God and one government. As the one God banished
the demons, the one emperor gains sway over his foes." [10]
Less enthusiastically, St. Augustine looked on the empire and

its component provinces and kingdoms as the instruments appointed by God to maintain social order on earth and protect the holy Church. In Book Five of his *City of God* he even paints the portrait of the ideal Christian emperor. To be sure, peace on earth was only a means to a spiritual end, the preparation of God's pilgrims for their final journey to heaven. Nonetheless, it had a dignity of its own. The state was good because its laws proceeded via nature from God himself, as the Stoics had always taught. But it must be admitted that for all these arguments, the Church did not entirely have its heart in the empire of the Caesars, nor did the Church save it from catastrophe.

Then, after the disappearance of the Western empire and the chaos of the sixth and seventh centuries, Christian thought underwent a much more thorough transformation. For many Christians, the earlier faith in the second coming of Christ at the end of time was channeled into the humbler task of building a new order on earth. As Ernst Troeltsch once observed, the very existence of this faith in the future imparted to Christianity a dynamism never possible for the piously resigned Stoic.[11] Christians sought to build a sacral civilization as a terrestrial monument to the greater glory of God. The task filled some eight or nine centuries.

Although it should go without saying that medieval realities only dimly corresponded to medieval ideals, the ideals, handed on from generation to generation, compel respect. Casting wistful eyes back to Rome, medieval man revered the idea of a world state. French and German statesmen vied to re-create the Roman empire all through the Middle Ages and on into early modern times; Charlemagne's empire and the Holy Roman Empire of central Europe were only the most spectacular efforts. At the same time, medieval man believed fiercely in the need for a single universal catholic Church. So far as Western Europe is concerned, he was able in this instance to translate his ideas into reality. The undivided Roman Church, with its vast literature and liturgy in Latin, its network of superb cathedral schools and universities, and its virtual monopolization in many countries of all the media of higher culture, did much more than any other institution to create, sustain, and integrate medieval civilization. World state and world church, secular and spiritual authority, together with the souls of the faithful all over Christendom, constituted in medieval theory the *respublica Christiana,* the Christian Republic, or the *corpus Christianum,* the Christian body politic. It was one organic whole, living under one law and one God.

Such at least is the impression gained from a first encounter with medieval social philosophy. The vision of the Christian Commonwealth inspired many of the best minds of the age, although explicit treatments of the theme are understandably rare. It was a view of things taken usually for granted. Closer study will also bring to light, however, many partially dissenting opinions. Few medieval thinkers denied the desirability of Christian unity, but acute controversy often marred the alliance of church and state. Some thinkers believed in a strongly unitary universal church with ultimate power over secular authority; others favored a weak church and a strong empire, reflecting the interminable contest during the High Middle Ages between the Holy Roman Empire and the papacy. Following Aristotle or the interests of princes, still others ignored the ideal of a universal empire altogether and wrote only in terms of the sovereign and semi-sovereign territorial principality. In all the enormous output of St. Thomas Aquinas, who in this respect as in most others echoed the newly rediscovered treatises of Aristotle, there is scarcely a word about the world state.

Plausibly enough, most of the keenest debate on the exact nature of the *respublica Christiana* took place after medieval society had achieved a fairly high level of sophistication and complexity, and was already on the verge or in the throes of internal disintegration. The books best remembered in this connection all date from the fourteenth and fifteenth centuries. With the death of the last Hohenstaufen emperor in 1254, the long history since Charlemagne of vigorous efforts by skillful rulers to re-create the Roman empire in Europe had come to an end, although the empire itself, as a feeble Germanic confederation, lasted until Napoleon gave it a French *coup de grâce* in 1806. In 1305 the papacy was transferred from Rome to Avignon in France, where it remained for nearly three quarters of a century the not entirely unwilling "Babylonian captive" of the French king. These two developments, followed in 1378 by the "Great Schism" in the Church and forty years of rival papacies, led to much bitter controversy over the best way to renew the organic unity of Christendom.

Perhaps the finest treatise on the *respublica Christiana* was written by the same man who created the greatest literary masterpiece of the Middle Ages: Dante Alighieri. His *De Monarchia*, 1310-13, burned by Pope John XXII in 1329 on a charge of heresy, took the position that God had appointed two men to govern mankind, the pope in the spiritual realm, the emperor in the secular. Each in his own realm was absolutely sovereign. To prove his case, Dante recalled that Christ had been born during the reign of the first Roman Emperor, Augustus Caesar. God's plan, then, was clear: just as the pope was the earthly successor of Christ, so the emperor was divinely appointed to succeed Caesar. Dante also defended the empire on metaphysical grounds. Starting with the thesis that Being in its highest form — a Greek way of saying "God" — exhibited perfect unity, Dante deduced that "in proportion as anything is far from Being in its highest form, it is far from Unity, and therefore from Good. Where Unity is greatest, there Good is also greatest." [12] The human race thus most nearly approximated divine goodness when it accepted one supreme ruler. There can be no better illustration of the medieval way of reasoning. As in the case of Chinese philosophy, the passion for a cosmos so orderly that clear and simple correspondences weave each order of being into a rationally meaningful pattern produces, in the weaving, a doctrine of cosmopolis.

Still, Dante had no desire to raise a political monolith. "Nations and kingdoms and states," he wrote, "have, each of them, certain peculiarities which must be regulated by different laws." Only "in those matters which are common to all men" should the human race be ruled by an emperor. The main business of the empire was to keep the peace, which the several nations obviously could not do alone.[13]

A few years before Dante, a German abbot, Engelbert of Admont, had already made most of the same points in his *De Ortu et Fine Romani Imperii*, "On the Rise and Fall of the Roman Empire." His arguments have a sweet familiar ring: "The whole constitution of this world, which is made up of things diverse, unlike, and contrary, cannot endure except through the concord of the diverse, the unlike, and the contrary." Since the diversity of nations is the cause of discord among peoples, there must "necessarily be some greater and superior power which will have force and authority to harmonize them, and to ordain and preserve concord among kingdoms and nations which are diverse from and hostile to one another." In His providence God had ordained the creation of an empire and an emperor to rule over it. But Engelbert's world state resembled nothing visible in fourteenth-century Europe. It was, writes Ewart Lewis, "a philosopher's empire, based on the ultimate unity of human nature and its purposes, comprehending all mankind as a single purpose consenting to a common law, carrying to its perfect logical conclusion the principle of order attained through hierarchical subordination." [14]

Engelbert's cosmopolis would have been a crusader empire, as well as an instrument for the pacification of Christendom. It would have promoted the conversion of the infidel and the recovery of the Holy Lands. Much the same project engaged the attentions of a French statesman, Pierre Dubois, who urged the French king in 1306 to establish a federation of princes uniting all Christendom for a concerted crusade to conquer the world. Dubois clearly had in mind French hegemony in Europe, and perhaps the project of a crusade was only an excuse to advocate vigorous internal reform within the French monarchy, to strengthen it against its Christian enemies; but it is at least significant that the excuse was necessary.

Other theories took other tacks. Anticipating quite bluntly the modern doctrine of national sovereignty, John of Paris argued against any analogy between temporal and spiritual government. Unity in the latter exists, as God's spoken will; in the former, it is impractical, un-Biblical, and contrary to Aristotle, the most revered of Greek philosophers in the later Middle Ages. The extreme papalists, like Tholommeo of Lucca, insisted that the Roman empire, on its collapse, had surrendered its authority to the papacy. For Tholommeo, the Roman Church itself was the fifth great world state in history, after those of the Assyrians, the Persians, Alexander the Great, and the Caesars. So far as facts are concerned, the Church, rather than the Empire, was indeed the "world state" of medieval Western Europe, although the efforts of the popes to meddle too energetically in the affairs of the separate kingdoms and principalities led, in the end, to the almost total ruin of its spiritual prestige at the close of the Middle Ages. The so-called conciliar movement during the Great Schism fought unsuccessfully to replace papal authority in the Church by a system of church councils.

But the clash of opinion should not blind us to the over-riding conviction of nearly all medieval thinkers that mankind was a single family acknowledging the spiritual supremacy of a single church under the judgment of a single omnipotent divine being. And in spite of the growing power of the national monarchies, it is also interesting to note that the last great medieval philosopher, Nicholas of Cusa, returned once again to the doctrine of a universal church and a universal empire.

The old Roman empire had two other heirs to its territory, after Western Christendom. From Constantinople the Byzantine emperors ruled an empire much reduced in size but carrying on many of the traditions of the Caesars. The great Justinian reigned all through the middle decades of the sixth century, codifying Roman law in definitive form, dreaming of a complete restoration of the ancient Roman *imperium,* recovering all of North Africa and Italy from the barbarians. But by the end of the seventh century, most of Italy was lost again, and the Arabs — soaring on the wings of Islam — had engulfed Africa and the entire Middle East. The Byzantine empire became a mostly Greek affair, in theory a highly centralized universal state in which the emperor wielded supreme power over church as well as government, but challenged so strongly by South Slavs, Persians, Arabs, and Turks on all sides that it led a hectic existence not conducive, apparently, to the production of much creative thought, other than theological. The chief centers of secular culture in the Middle Ages lay rather in Western Europe and in the third heir of Rome, the Islamic civilization created by Mohammed's Arabs in the seventh century.

No less likely people than the Arabs can be imagined as the builders of a universal society larger than any in the Western world in the seventh century after Christ. Islamic civilization was, in fact, much more than Arab. In establishing their rule over so many ancient centers of Hellenistic and Roman civilization, the Arabs inherited more of the thought of antiquity than the barbarians of Western Europe. To the still vital classical heritage, they added their own

virile monotheistic religion, itself based largely on Judaism
and Christianity, a desert people's zest for life, and two
powerful dynasties, Omayyad and Abbasid, which between
them united most of the Islamic world under one government for well over three hundred years. Their place in the
Islamic world was filled later in the Middle Ages by the
Turks, but not nearly so well.

The Islamic civilization also took as its own the classical
vision of world order and succeeded somewhat more impressively even than medieval Western Christendom in
giving it tangible form. Much of the credit goes to the peculiar starkness of Islamic unitarianism. The devout Muslim
has always rejected the subtle concepts of unity-in-duality
and unity-in-trinity so precious to the Christian metaphysi-
cian and theologian. He sees no rigid bifurcation of man
into matter and spirit, no fission of society into church and
state, no division of God into three persons. "There is no
God but the one God," he insists, and he means it. All men
are brothers, regardless of color or nationality, so long as they
worship the one true God. Mohammed interpreted his mission as the final reunification by book and sword of the sorely
divided world of his time. His book, the Koran, was no less
important than his sword in building the Islamic world state
of the early Middle Ages.

As Majid Khadduri points out, the medieval Islamic
political ideal for centuries after Mohammed's death continued to be a universal society, the *dar al-Islam* or "abode
of Islam," ruled by divine law. "The universal nomocracy of
Islam, like the *Respublica Christiana* in the West, assumed
that mankind constituted one supra-national community,
bound by one law and governed by one ruler." [15] It refused
to tolerate the existence of infidel polities, and waged war
against them as best it could; the *respublica Christiana*,
hardly to the credit of her gentler namesake, gave back as
good as she got, always loath to be outshone as a scourge of
rival world-orders.

Modern Prophets, 1600-1900

THE MODERN ERA needs no introduction. As the vision of *dar al-Islam* sank into near oblivion, desecrated by dynastic feuds, leaving behind it such imperfect vessels of the old Islamic dream as the Ottoman Empire, so the *respublica Christiana* gave way in turn to ecclesiastical schism, reformations and counter-reformations, and the rise of a constellation of fiercely independent nation-states which at first agreed to fight one another according to certain rules, and now wage war like the locust. "The consciouness," writes a German sociologist, "of belonging to a family of Western, Christian peoples, which in the Middle Ages had been upheld by knights and clergy, was alien to the bourgeoisie. . . . The concept of a supra-national occidental community lost its meaning with the decline of those social groups which had upheld it." [16] Bourgeoisie and proletariat alike have conspired to make of the modern nation-state one of the most perfect social machines in history, and certainly the most prosperous, but the unity of Western civilization as a whole has been irremediably shattered. With the expansion first of Western rule and now of Western ideas and technics to the entire planet, every other civilization has similarly been pulverized. This is the central fact of our epoch.

As the major trend in political philosophy has been toward the idolization of the national state and away from cosmopolitanism through most of modern history, so in other departments of Western thought. We have systematically, step by step, dismantled the medieval synthesis. Religion, science, and philosophy have each gone their separate ways, and each has broken up into dozens of sovereign sects, creeds, schools, and disciplines. This fragmentation has sometimes yielded rich harvests; modern Western civilization even in breakdown is amazingly fertile in many areas. But our achievements are as fragmentary as we ourselves are. Each national organism produces its own distinct and largely self-sufficient national culture, and each isolated discipline and sect produces its own microcosm of truth and beauty, often comically oblivious of all the others.

After a survey of classical and medieval cosmopolitanism, it may be anticlimactical to study the prophets of world order between 1600 and the end of the nineteenth century. But the search for a universal society has continued all through modern times, even if relatively few thinkers have joined in it. The smashing success of the nation-state system during the seventeenth, eighteenth, and nineteenth centuries did not intoxicate everybody. As a result, thinking people in the years of total crisis since the first World War have not had to start from scratch. An unbroken chain of cosmopolitan thought connects the contemporary movement explored in later chapters with its classical and medieval forerunners.

The first links in the chain were forged by some of the same seventeenth-century philosophers who helped dissolve the medieval synthesis. Seventeenth-century man was Janus-headed. On the one hand he looked to the past, dreamed of splendid harmony, believed in angels, and undertook pilgrimages to shrines. On the other, he tried to isolate religion and philosophy in separate leakproof compartments and constructed a strange mechanico-mathematical picture of the universe with Galilean and Newtonian physics which corresponds to nothing ever imagined in medieval science and subtly undermined the whole Christian world-view. Seventeenth-century man created several strikingly new philosophical systems, the first leaps forward in philosophy for centuries. But he also shared, more than he knew, the medieval passion for comprehensiveness and order. The result was a series of ingenious philosophies, mutually contradictory, but animated by what the French call *l'esprit de système,* a yearning for total explanation. Seventeenth-century man was effervescently confident of his ability to swallow and digest everything. He set out to integrate all knowledge, discover the whole clear and distinct truth about the mechanics of nature, construct infallible sciences of politics and behavior, heal the wounds of the Reformation, and find some way of ending or at least drastically humanizing war. By the end of the century, he had been successful enough in some of these things, and also in amassing wealth and power in such impressive national states as Stuart England and Bourbon France, to inspire people like Fontenelle to proclaim a doctrine of inevitable progress, for the first time in Western intellectual history.

The names are all familiar. At the beginning of the century, Francis Bacon in his *Dignity and Advancement of Learning* had heroically attempted a census of all the branches of scholarship and literature, to integrate all knowledge and unify human intellectual enterprise. Knowledge was power, he said, and with power man could shape the universe to his will. The Moravian educator Comenius saw even more deeply into the problem. He called his system "Pansophy," and claimed for it the power to reunite religion and philosophy, and thereby to integrate humanity itself. For the pansophist, since all created things were logically related, they could all be accomodated in a common system of knowledge. To quote his countryman Eduard Beneš, Comenius believed that it was necessary "to unify all human knowledge and science into one harmonious system which will ultimately lead to a general harmony on the human plane, and to collaboration between nations." [17] And more than collaboration. "We are all fellow-citizens of one world," he wrote, "all of one blood, all of us human beings. Who shall prevent us from uniting in one republic?" Given only spiritual and intellectual harmony, men could become "as it were one race, one people, one household, one School of God . . . one all-inclusive world-society by reason of common knowledge, common law, and common religion." [18]

In Holland, that most heterodox of men, a pariah among Jews and Christians alike, Benedict Spinoza, proposed a system of frightening simplicity. With Hindu philosophy, he insisted on the absolute unity of all being, and called every sensed object an aspect of God. But under the spell of seventeenth-century physics, he ended by seeing the God-world as a vast, purposeless machine, shuttling back and forth according to mathematically inexorable laws, never changing, and never changed. Spinoza had a keen sense of cosmic order, but his cosmos, with its ingenuous dependence on mathematical physics, lacked life. Still, here is a striking illustration of seventeenth-century man's hunger for unity, though on the metaphysical, rather than the sociological, plane. Had Spinoza's system won general acceptance, needless to say, it would have done much in its peculiar way toward restoring in Western man a consciousness of his integral unity with the cosmos.

But the drift of Western thought was all the other way as the century wore on. Theology and philosophy parted company permanently under the decisive influence of Descartes. Physical science seemed more and more to imply that the world was simply composed of discrete chunks of matter in motion, as precise as clockwork; and the British empiricists, from Locke to Hume, tried with some success in professional circles to reduce all human knowledge to the brain's interpretation of collisions between those same chunks of matter and the five senses, which would have the effect of making all attempts at a total explanation of the nature of things merely foolish. Though a man of the seventeenth century, Locke himself set a good example for empiricists by not indulging in metaphysical speculation at all.

In the later part of the seventeenth century, the search for harmony and synthesis continued, as best it could, mainly on the Continent, and there above all in the person of Gottfried Wilhelm Leibniz. In the words of an American philosopher, Leibniz "approached philosophy as a diplomatist might be expected to, seeking for each specific crisis a formula on which divergent parties might agree." [19] His metaphysical system rescued the cosmos from being a mere piece of machinery and gave it a semblance of organic unity by postulating that reality was composed entirely of "monads," incorporeal atoms, each a living soul, expressing itself through self-willed action and interacting with other monads through the agency of physical stuff, its un-self-willed material aspect. Each monad had its place in a great quasi-Aristotelian chain of being ascending by degrees to the ultimate soul, God Himself. "The universe is one vast choir . . . a concord more perfect than that music of the spheres dreamed of by Plato." [20] Leibniz was also a gifted mathematician, the discoverer of infinitesimal calculus; the founder of scientific academies which he hoped would integrate all knowledge; but what he wanted perhaps most to do, he could not. He could not translate his vision of cosmic harmony into terrestrial terms by reassembling the broken body of Western Christendom. This was his grandest project. An unattached Protestant, he tried his best for years to negotiate some sort of reunion of the Church of Rome and the various Protestant denominations. His lengthy correspondence with Bishop Bossuet, the most towering contemporary figure in the Catholic world, reveals how close he came. But Bossuet would not concede that the Mother Church was fallible, any more than Leibniz could concede that she was infallible, and there was no reunion, not even of these two doughty champions from the contending camps.

Leibniz died, a wasted man, in 1716, a year after Louis XIV, two years after the accession of the House of Hanover in Great Britain, and three years after the end of the War of the Spanish Succession, which all together round off the seventeenth century nicely and usher in the eighteenth.

The eighteenth century was a brilliant era for ruling houses and middle classes alike, at least until the revolutions of its last quarter. In intellectual life, love of science, optimism, tolerance, and reasoned skepticism were the prevailing attitudes. In some respects the eighteenth-century "Enlightenment," as it called itself, did restore a sense of unity to European thought and culture. "Enlightened" churchmen and laymen were remarkably free from "prejudice," and the doctrine of a natural religion revealed to men of reason everywhere through natural laws, on the analogy of physics, echoed for a time from pulpits, salons, and coffee houses. Schemes for a global or at least European league of nations became fashionable. Following hard on the seventeenth-century plans for a European confederation drafted by people as unlike as the French monk Crucé, the duc de Sully, and William Penn, came the immensely celebrated scheme of the abbé de Saint-Pierre, his "Project to Render Peace Perpetual in Europe," well publicized by Rousseau later in the century, and worked into a luminous philosophical framework still later by Kant. Like most such plans before and since, Saint-Pierre's called for a renunciation of war as an instrument of national policy, while at the same time guaranteeing the territorial status quo and the utter sovereignty of all member states. In the event of unprovoked aggression, the members would pool their armed forces to bring the offender to his knees, if he refused to accept the verdict of an international "Senate of Peace." In form and spirit the good abbé's project was fully realized in the League of Nations fathered

at Versailles in 1919, and lives on in the United Nations today. Like those worthy institutions, it belongs to the era of
the now tragically obsolete sovereign nation-state. But eighteenth-century Europe had not even a League of Nations, and
had to be satisfied with a still more paradoxical perversity,
the rapidly growing body of international "law."

But the typical eighteenth-century *philosophe* did love
humanity better than his *patrie,* most of the time, and in its
way the Enlightenment must be counted among the happier
periods in modern history. Only a well-mannered boy in
the eighteenth century, nationalism grew in the nineteenth
century to the proportions of a titan. The Industrial Revolution led to a rapid redistribution of wealth and a bitter class
war not fully settled even now. Christianity by and large lost
its struggle with secular science and philosophy, almost dis-
appearing as a vital spiritual force capable of unifying the
intellectual class. Atheism and agnosticism became, and remain now, the most fashionable points of view among thinking people.

Matthew Arnold accused his century of preferring anarchy
to culture, and in this he was generally right. The nineteenth century produced more prophets of world integration
than any other in history, but more than ever they were
voices in the wilderness, scattered and impotent, almost in-
audible above the din of a thousand competing ideologies,
religious cults, and schools of academic philosophy. It would
be misleading to give them much space here. In all the riot-
ous sprawling vitality of nineteenth-century letters, they seldom cut much of a figure.

There was Karl Christian Friedrich Krause, for example,
a latter-day Leibniz, who prophesied in 1811 a world federation with its center, incredibly, in Polynesia. He looked on
mankind as a biologically organismic entity and looked forward to the day when "men will not only become conscious
of their unity in God and in humanity, but . . . will practi-

cally and outwardly realize it in every sphere of life. . . .
Science and art, religion and morals, law and policy, will all
become, when they have reached their maturity, cosmopolitan, and will all contribute to bind together, to unify, our
earthly race into a city and kingdom of God." [21] But his more
influential rival Hegel proposed a similarly elaborate world-
scheme in which the national state, and particularly the
Prussian state, was the culminating point in evolution. At
the end of the century Germans could catch rare passionate
glimpses of a cosmopolis of supermen in the later prophetic
writings of Nietzsche, but other aspects of his thought won
much wider interest.

In France, after Napoleon's short-lived restoration of the
old Roman empire, the most articulate cosmopolitans were
Henri de Saint-Simon and his disciple Auguste Comte. Saint-
Simon offered a plan for world peace with a somewhat
stronger federal government than such plans usually involved.
Almost completely forgotten is Comte's still more ambitious
project for a "Western Republic" to unite Europe and
America and eventually serve as the nucleus for a planetary
society. It would have its own religion, the richly synthetic
"religion of Humanity" invented by Comte himself. Humanity, said Comte, was at its highest level of existence a Great
Being, much like Krause's racial organism, evolving through
space and time to world mastery. As "Positivism," Comte's
philosophy won many adherents in France and England during the second half of the nineteenth century, although for
most of them his high opinion of the unlimited powers of
science carried more weight than his philosophy of world
integration.

The majority of nineteenth-century thinkers sought and
found other foci of integration than the cosmic and human
world order. For socialists, it was the concept of the "working class," wrought into a crucified God by intellectuals ap-
palled by the seemingly flagrant social injustice of the earlier

stages of the Industrial Revolution. For the nationalists,
from Mazzini to Barrès, it was the sacred soil of the "mother-
land." For the racists, who must take responsibility for that
very nineteenth-century monster, Adolf Hitler, it was the
mystical doctrine of "pure blood." For the liberals, it was
"freedom," and later "democracy," although old-fashioned
liberals tended to love the former and fight the latter tooth
and nail. Many of these nineteenth-century ideologists were
at least lukewarmly "internationalists," too, but just as many
more despised internationalism, and of the older and purer
tradition of cosmopolitanism, they would have no part.

Toward the close of the century, the most articulate cosmopolitans lived outside the pale of Western civilization,
although they could not help but feel its influence. In Russia,
for example, many Orthodox thinkers, still sensing themselves members of the ancient body of medieval Christendom,
challenged Holy Russia to accept her messianic destiny
to restore the unity of Christendom. This "Russian Idea"
was a weird farrago of reaction, revolution, and national
hubris, but it inspired many honest, sensitive thinkers. The
same cultural renaissance that gave the world Tolstoy and
Tchaikovsky also produced Pyotr Chaadayev, dreaming of a
Christian world civilization unifying the creeds and insights
of the Latin West and the Greek East; Nikolai Fedorov, the
saintly scholar and librarian of the Rumiantsev Museum in
Moscow, prophesying the establishment of a kingdom of love
on earth, a universal fraternal state combining the spiritual
power of Christ and the technical power of Western science;
and the great mystic Vladimir Soloviev, preaching a single
organic church and the pan-unity of all knowledge and being.
For most of the Russian prophets, Russia herself was somehow appointed by destiny to lead the way to the new world
order.

But the most radical vision of cosmopolis in the late nineteenth century welled out of the oldest cosmopolitan tradi-

tion of all: the Confucian. The last major Confucian scholar
in the history of Chinese philsophy, K'ang Yu-wei, sketched
a book in the 1880's which he finished in 1902 under the final
title of *Ta T'ung Shu,* "The One-World Book," only recently translated into English by Laurence G. Thompson.
Embroidering liberally on the Confucian tradition, K'ang
overcame millennia of Sinocentrism to advance a doctrine
of global synthesis through a single unitary state. Such a
world would be able once and for all to abolish the "Nine
Barriers" to human unity. National states, class and racial
differences, family ties, regional mores, religions, and all distinctions based on sex and vocation would be ruthlessly eliminated. All men would be equal, all property held in common, all citizens cared for by the twenty ministries of the
omnicompetent world bureaucracy. The simplest rudiments
of privacy would vanish utterly. "The progress of mankind,"
he wrote, "towards complete Peace-and-Equality throughout
the world is like the rushing of water through a gully: nothing can check it." [22] He had a considerable following and influence round the turn of the century, before China followed
the modern Western path to nationalism under Sun Yat-sen.
In its total annihilation of all cultural diversity and individual freedom, K'ang's vision of world order may seem night-
marish in Western liberal eyes, but much of the Chinese way
of life since 1950 under communist rule bears it a startling,
even a disquieting, resemblance.

Crisis and Renewal:
The Twentieth Century

FOR THE most part nineteenth-century prophets of human unity were dreamers: saints and sages who preached to a largely indifferent and self-satisfied world. The twentieth-century prophets who follow them minister to an age stunned by crisis and torn with anxiety. In this new historical climate cosmopolitanism takes on new meaning. Before picking up the thread of our narrative, it is vitally important to fix firmly in mind the scope and gravity of the twentieth-century world crisis. In spite of the staying power of the idea of a world commonwealth, the framework of values that sustained Western civilization in all its metamorphoses from classical to modern times has today cracked and shattered. The fragments lie strewn impressively all around us, waiting to be reinforced with fresh ideas and hammered into a new structure built to a new scale; but Western civilization, as historians know it, is lurching to its death. The body cannot live without the soul.

The death of a civilization, to be sure, is not like the death of a people or an idea or a religion. Many of Arnold Toynbee's cleverest critics have failed to grasp what he, and most historians, mean by a "civilization," and this simple failure leads to much unpleasantly hysterical breast-beating about the "vitality" of Western culture and the "vigor" of the Western peoples. A civilization can disintegrate and still not necessarily or immediately destroy the people in it, or even their vitality. Without delving quite yet into the intricate question of just how many civilizations have actually existed in history, or whether a certain pair of civilizations is actually only one, or whether a certain one is actually a pair, the term "civilization" can be defined as a system of ideas, ways of life, and symbols characteristic of a relatively self-contained group of peoples living in more or less continuous historical contact with one another and radiating from a single or several closely related geographical centers. Because civilizations rise and fall, collide and fuse, shift from their original centers, and even sometimes simply do nothing at all for centuries on end, historians searching for thoroughly logical, air-tight definitions of the civilizational phenomenon will never find any. But if one is to make any sense at all out of the larger patterns of history, he must resort to the concept of a "civilization," or some near equivalent.

In the case of Western civilization — and a similar analysis could be made of all the others — the last several centuries have obviously resulted in revolutionary changes. The old geographical boundaries of the West have ceased to be meaningful. No longer is the West "relatively self-contained" or Western Europe its center. Ways of life have altered almost unrecognizably, under the impact of machine technology. Some of the old symbols persist, but many new ones have been imported or invented. And most clearly of all, the world-view of the classical and Christian Western heritage has been discarded by most of the people on whose high intelligence and deep faith the inner spiritual integrity of any civilization has always seemed to depend. Perhaps the West, and the world, can now suddenly dispense with inner spiritual integrity. Perhaps civilization itself is obsolete, and humanity is ready for apotheosis. This would simplify matters immensely. But the historian cannot afford to work on these premises, nor should any other ordinary mortal.

What, more exactly, was the world-view which sustained the West until recent times? There have always been tangled threads and clashing colors in the fabric of the Western world-view. The Judeo-Christian tradition has not always harmonized with the Greco-Roman. But the pattern stands out clearly enough, to the detached observer. To summarize it, is to see at once how little of it survives intact in our century.

We once believed in a transcendental supreme being, addressed in its personal aspect as God. We believed that God created the universe as a cosmos, and not as a chaos: an orderly, meaningful, purposeful system of being, regulated in at least its observable modes by a divinely ordained body of natural law. Today, says William Barrett, through revolutions in science, theology, and economic life, "the central fact of modern history in the West" is the decline of religious faith. Religion had served for centuries as a "psychic container," as "a solid psychological matrix surrounding the individual's life from birth to death. . . . In losing religion, man lost the concrete connection with a transcendent realm of being; he was set free to deal with this world in all its brute objectivity. But he was bound to feel homeless in such a world, which no longer answered the needs of his spirit." And modern natural science, preoccupied with the problem of the mechanical and mathematical aspects of the cosmos, "stripped nature of its human forms and presented man with a universe that was neutral, alien, in its vastness and force, to his human purposes." [23] Gerhard Szczesny, in his new book *The Future of Unbelief,* says bluntly what has needed saying for some time, that not even the recent flurry of reverent interest in Christianity awakened by modern man's sense of his inadequacy, has "altered the fact that the real content of the Christian doctrine of salvation, for a dominent type of modern man, has become completely unacceptable." [24]

We also believed that mankind was an integral part of the

cosmos, and through the gift of reason had an open channel of communication with God and ready access to knowledge about the true nature of things and the true laws of nature. We believed that man, under divine and natural law, was obliged to love his fellow man, and deal justly and honestly with him, and we shared a reasonably articulate body of ideas about what constituted justice and honesty. Today, under the devastating impact of Hume, Kant, Kierkegaard, Nietzsche, Mach, Russell, Wittgenstein, and Heidegger — to name just a few of the men of the last two hundred years who have brought philosophy to its contemporary impasse — we no longer believe there is any necessary correspondence between the world-as-it-is and the world-as-we-see-it. The analytical philosophy now ascendant in the Anglo-Saxon world has carried the empiricism of Locke and Berkeley to its perhaps final, irreducible conclusions. Man, say the twentieth-century empiricists, experiences something of the world, but he knows it only partially in a limited and fallible way. Final truth, as such, is inaccessible. "All human knowledge," writes Bertrand Russell, "is uncertain, inexact and partial." Nothing is sure, except that nothing is sure. "To this doctrine we have not found any limitation whatever." [25] Because even most of the traditional philosophical questions, from the ultimate nature of being to the problem of good and evil, turn out to be "non-cognitive" and therefore "meaningless" to the professional philosopher, he limits himself in the end to the modest, though important, task of learning and teaching how to think logically.

On the Continent of Europe, a more humanistic emphasis persists, but for the good existentialist, at least, there is a great gulf fixed between the subjective, valuing, acting self, and the objective world of dead, dumb material stuff. The twain meet, but the only result for the former is a nauseating realization that he is contingent upon, and will ultimately crumble into, the latter. What it all means, no man knows.

Witness Camus: "Of whom and of what indeed can I say: 'I know that!' This heart within me I can feel, and I judge that it exists. This world I can touch, and I likewise judge that it exists. There ends all my knowledge, and the rest is construction." [26] Everything, he writes, is permitted, in the sense that there is no knowable scale of values. All experiences are of the same grade, and while a man may be held "responsible" for what he does, he cannot be "guilty" of doing it. If nearly every serious student of modern thought would agree with Paul Tillich that "twentieth-century man has lost a meaningful world and a self which lives in meanings out of a spiritual center," [27] nearly every twentieth-century European writer of any stature, from Kafka to Camus, has proved it in his life and work.

We also believed that man had inherent dignity as a rational being, and freedom enough either to obey or to defy cosmic law — in the special Christian terms, to do God's will or to sin. Today, biology has located man among the higher apes; Pavlovian psychology has reduced him to a machine, and Freudian psychoanalysis to a jungle of instincts and irrational inhibitions in which the conscious reasoning ego only barely survives.

Finally, we believed that society and government were right and proper, serving divine ends, and obligated to follow the dictates of natural law. We believed that institutions should be so established that men in every part of our civilization could live together in harmony, in a unified world order. But Western liberalism since Jeremy Bentham has largely repudiated the whole concept of natural law, to insist that governments are simply conveniences for mutual security and pleasure; and for the integral nationalist, la patrie is above all laws. The pursuit of individual comfort, group benefits, and national advantage has absorbed nearly all our political energies and idealism for many generations, leaving little for the wider tasks of civilization-building.

These were the ideas and values which men, all through the formative stages of Western civilization, accepted almost as readily as they accepted the basic facts of life and death. Some still find champions, but the majority of the intellectual leaders of the West can no longer live with the classical-Christian world-view handed down from the Middle Ages. Even if they believe with their mouths, they doubt and deny in their hearts. And meanwhile, whether directly related to this spiritual crisis or not, every civilization has been caught up in a maelstrom of revolution at the socioeconomic and political level which threatens to terminate the whole human adventure.

It is in this context of civilizational breakdown and world crisis that the prophets of world order in our own century must be studied. They are not a mighty host. Nor have they developed any miraculous immunity to the spiritual sickness of the century. They are not innocents, unscarred and unafraid. But at the same time they do not automatically assume that every element of the great traditional value-systems of East and West need be scrapped in favor of a cheerless agnosticism. They are willing to occupy the difficult middle ground between faith and knowledge, between the conservative impulse and rebellion. And if, as they think possible, the emergence of an organic world civilization turns out to be the next stage in human evolution, their work is the most promising sign of renewal in our time. If they are wrong, even that greatest conceivable blessing in the wildest dreams of Cold War news analysts, a permanent thaw in Soviet-American relations, might decelerate only a little the *dégringolade* of civilization.

For a history of thinking on world order, the twentieth century falls into two sharply contrasting periods, thirty lean years and thirty fat. Down to the onset of the Great Depression, the intellectual leaders of Europe and America were mainly engaged in trying to demolish what survived of the Western tradition sketched above. They drafted all their battle plans and had all their chief tools and weapons of war in mass production. Much of this was both inevitable and salutary. It would not be possible to imagine events taking any other course. Everything since at least the seventeenth century points in this direction. In fact, apart from those few splendidly genteel scholar-statesmen who gave Europe her Hague Court and her League of Nations, institutions which the Great Powers skillfully used to beguile and hamstring a whole generation of well-meaning internationalists, the only outstanding prophet of world order in the first third of the century was the now almost forgotten English journalist and jack-of-all-literary-trades, H. G. Wells.

Wells is chiefly interesting as a transitional figure *par excellence* between the main currents of late nineteenth-century thought and the astonishing upsurge of cosmopolitan prophecy in the last thirty years. His direct influence on most of the prophets whose ideas will be discussed in the next three chapters is probably negligible. There was never full *rapport*, in any case, between his generation and the young men of 1914. But he deserves at least brief attention even today because, much more than any other single thinker, he created the frame of public mind which has helped make possible a hospitable reception to the ideas of the current crop of protagonists of world integration.[28]

During the first twenty years of the century Wells was one of the two or three best known British novelists and political writers in the Western world. But all his life he presents the rare picture of a man whose roots lie firmly embedded in one epoch, and yet who manages to go on working creatively long into another. Before the first World War, he wrote dozens of scientific romances, sociological novels, and socialist tracts illuminating the breakdown of the Victorian *ancien régime* and preaching a gospel of science, progress, and socialism

which found a ready audience among young people in Britain and abroad. He rejoiced in the steady advance of technology, and gratefully held it responsible for the decay of the
old order, although in books like *The Time Machine,*
1895, he dissociated himself from Herbert Spencer's doctrine
of inevitable progress. Technology could be misused.

But unlike nearly all his contemporaries, Wells even before
1914 included in his indictment of the old European order
the nation-state system. Science and technology had ren-
dered it just as obsolete as hereditary monarchies and uncontrolled laisser-faire capitalism. As early as 1902 in a series
of *Anticipations* he predicted a colossal world war among the
nations which, he hoped, would end in the seizure of real
power throughout the world by a new breed of men conscious of the fatal futility of nationalism and tough-mindedly
prepared to reorganize the world in a "larger synthesis."
These men would come from many walks of life, but mainly
from the technically trained middle classes — engineers, scientists, and doctors. Their expertise would make them indispensable to the warring governments, and step by step they
would exploit this advantage and take the reins of power into
their own hands. Wells followed with a detailed account of
the world state in being in his novel *A Modern Utopia,* published in 1905.

After the first World War, which moved him profoundly,
Wells burned his literary boats and set out on a messianic
campaign to preach what he now called an "Open Conspiracy" to by-pass existing governments and establish a socialist
world state. He sometimes proposed, as in his scientific
romance, *The Shape of Things to Come,* that it might take
another even more catastrophic world war to jolt mankind
into an acceptance of the need for world government. But,
meanwhile, in a long string of encyclopedic "outlines" of
knowledge,[29] mostly mediocre novels, and hastily assembled
prophetic books, he continued to plead the case for a world
state and a conspiratorial movement to achieve it. Except

for a few youthful British admirers who quarreled among themselves, no conspirators ever materialized.

The second World War and the postwar settlement broke Wells' spirit; after damning humanity to extinction in a queer jeremiad entitled *Mind at the End of Its Tether,* he died in 1946. The world society of his prophecies would have been in some ways as authoritarian and communistic as the *ta t'ung* of K'ang Yu-wei. Like K'ang's cosmopolis, it was a kind of leviathan, although its government consisted more of psychologists, educators, industrial managers, and scientists than of mandarins. With a Victorian radical's exaggerated idea of the intellectual potentialities of the natural and social sciences, and a Victorian radical's basic contempt for religious tradition and non-Western civilizations, Wells constructed his vision of world order out of a fairly narrow range of values. But no one else of his stature was producing visions of world order at all during the first third of the century.

Then, since the mid-thirties, a generation of thinkers whose minds were formed entirely in the twentieth century has written a fresh and vitally significant chapter in the history of cosmopolitan prophecy. The tradition Wells kept barely alive in the early decades of the century is once more a powerful force in modern thought. It has by no means drowned out the clamor of nihilist despair or achieved anything like ascendancy in the contemporary intellectual class. But in view of the stupendous obstacles which loom in the way of any movement proposing to salvage organically meaningful values from the past and project the vision of a still more organic future, the existence of a party of devout cosmopolitans in mid-century is almost a miracle. It may be useful to point out briefly the great landmarks in this latter-day cosmopolitanism, to see the movement in its over-all dimensions, before plunging into closer analysis in later chapters.

Most typically, recent prophetic books have taken the

form of broad historical surveys, explaining the patterns of
the past and out of a study of evolutionary or civilizational
trends urging and sometimes even predicting the integration
of mankind in a stable planetary society. Wells himself had
set a strangely successful example in 1919-20 with *The Outline of History,* which rounded off a thousand pages of narrative with the vision of a unified mankind reaching out for
the stars. In 1934 his countryman Arnold Joseph Toynbee,
much impressed by *The Outline of History*[30] and even more
by Spengler's oracular *Decline of the West,* issued the first
volumes of his *Study of History.* Toynbee's professional colleagues have by and large found him indigestible, if not positively a pious fraud, but as a prophetic book, *A Study of
History,* now complete in twelve large volumes, is the most
widely read plea for a world civilization written in this
century, no matter what its success or failure in fathoming
the pattern of the past.

In 1937-41 came Pitirim A. Sorokin's massive *Social and
Cultural Dynamics,* followed closely by a long series of less
technical prophetic books, attacking the problem of civilizational crisis and renewal from the sociologist's point of
view. More recently, several professional philosophers have
taken up the task of producing broad, interpretative studies
of history which are also propaganda, in a sense, for world
integration, from the German existentialist Karl Jaspers to
the American Christian idealist William Ernest Hocking.
Another major American writer, Lewis Mumford, who prefers to call himself a "generalist" rather than a "specialist,"
has contributed several books to the literature of world
history and world crisis since the early Forties, each climaxing
in a vision of cosmopolis as rational and eloquent as anything published in this century. Mumford's German counterpart is Erich Kahler, another outspoken "generalist," best
known in the English-speaking world for his study of history conceived as a "biography of humanity," *Man the Meas-*

ure. Great professional biologists have made use of the still broader perspectives of the history of life to argue for world integration as the next stage in human evolution: in France, the late Pierre Teilhard de Chardin; in Britain, Sir Julian Huxley. And clearly, the deep sense of historical mission which permeates such world movements as Roman Catholicism, the Bahai Faith, and international communism, each in its way a project for world integration, immensely strengthens their appeal to the spiritually starved infidel.

But the idea of a world civilization reaches contemporary minds in many other forms. The historical approach lends itself best of all to the canvassing of large trends and the study of civilization as a whole. More specialized work has been done, for example, on the problem of world philosophical synthesis. Since 1939 a group of Asian and Western philosophers has convened at the University of Hawaii every ten years to undertake the rugged job of harmonizing Eastern and Western approaches to philosophy. In *The Meeting of East and West* and several other recent books, F. S. C. Northrop of Yale University, a leading participant in the Honolulu meetings, has proposed ways and means of bringing into dynamic integration the various methods of truthseeking in which different cultures have specialized, often to the exclusion of every other, throughout history: ideological synthesis, he argues, is the necessary precondition for any true world order. Following Comenius, such thinkers as the British scientist Lancelot Law Whyte and Oliver L. Reiser of the University of Pittsburgh have stressed the vital importance to world order of the systematic integration of knowledge, the creation, in short, of what Wells used to call a "world brain," on the premise that human beings cannot unite on the cultural and political level unless they share a dynamically unified picture of the world as modern science knows it. This in turn presupposes, so the argument runs, an *a priori* conviction of the metaphysical unity of being.

Others have emphasized the need for a harmonization or synthesis of the great world religions, insisting that man is foremost a religious animal, and that no world civilization is possible without a world community of spirit. Toynbee and Hocking have each contributed a good deal in this department; also, among others, Carl Gustav Jung, Sir Sarvepalli Radhakrishnan, Gerald Heard, Erich Fromm, and Charles Morris. Here the sharpest division not unnaturally comes between those who envisage only a gradual growing together of the existing positive religions and the more radical humanists who reject all the positive religions in favor of a new world faith of life-affirmation. But the area of agreement among twentieth-century cosmopolitan thinkers on the possible metaphysical and ethical content of any world faith or related system of faiths is surprisingly large. When twentieth-century people with open minds allow constructive impulses to gain the ascendancy over fear, doubt, and despair, they apparently *can agree* on cogent definitions of good and evil, law and freedom, and the collective goals of civilization.

Still another school of thought takes the strictly economic and political approach to human unity. Followed to the exclusion of every other point of view, this might be a dangerously naïve approach; but few contemporary prophets of world order would deny that, at some stage in the evolution of a world society, far more political unity must be achieved than now exists, to consolidate by law the progress registered in other areas and prevent total war. The movement for a world government which thrived so well in the five plastic years between Hiroshima and Korea has slowly declined since then, but it produced a large literature of constructive thought, and it revealed the mass support still potentially available for another deeper and better organized thrust in the future. On another level, the concrete progress toward West European, Arab, black African, and Latin American unity since World War II illustrates tendencies working against the nation-state system which may one day over-whelm it entirely, and prepare the ground for wider syn-theses.

But the exponents of a world government, both those who want one established now by direct political action, and those who believe it can be reached only indirectly, differ in many crucial details on the amount of universal govern-ment the world needs. That the world state will not be a loose confederation of autonomous villages, most would agree; and only a handful favor a highly centralized state even remotely like K'ang Yu-wei's *ta t'ung*. But the golden mean between the two extremes is hard to arrive at. Nearly all the prophets who have fitted their vision of cosmopolis into a broad historical framework have had something to say about the form of the world polity, as compared with earlier attempts at a universal state in history. All the same, if there is to be a world state, it will most likely take whatever shape is possible and desirable under the exigencies of the moment. Detailed proposals for a world constitution are perhaps use-ful only as a form of propaganda.

In Chapter Two below, the twentieth-century prophets of world integration are studied first of all in their role as historians, tracing the outline of the past, diagnosing the pres-ent world crisis, and foreseeing a world civilization. The next two chapters will examine more specialized aspects of civilization-building, as seen by contemporary thinkers: the intimately related problems of intellectual, spiritual, eco-nomic, and political integration. In Chapter Five we shall be in a position, hopefully, to assess the limits and uses of cosmopolitan prophecy in the twentieth century, and indulge in some prophesying of our own.

For in the last analysis, man has only his future. Even the purposes to which he will put his past, are part of his future. On the sands of time not one footprint can be erased, but the future is open country. Within the unknow-able final limits of human nature, we shall go where we please, as far as we choose to see. The ultimate function of prophecy is not to tell the future, but to make it. If our present generation of prophets succeed in their work, they will be doing for the world civilization what Moses did for the children of Israel, Confucius for the Middle Flowery Kingdom, Jesus of Nazareth for the *corpus Christianum,* and Mohammed for the House of Islam.

Two

History as Prophecy

The Vogue of Clio

ARNOLD TOYNBEE credits "all civilizations so far known" with the ambition, conscious or unconscious, of establishing a world order "in which the whole of mankind will be able to live together in harmony, as members of a single all-inclusive family." [1] None has wholly succeeded, but each has tried. Chapter One explored this vision over a span of twenty-five centuries from the point of view of the history of ideas. The next job at hand is to study it from the point of view of twentieth-century ideas of history. Most recent prophets of world integration, including Toynbee himself, insist on fitting their vision of world order into a massive historical and sometimes even biological framework, in which cosmopolis becomes the next stage or the chiliastic fulfillment of history. The coming world civilization is not construed as a sort of benign catastrophe erupting out of nowhere, imposed on man by a senseless flurry of events. It becomes part of a larger pattern of meaning. It achieves for a few perhaps — and this would be dangerous — an aura of inevitability. But taken all together, these prophetic studies of history offer the best possible introduction to recent thinking on the problem of world order.

The use of history to sustain and organize a vision of world integration is only one spectacular example of Western man's obsession, since the early nineteenth century, with the art

and science of history. Applying his critical faculties, tough-
ened by the methods of modern natural science, to the complex problems of what happened and why, on every continent
as far back as the records reach, he has managed to heap up
incredible masses of data. Collectively we know ten or
twenty times as much about the total human past as any
single civilization knew just a century ago.

Clio even threatens to usurp the functions of Athene. The
philosophy of absolute idealism propagated by Hegel and
his numberless disciples in every country throughout the
nineteenth century was, fundamentally, a theory of history,
professing to trace the unfolding of the "World Spirit"
through historical time. Borrowing Hegel's enthusiasm for
history, but not his metaphysics, Karl Marx did much the
same thing for man conceived strictly as an economic animal.
Many of the philosophical systems inspired by the biological
theory of evolution, from Spencer to Bergson, have been, in
effect, philosophies of history. A conspicuous recent American example of history-mindedness is the career of Will
Durant, who began his adult life as a philosopher and pop-
ularizer of philosophy, and has now spent his last thirty years
writing a colossal *Story of Civilization* in many volumes,
pleading that one can "learn more of the nature of man by
watching his behavior through sixty centuries than by reading Plato and Aristotle, Spinoza and Kant." All philosophy,
he adds, quoting Nietzsche, "has now fallen forfeit to history." [2] Nor is anyone likely to forget Mussolini's epigram
that "outside history, man is nothing."

The Italian humanist Mario Rossi goes so far as to argue
that our historicism, our philosophies founded on the conviction that history is the ultimate reality, may be destroying
Western civilization. "By making even truth and falsehood,
right and wrong, good and evil, relative to the passing moods
of man in a certain moment of history, historicism under-
mines faith, love of truth, honesty. It fosters the moral
decay of mankind." [3] This is surely an exaggeration. "His-

toricism," far from being a cynical philosophy of flux and
negation, as Rossi implies, is only another form of modern man's desperate search for meaning in the world. It
has contributed to, and also grown out of, the collapse of
the traditional value-systems in Western civilization. In its
most doctrinaire dress, it seeks to supply a potent substitute
for the older traditions. It has given the Marxist a timetable
for revolution and conquest. It has breathed life into all
the varieties of fascism, by finding in the history of a nation
or race the true meaning of existence. It has given the
idealist philosopher a new way to approach reality, wholly
different from anything attempted before. And in the specific context of the last quarter century, although historicism in any form is now anathema among most professional
philosophers, a less dogmatic variety of historicism has
strongly attracted many prophets of a world civilization.

One point must be made at the outset. Most of the prophets studied here have not been so fatally fascinated by history
that they would qualify as historicists in the way Rossi defines the term. They do not believe that history is the sole
ultimate reality. They look on life historically, because
time is the fluid medium in which man has his being and the
past is often a useful guide to the future; but most of them
emphatically do not reject other approaches to reality. They
are not blasé historical relativists. Nor are they for the most
part dogmatic about their findings, after the poor example
of Hegel. All the same, it cannot be a crime against civilization to suggest — to prove would be impossible — that the
history of life on earth adds up to more than a mere sequence
of events. Far from threatening the values of civilization,
historicism in the looser sense of a determination to find
meaning in history only resurrects in a new guise one of the
most spiritually valuable elements in the Western world-
view. Its appeal to twentieth-century prophets of world order is eminently sane.

The Biological Key

THE MOST ambitious view of history begins not with the first written records but with the emergence of life on earth. Paleontology establishes beyond any reasonable question the unbroken continuity of life for hundreds of millions of years, and the common ancestry of all living creatures, including man. Biological historicism, to coin a phrase, has taken the form in recent decades of the idea that a world civilization is the purpose — or the next purpose — not just of history, but of the whole evolutionary process, which includes history. World order in this perspective becomes a requirement of nature, and a part of her design for life. As human history is the climax, until now, of all evolutionary advance, so the unification of man will be the climax of history and through history, of life.

Although attempts to find a purpose in evolution are as old as the theory of evolution itself, professional biologists since the triumph of Darwinism have tended to prefer, with T. H. Huxley, to find an impassable gulf between human ethics and the laws of evolution, or simply to dismiss the whole problem of purpose as outside their competence. But recently there has been a trend in the other direction. While philosophers increasingly shy away from the possible implications of biology for their discipline, biologists are turning to philosophy. Scientists as eminent as Pierre Teilhard de Chardin and Pierre Lecomte du Noüy in France, Sir Julian Huxley and C. H. Waddington in Britain, and E. W. Sinnott in the United States have each produced major books in the past twenty years which come unambiguously to grips with the meaning of evolution for human ethics and goals.[4] Their findings tend to be positive. They discover in the patterns of evolution a purposeful trend toward complexity of organization, individuation, intelligence, and spirituality; and from these trends they derive criteria for distinguishing between present good and evil, and goals for future progress. None of these systems would hold up for a minute if it were not taken on faith that men *should* somehow derive their values from the directional flow of evolution. The non-biologist is not likely to assume this so readily as the biologically trained observer, especially if he remembers that only three quarters of a century ago, most systems of biological ethics described incessant murderous competition to survive at no matter whose expense as the chief "law of evolution." But it is just as sound a hypothesis to suppose evolution purposeful as to suppose it otherwise, in the absence of any possible final proof one way or the other; and many of those who nowadays assume it to be purposeful are offering a world-view much more likely to lead to man's survival than — for example — the atheistic existentialists, who dogmatically divorce man from nature and find no guidance at all outside the forlorn freedom of selfhood.

Of all the biologists looking for a key to the significance of life in their science, the two best known today are also the two who have done most to keep alive the idea of world order: Sir Julian Huxley and the late Pierre Teilhard de Chardin. Sir Julian, a grandson of T. H. Huxley and the brother of Aldous, is a dedicated exponent of atheistic humanism, a biologist of world distinction, and the author of several important books on evolution and evolutionary ethics. Father Teilhard was simultaneously a Jesuit and a paleontologist, whose major works, and especially *The Phenomenon of Man,* could not be published until after his death in 1955, because of the attitude of his Order. The two became good friends in later years; their science brought them to a meeting of minds rare among men whose religious commitments differ so crucially.

Huxley grew up in his grandfather's shadow. His critics might argue that he never got out from under it. Like his old friend and colleague H. G. Wells, his roots are struck deeply in the mental world of the late nineteenth century. As a young man one of the decisive moments in his spiritual development occurred, he says, when he read in an essay by that eminent Victorian, Lord Morley, that "the next great task of science will be to create a religion for humanity." [5] This is a typical Victorian notion, thoroughly unfashionable today, but Huxley has spent much of his career trying to revive it and give it new meaning.

Taking the broadest possible view of reality, he divides the evolutionary process into three great stages or sectors: the inorganic, in which progress is confined largely to the building up of more complex molecular structures; the organic, or biological, in which, in addition to increasing complexity of organization, cumulative progress takes place in mastery and awareness of the environment; and finally the psychosocial, or human, sector. Each sector has its own methods. In the biological sector, the method is natural selection of genetic variations; but in the human sector, natural selection has been replaced as the main technique of progress by social organization, especially the transmission of cultural achievement through education.

Although the entire evolutionary process is strictly continuous, the steady onward-moving translation of the same "world-stuff" to higher and higher levels of achievement, its human sector is unique. Most important of all, man stands alone, as the only surviving agent of evolutionary advance in this era. "During evolutionary time the avenues of possible progress have become progressively restricted, until today only one remains open." Man, as it were, has "been suddenly appointed managing director of the biggest business of all, the business of evolution." [6] The plants, the invertebrates, the lower vertebrates, and even the mammals are no longer capable, so far as we know, of any major evolutionary breakthroughs. They have all ended in biological blind alleys that bar further significant change. Man alone goes on evolving, and at a rapidly increasing rate of speed. His capacity for rational thought, artistic and spiritual experience, and psychosocial control over his destiny opens up endless possibilities for further advance.

The burden of serving as "the agent of the evolutionary process on this planet" would be unbearable if evolution did not supply us with standards and goals, but it does. It offers guidance, says Huxley, in three broad areas, if we simply extrapolate the main trends of evolutionary progress into the future. First, we must strive to the utmost to exploit all our possibilities, because evolutionary advance has always been basically a realization of new powers through progressive change. In the case of mankind, obviously the greatest possibilities lie in the realm of the mind, our most distinctive possession. Second, since there is a clear trend in evolution toward steadily higher degrees of individuation, or individual uniqueness, and "the developed human individual personality is . . . the highest product of the cosmic process," we must do everything possible to maximize individuality and make possible the fulfillment of individual talent. Finally, since "human individuals cannot realise their possibilities except as members of social groups," and social organization "operates by the pooling of experience and co-operative action in a cumulative tradition," it is clearly preferable "that there should be a single universal pool of experience and action, not a number of isolated or even competing and hostile ones." Through a "world orchestration of cultures" the work of evolution "can become a single joint enterprise of the human species as a whole." [7]

Getting down to immediate needs, Huxley describes the present crisis as a "world revolution" and "a race . . . between disintegration and reintegration." Out of the wars, cultural confusion, and rapid socioeconomic changes of the twentieth century must emerge a world civilization, "the creation of a single unified pool of tradition, organized politically in a single unified World Government." [8] Huxley's socialist leanings impel him to see no possibility for full development of individuality without a planned economy and a welfare state, but all government controls can be justified only if they promote the free development of human personality. Most important of all, the world civilization must give birth to a new universal religion or idea-system. Idea-systems "play the same sort of role in cultural evolution as do skeletons in biological evolution: they provide the framework for the life that animates and clothes them, and in large measure determine the way it shall be lived." [9] The need now is for a naturalistic religion, which Huxley calls "evolutionary humanism," capable of doing for the human will and spirit what science itself is doing for the human intellect. Science is universally accepted by all cultures; the same degree of universal acceptance must be won for a religion based on science.

Sir Julian had a unique opportunity to try his ideas out on the world conscience in 1946 when he became executive secretary of the Preparatory Commission for the United Nations Educational, Scientific, and Cultural Organization. In a pamphlet not sponsored by his commission, he pointed out that the proposed organization could not function unless it adopted some sort of comprehensive philosophy, based not on sectarian theologies or competing ideologies, but on the universal facts and methods of the natural sciences.

Although the "world scientific humanism" outlined in the pamphlet was a great deal less sweeping and outspoken on controversial issues than the new religion suggested in Huxley's books, it ran into implacable hostility on all sides. A Yugoslav delegate immediately challenged it as not being scientific enough, because it ignored Marxist dialectical materialism, which to any orthodox communist is the supreme science. The American representative, William Benton, noted that if Unesco adopted Huxley's platform, it would violate its pledge to respect the democratic freedom of every culture to develop along its own lines. Neither the Preparatory Commission nor Unesco committed itself to any philosophy at all, which is routine for an organization representing sovereign governments fanatically opposed to human unity; but Sir Julian did go on to serve as Unesco's first Director General. His failure is instructive, but it has not shaken his conviction that mankind will sooner or later have to find a new religion.

The more than faintly Victorian overtones of Huxley's biological historicism prevent his message from being taken seriously by many modern intellectuals, especially those outside the discipline of the natural sciences. No such handicap has hobbled the books of Teilhard de Chardin. Their publication since his death in 1955 has touched off a revival of interest in the biological approach that would have seemed incredible just ten years ago.

Some of Teilhard's great current popularity stems no doubt from his personal qualities and the sometimes pathetic facts of his life. He remained to his dying breath a good Catholic in his own eyes, but a virtual heretic in the eyes of his ecclesiastical superiors. The tensions between Catholic orthodoxy and evolutionary science could not but take their toll of his spirit. They have also tended to give his life a dramatic character of the sort that sells books. Teilhard was undoubtedly a complex man: a passionate mystic, a theist, a Jesuit, a scientist, an evolutionary humanist, and a prophet of world order. It would be a jaded century indeed that could resist him.

With Huxley, Teilhard looked on the evolutionary process as continuous but passing through three distinct stages, the evolution of matter, of life, and of man. As matter surrounded the solid core of the earth with air, water, and crust, so life surrounded it with a "biosphere" of self-reproducing creatures all intimately related to one another, and man's brain has surrounded it with a "noosphere," a living envelope of thought as different from protoplasm as protoplasm is from inanimate atoms. "Everything precious, active, and progressive originally contained in that cosmic fragment from which our world emerged, is now concentrated in and crowned by the noosphere." [10] Mankind is today the sole vehicle of evolutionary progress, and in man the world has found its soul.

All through the process of evolution, Teilhard detected two basic trends which he insisted on coupling, although they seem at first blush antithetical. On the one hand, all the stuff of the universe, from the merest submicroscopic grains of matter to the human person, demonstrates in evolution a tendency toward "complexification." Atoms form molecules, molecules form cells, cells combine to produce many-celled creatures, and so forth; and these increasingly more complex forms of organized cosmic stuff converge upon themselves to yield syntheses far greater than the sum of their component parts. At the same time, there is also a marked trend toward "individuation." Individual members of a species grow in importance in relation to their species, as it evolves, until at last, in mankind, the "phenomenon is precipitated" and "personalization" occurs, the birth of the self-conscious, self-directed person.[11]

Out of these different but persistent tendencies Teilhard deduced the next stage in human evolution, if man is to succeed in realizing his cosmic destiny. Through an ultimate complexification, he would achieve "an organic super-aggregation of souls" uniting all minds everywhere; and through an ultimate personalization, this super-being would become itself a person, a "hyper-person," an organic synthesis of persons not deprived in any sense of their personality, but fulfilled through union. For Teilhard, this was the "Omega Point," the goal of evolution since the beginning, and clearly deducible as such from trends already well established.

Looking at the world of his own time, he could see the dawn of a world civilization — if so prosaic a phrase can be used interchangeably with Teilhard's "hyper-person" — in a preliminary stage of convergence which he labeled "plane-tization." Anthropology and history, he wrote, showed a steady rise in the scale of human interaction. "Originally and for centuries there was no serious obstacle" to the diffusion of mankind "over the surface of the globe. . . . Then, from the Neolithic age onwards, these waves began . . . to recoil upon themselves. All available space being occupied, the occupiers had to pack in tighter." Through a steady rise in population levels, intermarriage, trade, and war, men did not lose touch with one another, which accelerated their progress. Then, in the last century, "in the modern parox-ysm," through the invention of rapid mechanical transporta-tion and electromagnetic wave communication, mankind has converged until it is now "an almost solid mass of homi-nised substance." Unlike every other species in evolutionary history, mankind "has succeeded, not only in becoming cosmopolitan, but in stretching a single organised mem-brane over the earth without breaking it." The moral of this planetizing revolution in human intercourse is perfectly clear, with or without the lessons of Teilhard's biology. "Something will explode," he wrote, "if we persist in trying to squeeze into our old tumble-down huts the material and spiritual forces that are henceforward on the scale of a world." [12]

But "there are no summits without abysses." Drawing as

much on Christianity as biology, Teilhard foresaw more than one possibility for mankind. If we can achieve world synthesis, "hatred and internecine struggles will have disappeared in the ever-warmer radiance of Omega." But "evil may go on growing alongside good" as in the past; the noosphere — human thought — may never attain organic unity at all, and may instead divide into hostile fragments, so that only a small portion of humanity can win through to whatever lies ultimately in store at the end of time." [13]

Nonetheless, Teilhard remained an optimist. He believed passionately in the power of love, the vital energy of the personal God whom he continued all his life to worship as the author of the whole evolutionary process and also as its final cause. "The World would not function," he wrote in 1937, "if there were not, somewhere outside time and space, a cosmic point of total synthesis." God's love draws the stuff of the universe by evolution up through dumb passivity to thinking personality and so to Himself. If the human race reaches the Omega Point, it may find itself — the implication is ever-present in Teilhard's mystic vision — in the presence of God. The hyper-person evolved in time will somehow converge with the hyper-person outside of time, God Himself. [14]

Meanwhile, the history of life is decisive on one point. "There is only one way which leads upwards; the one which, through greater organisation, leads to greater synthesis and unity." The human consciousness must expand beyond "the broadening, but still far too restricted, circles of family, country and race" to discover the unity of the world. "The Age of Nations is past. The task before us now, if we would not perish, is to shake off our ancient prejudices, and to build the Earth." [15]

Teilhard's thought is rich in suggestive metaphors and graphic neologisms. Like any system of ideas tinged with mysticism, it is also difficult to summarize or even evaluate.

But taking into account the immense distance between even the most liberal Jesuit and even the most tolerant atheist, one is tempted to see in Teilhard a world-view almost identical in substance with Sir Julian Huxley's. Teilhard had very little to say about the practical and material shape of a unified world, Huxley with his rather narrow conception of theology refuses to speculate about final causes and purposes in the universe. Yet they are virtually at one on the subject of a world civilization. Both see it as a requirement of nature and the next stage in human evolution.

The biologists are not alone in constructing evolutionary philosophies of world order in our time. A few professional philosophers have contributed systems of their own in spite of the hostility rampant in their profession to metaphysical filibustering. George Perrigo Conger, of the University of Minnesota, has an interesting book, mimeoprinted in 1949 by the University library on no fewer than 878 quarto pages, entitled *Epitomization,* which is one of the most ambitious attempts to bring all phenomena into the compass of one comprehensive scheme since Hegel. The supreme principle governing the whole universe, according to Conger, is the tendency of phenomena to form loose aggregates which then combine in higher, organic integrates, and so on, unless disintegration occurs, up the scale of evolution to steadily more complex integrates. Evolutionary progress takes place whenever integrates combine to form permanently viable higher integrates. Somewhat like Huxley and Teilhard, he divides the totality of things into three realms of being, each an epitomization of the one below it, from the "cosmogonic" realm of evolving matter through the "biotic" realm of evolving life to the "neuropsychological" realm of evolving thought. And like Huxley and Teilhard, he envisages the ultimate synthesis of humanity in a "planetary culture" integrating the civilizations of East and West.[16]

Still another example is Hugh Miller of the University of

California, in his vividly styled plea for a world civilization, *The Community of Man*. Unlike Conger, he agrees with the logical positivists that philosophy must limit itself to logic and arithmetic, surrendering to science everything connected with "empirical knowledge," the knowledge derived from experience and subject to change at any time because of fresh experience. But this does not make ethics or the need for ethics obsolete. It simply transfers them to the province of science. Specifically, it is the duty of evolutionary science, and only that science, to supply mankind with tentative goals for further evolution. Biology teaches us that existence and increase, maintained through adaptability to change without fixation of type, are the supreme goods of life. Evolutionary history is littered with overspecialized species which dropped out of the running because they lost their capacity for further adaptation. Man must meet new challenges to his continued growth through deliberate creative response; but he must avoid fixation and stagnation. Miller suggests that the chief cause of the failure of civilizations, as of species, is their reluctance to keep growing, their petrification in fixed forms of life and inflexible dogmas, and their eventual fragmentation into a congeries of local breeding populations no longer in touch with one another. Progress demands maximum variety of contact, to insure maximum adaptability and growth. Society's "vital movement is outward, toward all men, bringing families and peoples into larger group association. Civilization must recover the kinship of that association which originally established man on earth, and which was then temporarily dispersed into clan and tribe and race. . . . Civilization is mankind made kin again, and kind." The next step in man's evolution must be "a world society embracing mankind," in which all the traditional cultures are "woven into the great society of the future." [17]

Cycles and Millennia

THE BIOLOGICAL approach to the idea of world integration, at least in the published writing of Huxley and Teilhard, has won public interest only in the last several years. It is a good place to begin, because the biologist-prophet views cosmopolis from the broadest possible perspective in time; but the prophets who made the earliest really significant impact on twentieth-century thought, and may still have the widest audience, are two leading exponents of the so-called cyclical theory of history, Arnold J. Toynbee and Pitirim A. Sorokin. Even Toynbee and Sorokin did not make altogether clear their intent as prophets until fairly recently, so that both are still better known as philosophers of history than as prophets of world order. But all things considered, future generations are not likely to take their theories of history seriously. There are just as many patterns of the past as historians enterprising enough to discover them; each era must shape history to its own needs. What matters for the moment is the high prophetic content of nearly all the work of Toynbee and Sorokin since the late thirties, and its prominent place in the recent history of cosmopolitanism. For the astonishing thing is that the next turn of the wheel of history in these seemingly cyclical theories will not necessarily find us back once again in the forest primeval. Both prophets hold out, instead, the possibility of something very much like the

Millennium, and perhaps even an absolute transcendence of the whole cyclical rhythm of the past.

The cyclical idea, that states or civilizations, like individual organisms, pass through a predestined life-cycle from "birth" to "death," can be traced all the way back to the historians of ancient Greece, and even earlier. Revived in modern times by Vico during the Enlightenment, it was used by the great Slavophil Danilevsky in the nineteenth century to predict the approaching collapse of Western Europe and a time of greatness for Holy Russia. Ernest Millard further exploited cyclical theory in France shortly before World War I, and Oswald Spengler applied it to the predicament of twentieth-century man in his murky, interminable, Wagnerian prose-poem, *The Decline of the West,* first published in 1919-22. What particularly gripped Spengler's spellbound readers in the twenties was his then daring thesis that modern Western civilization had long passed its prime and was now descending into wintry old age, from which there was no escape but death. The prewar doctrine of inevitable progress was neatly transformed into a doctrine of inevitable decay.

But since Toynbee and Sorokin, the cyclical concept of history has been put to radically new uses that preserve its obvious merits, and yet subordinate it to a life-affirming vision of world order. The gap between Spengler and Toynbee, in particular, has steadily widened with each new batch of volumes of Toynbee's *A Study of History,* until by now it is almost as wide as the gap between Spengler and Wells.

Toynbee was born in 1889, the nephew of another Arnold Toynbee, the economist who coined the phrase "Industrial Revolution," and Paget Toynbee, the philologist and Dante scholar. He had a sound classical education and teaching experience in ancient history at Oxford, worked for the British Foreign Office during both world wars, and served for many years as director of studies at the Royal Institute of International Affairs. He began planning *A Study of History* while teaching at King's College in the University of London shortly after the first World War. The first three volumes were published in 1934, the next three in 1939, four more in 1954, an atlas in 1959, and a volume of "Reconsiderations" in 1961. There are at least three Toynbees, then: the respectable professor of Greek history, the patriotic director of foreign affairs research, and the prophetic metahistorian. Each has been eminently successful, but the third has become one of the twentieth century's greatest thinkers, and certainly its most popular and controversial historian, at least in the English-speaking world. He has already provoked hundreds of important critical articles and books. His adversaries rise up from every quarter to do him battle. Most fight fairly. A few, notably Jewish scholars and one or two brash young British dons, have all but descended to character assassination on behalf of their respective tribal gods.

So many people have read D. C. Somervell's expert abridgment of *A Study of History* or summaries of Toynbee's original argument in books like De Beus' *Future of the West* and Sorokin's *Social Philosophies of an Age of Crisis,* that it is hardly necessary to dwell in any detail on the first six volumes of Toynbee's *magnum opus.* But the six volumes which have appeared since 1954 alter many of his theses substantially, make him much more than ever a prophet of world integration, and so deserve more careful attention here. One of his least acknowledged and most admirable qualities is his willingness to keep an open mind. He has not petrified. This has become especially obvious since the publication of the twelfth volume, in which he devotes more than six hundred pages to a closely reasoned re-examination of the whole architecture of *A Study of History,* in the light of the comments of more than two hundred of its critics.

The purely cyclical features of Toynbee's system can be disposed of quickly. In the first ten volumes, he identified twenty-three full-blown civilizations, each self-contained enough to be studied more or less separately. Now, in the twelfth volume, he distinguishes twenty-eight, thirteen "independent" and fifteen "satellite" civilizations. Each has run, or is running, through a comparable life-cycle, which at first he thought corresponded to the history of the Hellenic civilization of classical times. He has now streamlined and given more flexibility to his civilizational life-cycle by adding to his Hellenic model some variant features from the history of Chinese civilization. But the stages which must be passed through are still the same: genesis, growth, breakdown, time of troubles, the universal state, and final collapse leading to genesis again.

But this is merely the "normal" pattern of the historical past. Especially since the volumes published in 1954, it has become quite clear that Toynbee's study of the life-cycles of past civilizations is only part of a much broader interpretation of the human experience. He freely confesses that Christopher Dawson is right in detecting in the 1954 volumes "a change from a cyclical system to a progressive system." [18]

First of all, Toynbee no longer feels that his twenty-odd civilizations are the only intelligible units of historical study. In their disintegrations, they also give rise to "higher religions," of which he now recognizes at least six: Hinduism, Zoroastrianism, Judaism, Buddhism, Christianity, and Islam. These higher religions disengage the "spiritual presences higher than man" from "the highly integrated life of some particular local community," with the supremely important result that the realm of God, or absolute spirit, "comes to be thought of as being coextensive, not with some local state or some regional civilization, but with the entire Universe, while Its worshipers come to feel themselves members of a church that, in principle and in intention, em-

braces all men." [19] The higher religions suggest the existence of a world spiritual order infinitely greater than the
merely social and political order of the universal state,
with all its human failings and instability. These higher religions are a new species of society. They survive the disintegration of the civilizations which beget them, and they
have an organic life of their own. Because they seek to answer the most important questions men can ask about existence, they are intrinsically more important, and more
worthy of study, than civilizations.

But most of Toynbee's critics have jumped from these
ideas to the conclusion that Toynbee is, for better or worse,
an incorrigibly otherworldly soul, who fixes his eyes on the
hereafter and dismisses all ideas of earthly progress as the
provincial illusions of mammon-worshiping Westerners.
He does write off as nonsense "the use of the word 'progress'
in the absolute"; progress may occur in an infinite number of
fields, and obviously never does at the same time in all fields
or continuously in any.[20] But he maintains, on the one hand,
that there is an over-all record of progress in the religious history of mankind, and, on the other hand, that through the
transfiguring power of the higher religions and much luck
and perseverance, mankind may transcend the age of civilizations altogether and enter a wholly new phase of life
in which the treadmill of civilization cycles is left behind
forever. This millennial vision may prove, in the end, to
be Toynbee's supreme contribution to twentieth-century
thought.

The best approach to Toynbee's vision of cosmopolis is
through his many attempts, in A Study of History and elsewhere, to explore the prospects of Western civilization.
There are, he says, indications that Western civilization may
be repeating the well-established patterns of the past, although modern Western observers lack enough perspective to
be sure. Many of the familiar phenomena found in disinte-

grating civilizations recur in ours. The Western body social
shows every sign of having experienced its "breakdown," the
collapse of harmonious relations between governing minori-
ties and governed majorities. Authoritarian and totalitarian
regimes maintained by force and terror, the "proletarianiza-
tion" of the working classes, the profusion of "displaced
persons," are all exhibits in evidence. There may also be
telltale signs in the spiritual realm: the rise of a morbid
sense of drift and sin, promiscuity in styles of art and
thought, the outbreak of pathological movements designed
to rescue civilization by plunging it backward into some
idealized segment of the remote past or by jolting it forward into a synthetic, rootless future. Toynbee has discovered these phenomena in all other disintegrating civilizations, and they seem to be cropping up again in the history
of the West.

If the West has already broken down, the crucial moment might have occurred in the sixteenth century, during
the Reformation which split Christendom into competing
camps and touched off a long series of fanatical wars of religion. In this event, we would now be stumbling through our
"time of troubles," in search of a conqueror to unify all the
contending Western states in a single empire. Napoleon
nearly succeeded in the early nineteenth century, Germany
in the first half of the twentieth. But their failures are significant. "Each time the Western World had expanded, before the attempt was made, to dimensions that made the
attempt a forlorn hope." [21] Napoleon could not swallow all
continental Western Europe and also conquer a British Empire which had become a global sea power and a Russian
Empire which had been attracted from outside into the orbit
of Western civilization since the days of Peter the Great.
Germany also failed, and for much the same reason. She had
to contend, not only with the British and Russian empires,
but also with a new outpost of Western civilization in the

Western hemisphere, the United States of America. The job proved overwhelming for both would-be conquerors.

And this raises the important point that Western civilization has begun to veer in recent centuries away from the pattern of the past in several unprecedented respects. We have had unique experiences, which do not surprise Toynbee, since he has always maintained that his model for the life history of civilizations is merely a provisional hypothesis offered in the empirical spirit of Western science, and that in any case "the outcomes of human choices, purposes, and plans are unpredictable intrinsically, however fully we may be informed about the relevant past facts up to date." By the very nature of man as a spiritual being with the power of free choice, recurrences of events were never inevitable in the past, "nor do I believe that any of them, or any others, are bound to repeat themselves in the future." [22]

Briefly, what makes Western history unique is the "spiritual revolution" which the West passed through toward the end of the seventeenth century, the revolution which gave us modern science, liberalism, and the rudiments of democracy; and then the technological revolution of the eighteenth and nineteenth centuries, which armed Western man with incredible material power, permitting him to extend greatly his control over non-human nature, to explore and temporarily subdue the whole planet, and influence decisively the lives of all non-Western peoples. Western technology, institutions, and moral ideas are effecting at least a superficial Westernization of all non-Western societies. For the first time in history, the peoples of the whole world are in direct and daily contact, so that "the minimum political unit and the minimum effective unit of the industrial system is now the whole planet and all mankind." [23]

But in Westernizing the world, the West has not been able to conquer it, as Rome conquered the known civilized world in her day. Technology is "difficult to invent but relatively easy to acquire from its inventors by mimesis," [24] and the non-Western world, beginning with Russia and Japan, has made haste to do just that. All the material blessings and all the military might accruing from Western technological progress lie now within the reach of the whole non-Western world. The West's last chance to establish a universal state by conquest was forfeited by the United States between 1945 and 1949, when she combined world industrial leadership with a world monopoly of nuclear weapons, but refused to ape the Caesars. Since nuclear technology has "now armed a perpetually reborn Original Sin with a weapon potent enough to enable a sinful Mankind to annihilate itself," [25] and several rival powers possess nuclear arsenals, the establishment of a universal state by conquest is too impossibly dangerous to be risked by sane statesman. The only way out of the crisis lies in another direction, and, if taken, it will put an end forever to history as we have known it, and inaugurate a new era in the experience of mankind.

This trans-historical solution becomes clear in the light of Toynbee's attitude toward the universal states of the past. He looks on them with more approval than might be expected, considering the unhappy role they play in the disintegration of civilizations. When created by force, as they always are, they do make fatal mistakes. But he finds in them intimations of a better future, all the same. In fact, just like the higher religions, which put man in contact with the spiritual ground of the cosmos and make all men brothers, they are "symbols of the ideal unity of mankind and auguries of a future practical achievement of this unity once for all on a literally world-wide scale." The universal states in history despite their shortcomings were "so many preparatory exercises for the eventual establishment of a literal universal state." [26] The way out of man's present dilemma, therefore, is the creation of a world polity to bring into final union the rapidly coalescing peoples and cultures of the planet. But not by force. The use of violence to achieve order is against the ethical insights of the higher religions, and in the nuclear age it is not even practical. The world state of the future must be forged by federation, by voluntary association, and in a spirit of love and good will. When there is an authentically worldwide civilization, with the higher religions in harmonious alliance or even unified into one still higher world-faith, with a world authority to keep the peace, the age of the civilizations will be over. The "vain repetitions of the heathen" will end at last. "This *union sacrée* in the face of imminent self-destruction will be, if it is achieved, man's finest achievement and most thrilling experience up to date." [27]

It will not, of course, be man's last great experience. Toynbee does believe in the existence of a higher realm of being in the cosmos, and man's supreme task is to achieve communion with it. But this does not absolve him of his terrestrial responsibilities. Toynbee does not see reality as radically bifurcated into a "this-world" and an "other-world." This world, he writes, is "one province" in the Kingdom of Heaven, and life here below has, or should have, a profound spiritual significance of its own directly related to the more intense reality of the divine presence itself. The meaning of existence lies both inside and outside of time, because ultimately the cosmos is one.[28] The higher religions will help man to create a world civilization, and in turn the world civilization will enable man to fulfill the will of God on earth, whatever it may be.

In the final analysis, then, as a prophet Toynbee is not content to ride the carrousel of the civilizations with the cyclical historians who preceded him. He is no Danilevsky, no Spengler. His thought is deeply and perhaps unconsciously suffused with the modern Western gospel of evolution. Three times in *A Study of History* he compares

the situation of mankind in the present age to a climber's pitch. Below us lies the ledge that our pre-human ancestors reached in

the act of becoming human. In the Age of the Civilizations mankind has been making a number of attempts to scale the cliff-face
that towers up from the ledge reached by Primitive Man. The
next ledge above, unlike the ledge immediately below, is invisible
to climbers who are striving to reach it. All that they know is that
they feel compelled to risk their necks in the hope of gaining this
next ledge and in the faith that the endeavour is worth while.[29]

No man can foresee what a unified human race, living together in cosmopolis, may achieve, God willing. Lo — as
Nietzsche might have added — the Superman!

For the late Philip Bagby, the apocalyptic visions in the
later volumes of *A Study of History* show that Toynbee "is
primarily a prophet — a prophet disguised as a 'modern
Western student of history.' " [30] Toynbee emphatically re-
pudiates the tag of "prophet," but in the looser sense of the
term, not as an oracle uttering the very words of God or "telling" the future by some infallible power, he is surely a
prophet, and the only sort we twentieth-century mortals are
likely to have among us. His further thoughts on the integration of knowledge, the harmonization of the higher religions,
and the probable nature of the world state in its first stages
will be examined in later chapters.

Other meta-historians inclined to the cyclical approach
have also pointed the way to the salvation of mankind from
the endlessly turning wheel of the civilizations, but few have
struck so nice a balance as Toynbee between the "here" and
the "hereafter." The late Nikolai Berdyaev, for example,
wrote voluminously about the achievement of a "New Middle Ages," a new epoch in which the "Russian Idea" of
brotherhood would unite the peoples of earth in a universal
order through the ministry of the ecumenical church of
Christ. But Berdyaev was too steeped in the Russian and
Christian messianism of the nineteenth-century Russian
Orthodox renaissance to share fully in the world perspectives

of twentieth-century thought. His writing lacks the very "ecumenicity" he always treasured, and his vision of the possible future betrays a passionate otherworldliness, a mystic craving for the absolute that might — if we all shared it — effectively prevent mankind from fulfilling its creative mission on earth. Man is not yet ready to take wing and join the angelic hosts.

But in Berdyaev's younger compatriot, Pitirim Sorokin, cyclical meta-history has once again produced a prophet of world order of Toynbee's type, and perhaps even of his stature. In the four volumes of his *Social and Cultural Dynamics,* 1937-41, and the half dozen shorter prophetic books based on it which have appeared in the past twenty years, Sorokin has exhaustively diagnosed the crisis in what he calls the "sensate culture of the West" and drawn on his sociological interpretation of history to find a life-affirming formula of response that in at least one sense clearly transcends the pattern of the past.

Sorokin is a complex and difficult man. Born among miserably poor peasants in northern Russia, and orphaned at ten, he managed against all odds to obtain a university education and join the Russian intelligentsia in the years just prior to the Revolution. In spite of vigorous involvement in anti-Bolshevik politics in 1917-18, he was able to teach and publish in Petrograd until 1922 when, with Berdyaev and others, he was arrested and expelled from the country. He came to the United States the following year. In 1930-31 he founded the sociology department at Harvard, retiring from active service in 1955.

Although he is just as tender-minded as Toynbee, Sorokin has never really allowed the cyclical rhythm of history to nauseate him, as it obviously does Toynbee. They approach the past very differently, and as a result each sees things the other misses. For Sorokin the largest authentically intelligible unit of historical study is the "cultural supersystem" rather than the "civilization." The supersystem is a galaxy of local cultures held together by common fundamental premises concerning the nature of ultimate reality or value, whereas civilizations are merely geographical expressions, where swarms of often unrelated sociocultural phenomena mingle and ferment. Only the cultural supersystem can have a life-cycle, because it alone has organic life.

Sorokin distinguishes three major phases in the life-cycle of cultural supersystems, each based on a different set of fundamental premises. In the "ideational" phase, ultimate reality is defined as absolute spirit or deity, and truth is regarded as above reason and above the senses. A good example of an ideational supersystem would be the Christian culture of the early Middle Ages. In the "sensate" phase, its dialectical opposite, ultimate reality is defined as the tangible material world revealed to the sense organs; and this has been the dominant attitude in the West since the seventeenth century. Finally, somewhere between the two extremes, is the "idealistic" or "integral" phase. Here the emphasis is on a balanced, rational synthesis of both "ideational" and "sensate" reality and knowledge. The idealistic phase is illustrated by the cultures of classical Greece and the High Middle Ages in Western Christendom.

Sorokin insists that all three phases are capable of creating a magnificent and highly integrated culture, but because no one of them is able to satisfy all men or achieve all truth or realize all human creative possibilities, they eventually exhaust their resources and become sterile. Twice in Western history, and perhaps a number of times in non-Western history, the phases have alternated according to a precise sequence: first ideational, followed by idealistic, and then sensate. The cultural supersystem itself need not die, as in Spengler's organismic theory, but can continue to run through all its phases indefinitely.

In Sorokin's view of history, then, the "vain repetitions of the heathen" are not vain at all, and the whole spectacle is intoxicatingly wonderful, like a three-ring circus. The only drawback is the inevitable period of uncertainty, chaos, disintegration, and cultural sterility which ensues when a supersystem is undergoing a change of phase. We in the West live in the twilight of a sensate phase which produced in its best years a Shakespeare, a Rubens, a Goethe, and a Beethoven, but is now capable of turning out only the vulgar, the crude, and the flamboyant, or at best the brilliantly, incoherently eclectic. The rise of dictatorships, widespread organized crime, total warfare, ruthless imperialism and capitalistic profiteering, huge increases in divorce and suicide and mental illness, and the breakdown of all values spring inevitably from the bankruptcy of sensate culture. Since the "previous system of basic values is now largely disintegrated" and "a new system of values has not yet been built," we are faced with "social, mental, and moral anarchy." [31]

Ordinarily, one might expect the sensate phase to be replaced, after much distress and confusion, by an ideational phase, its exact opposite. But Sorokin is not sure. The prophetic impulse to impose one's own passionate preferences on the future gets the better of him. In all his discussions of the coming order, and especially his latest, he clearly indicates that his hopes are pinned on a kind of world that differs in several important ways from a simple return to another ideational phase of Western culture, such as Berdyaev's new Middle Ages. First, he notes that the creative leadership of mankind decisively shifted in the last few hundred years from Asia to Europe, and is now shifting from Europe to "the wider area of the Pacific and the Atlantic, particularly the Americas, Asia, and Africa." Moreover, progress in the technology of communication and transportation has transformed mankind into a single community of peoples. "Mankind has largely passed from a multitude of causally independent groups often entirely isolated from each other, frequently knowing nothing of each other, to the stage of one unified, universal interdependent whole." [32] The implication is plain, although nowhere explicitly drawn in Sorokin's work, that the cultural supersystem which emerges from the death agony of Western sensate culture will somehow envelop all humanity, perhaps by fusion with the non-Western cultures. In any event, there is to be a world government, with total and universal disarmament.

But Sorokin likes both sensate and ideational culture too well to wish a period of lopsided ideational culture on posterity. What he would clearly prefer is the emergence of an idealistic or integral phase, in which the values of both ideational and sensate culture are harmoniously integrated. He himself subscribes to what he terms an "integral" theory of truth, a belief that reality is an "infinite manifold" understood as a whole only when intuition, reason, and sense perception are all exploited to the utmost: this is precisely the basic premise of the integral phase of culture, as he defines it. [33] Such a culture on a world scale would approach closely Toynbee's idea of an ecumenical, trans-historical civilization, although Sorokin apparently has no hope that it could last forever.

Finally, Sorokin believes with a messianic passion in the power of love, or "creative altruism," as he calls it, to transform human life fundamentally. He continues to talk of cycles, but he urges on us changes so far-reaching that his cycles all but fade in their stronger light. In 1949, with the help of funds from the Eli Lilly Endowment, he founded the Harvard Research Center in Creative Altruism, for the scientific study of ways and means of maximizing the production and distribution of "love-power." [34] The Harvard project, and others like it, will enable man in time to tap to the full his creative capacity for love and make possible the reconstruction of humanity. Governments will be composed of scientists, sages, and saints, just as they were "in an imperfect form" at certain times in history, and now may be soon again, "in an ennobled form." [35] The world government will enforce total disarmament, and most of man's aggressive instincts will be channeled into a pan-human war against disease, natural calamity, ignorance, poverty, and strife. "If mankind can avoid the irretrievable catastrophe of greater world wars, the dawn of a new magnificent order in the human universe is waiting to greet the coming generations." [36]

Here, then, is another cyclical historian who approaches the human predicament in a spirit that suggests the old-fashioned Western dream of progress, although in a clearly Russian accent. On the one hand, he remains a dogged cyclicalist; he clings to his thesis that no phase in the cycle can go on indefinitely. On the other hand, he calls on mankind to establish a splendid new world order, combining the best in both ideational and sensate culture, ending the horrors of war, and replacing the self-centered societies of the past with a universal community of love. Even if Sorokin must predict the return in time of another purely sensate culture-phase, which would inevitably disintegrate into something as hectic as the modern world, the practical effect of his social philosophy is to urge on man much the same goals and values as Toynbee preaches. No world has even been remotely like the world of Sorokin's vision. It is not the historical Athens, the historical Middle Ages, or the historical Renaissance: it is the Millennium.

Lines and Spirals

THE GREAT Enlightenment doctrine of progress, the gospel of man's perfectibility, comes back brazenly in the biological historicism of Huxley and Teilhard, and it creeps in by the back door in the cyclical theories of Toynbee and Sorokin. But the biologists are not proposing theories of *history* in the strict sense, and the cyclical historians are still convinced that civilizations have *so far* developed in a cyclical pattern, whatever ecstatic visions they may have of the possible future. Several modern prophetic meta-historians of their generation go even further toward rehabilitating the idea of progress. For some of them — William Ernest Hocking, Karl Jaspers, Lewis Mumford, Erich Kahler — human progress is basically linear or spiraliform, and a world civilization is simply the next likely stage in this steady onward movement of mankind through space and time.

Of course these more straightforwardly progressive ideas of history are not theories of inevitable progress. They discover no cosmic guarantees even of human survival. The experiences of the twentieth century are too decisive to allow the most optimistic prophet the luxury of simple faith. Another characteristic of recent progressive meta-historians is a tendency to incorporate cyclical features into their reading of the past, giving to linear progress the form of a spiral. This leaves the prophet free to borrow useful insights from Spengler, Toynbee, and Sorokin, and still foresee without methodological embarrassment the possibility of an organic world civilization as the next epoch in history. The major theme in all these progressive theories is the cumulative progress of the species as it evolves from stage to stage through history. No repetitive experiences en route can fundamentally alter the fact of progress.

Among the rehabilitators of progress, William Ernest Hocking is the oldest and the youngest: oldest in years — he was born of Massachusetts Puritan forebears in 1873 — but the last to join the ranks of the prophetic meta-historians, which he did only in 1956 with a succinct and beautiful book entitled *The Coming World Civilization*. Thirty years a professor of philosophy at Harvard, a Christian Idealist of the old school, a student of comparative religion, an important lay leader in the Christian missionary movement, Hocking has all the credentials of old-fashioned respectability in American learning and letters. But his continued growth and productivity as a thinker rescue him from mere respectability.

As meta-history, *The Coming World Civilization* takes the form of an essay on Toynbee, and at the same time it illustrates all the trends in the newer progressivism: the acceptance of certain cyclical patterns in the past, the stress on cumulative progress, and the resounding conclusion that man can, may, and must achieve world unity in the next stage of history. Hocking concedes to Toynbee the existence of isolable phenomena in history such as "civilizations," and a certain historic rhythm of rise and fall. Civilizations generate their own poisons; they cannot persist intact forever. Nonetheless, "some human achievements stay achieved, though their significance is continually revised by the emergence of novelty around them." As a whole, history does not repeat itself. Civilizations do not perish entirely. Beyond the rhythms of rise and fall "there is in history a

certain tough cumulativeness at two levels — levels at
which mankind cannot forget — the level of technic and the
level of insight." [37] The practical arts, science, mathematics,
literature, and religion are not, for the most part, lost with
each *Untergang* of empire. This "rising level of the 'unlos-
ables' " more than compensates for the collapse of civilizations. The cumulative progress of religion since the Stone
Age is the most important for man's future, and Toynbee in
his 1954 volumes agrees with this point entirely. But man
has also made significant progress in many other areas of life;
to ignore these, as Toynbee by his own recent confession
does, is to distort the whole meaning of history.

Today, through "the simple existence of the arts of unlimited human communication," a great exchange of "un-
losable essences" is in progress between East and West which
will culminate soon in a single world civilization. "Our present period is one of general and reciprocal osmosis of
thought, technique, art, and law. . . . These processes can
neither be stopped nor undone; the lines that have 'gone
forth into all the world' cannot return to their origin." [38]

But for Hocking as for Toynbee, the world civilization
must be in a real sense a sacramental civilization. He op-
poses the idea of a unitary world government which would
project the spiritual emptiness of our modern secular culture
into the future and build a dehumanizing, depersonalizing
global leviathan alien to man's creative mission. Man's survival and progress require a world religion able to infuse
the peoples of the world civilization with an understanding
of man's spiritual nature, his fraternity, and his unity.*
The task of mankind is to transform "this human history
into the pattern of a divine community . . . even though
the city to be built, already present in its conspectus . . . is
still in its architecture out of sight." To realize this purpose,
"the religions may, and will, ultimately unite." [39]

* For a full discussion of Hocking's concept of a world religion, see pp.
158–62.

Hocking's European counterpart, perhaps, is Karl Jaspers. Both are philosophers in the grand tradition; both owe much to Plato, Christianity, and Kant. But whereas Hocking grew up in an academic atmosphere saturated with neo-Hegelian Idealism, Jaspers came to philosophy relatively late in life, from a promising career in psychology and psychiatry, and then under the influence not only of idealism, but also of those two tempestuous forefathers of European existentialism, Kierkegaard and Nietzsche. In 1922, at the age of thirty-nine, he settled at the University of Heidelberg, where he was something of a maverick for fifteen years: a philosopher with an M.D., and therefore an outsider; a lonely defender of academic freedom in an era of pathological nationalism and Nazism; often called an existentialist, but of a totally different life-orientation from Sartre and Heidegger; and the husband of a Jew. He was finally deprived of his professorship in 1937 by the Nazis and after the war accepted an invitation to take a chair in philosophy at the University of Basel, his home since 1948.

Jaspers is that rare twentieth-century German, a "Good European," who refuses to acknowledge that all institutions, all cultures, and all men are the property of national states. "To be, first of all, a man," he writes, "and then, out of this background to belong to a nation," [40] is the rule by which he tried to live during the difficult years of the Nazi era, and he has never broken it.

As an existentialist, a label he himself does not use, Jaspers' chief work is a three-volume study published in 1932 with the simple title *Philosophie,* not yet available in English. To speak precisely, Jaspers is an independent thinker attached to no school, but in whose work many important existentialist insights are embedded. He recognizes with all "existentialists" that the inner human self is both free and objectively unknowable; and he rejects the notion that man is on such intimate terms with the cosmos that he can know it in any final or total way. But he builds up from these essentially negative propositions, where the existentialism of common parlance ends, to an ethic and metaphysic of great richness and complexity, articulated unfortunately in a German just as opaque as Kant's or Hegel's. *Caveat lector.*

As a meta-historian, Jaspers' great contribution is a book first published in German in 1949 and translated into English in 1953 as *The Origin and Goal of History.* To learn the structure of world history, he writes, has become imperative in an age of world perspectives. Spengler and Toynbee deal with history as a succession of integral cultures, which "develop like organisms, as independent life-forms having a beginning and an end, being of no concern to one another but capable of meeting and interfering with each other." But Jaspers' outline of history is based in a wider vision, on the conviction, which he takes as "an article of faith," that mankind has "one single origin and one goal," both equally unknowable in concrete fact, but expressed symbolically in the Christian myths of Genesis and Apocalypse.[41] In his schema of history, the separate civilizations and cultures become only instruments of man's progressive development from his common origins in the remote past to his common destiny in the unforeseeable future.

Mankind as a whole, says Jaspers, started out on a totally new basis four times in the past, at each critical moment achieving a new dimension of humanity. The first great breakthrough occurred when man learned the arts of speech and the use of fire and tools in the "Promethean Age" of prehistory, the second when he built the first river-valley civilizations of antiquity, the third during the "Axial Period" from 800 to 200 B.C. when he created the first universalized and spiritualized traditions in religion and philosophy, in China, India, the Near East, and classical Greece. The fourth turning point in history is our own "Age of Science and Technology" which the West entered between the sixteenth and eighteenth centuries, and which with Western help the whole world has begun to enter in recent years. This has not been an age of spiritual revolution, but it has inaugurated a whole new cycle in human affairs, just as the invention of tools and the use of fire and speech in prehistoric times made possible the long cycle that produced civilization itself and the great religions. Perhaps, Jaspers suggests, the human adventure consists of two "breaths," each beginning with a technological, and culminating in a spiritual, revolution. In that light, our present era is a "new Promethean Age and may lead, through constructions that will be analogous to the organisation and planning of the ancient civilisations, into a new, second Axial Period." [42]

The two "breaths" differ in one salient respect. "Whereas the first breath was, as it were, split up into several parallel ones, the second breath is being taken by mankind as a whole. . . . What happens in the future . . . will be universal and all-embracing; there can be no more limitation to China, Europe or America." In this basic transformation of the scale of history, "a total metamorphosis" has taken place. "The essential fact is: There is no longer anything outside. The world is closed. The unity of the earth has arrived. New perils and new opportunities are revealed. All the crucial problems have become world problems." Henceforth mankind steps out of the age of "history" as we know it, into the age of "world history," "the one world of mankind on the earth." [43]

But the end of "history" has also brought with it an age of unprecedented anxiety. Modern Western technology is no unmixed blessing. Jaspers, in his *Die geistige Situation der Zeit,* published in English as *Man in the Modern Age,* offered as long ago as 1931 one of the first thorough investigations into the crippling impact of modern science and the technics of mass production and mass consumption on the human soul. The diagnosis has been repeated in many books since, by many hands: a loss of faith in man as a spiritual being, preoccupation with technical means instead of spiritual ends, mass conformity and depersonalization, and a consequent leveling and flattening out of culture, thought, and life in general. This crisis goes on unabated, in the midst of our transition to an age of global interdependence. To it must be added a deeper spiritual agony wrought by the failure of the positive religions and the long series of devastating critiques of human reason that began with Hume and Kant.

Now, since 1945, technological man has committed one more atrocity, which may be his last. He has set free the power of the atom, and made it a weapon for waging total war. Just as, for the first time, technology has given all men everywhere a common future by abolishing distance, so it has presented man with the possibility of turning his planet into a mass grave for the whole species. Jaspers views this possibility as a probability in his latest book, *The Future of Mankind:* "on purely rational reflection it is probable that it will happen. . . . There is not much time. At most, it is a matter of decades, and perhaps the time is shorter. Perhaps the decisive moment is close at hand." [44]

The only hope for mankind is a change of heart, "the resolve of the human being in whom a change is wrought by extremity." It could not happen in ordinary times, but now there is a chance. Individuals everywhere must come to the decision that only individuals can reach. "Encompassing reason" must guide ethical choice and personal sacrifice to prepare humanity for the necessary alterations in its sociopolitical and cultural superstructure. If this resolve is forthcoming, if men see, feel, and act, Jaspers envisages the evolution of a new world order in which "human community" will be "realised in every phase of intercourse." [45] The great cultural traditions, without losing their identity, will engage in unlimited communication. The nations, without surrendering their autonomy, will associate freely in a world confederation to prevent war. There will be no monolithic world religion, world philosophy, or world state, no compromise of authentic freedom for the sake of unity, but the world will be in the fullest sense a community. Men, in Jaspers' favorite expression, will "communicate" with one another. He has recently made a substantial contribution of his own to this kind of world communication in *Die grossen Philosophen,* a study in depth of the seminal thinkers in the histories of Eastern and Western philosophy.[46]

But Jaspers nourishes no high optimism about the human prospect. We live in a world of despiritualized masses who have sold their freedom for soulless comfort and hollow security, and we live in a world under the shadow of the threat of nuclear annihilation. This second Promethean Age in history has opened up the possibility that a free, united, and creative humanity may continue man's spiritual pilgrimage and reach new peaks of self-realization through self-transcendence. But it has not itself unlocked the new spiritual energies needed for a resumption of that pilgrimage. The inner change remains unaccomplished.

The existentialist thread in Jaspers' thought reminds him constantly of what some prophets of world order fail to stress, that the vital nexus between crisis and renewal is the whole, unique, dynamic, willing self, which struggles to maintain its integrity against the grueling mass-forces in modern life and yet also acts both to realize its humanity by communion with other selves and to secure its very existence by reunion with the divine ground of all existence. To worship "Humanity" and yet ignore the millions of unique human selves who give it all the existential life it has, is a kind of idolatry.

Still another prophet of world integration who, like Jaspers, shows profound concern for the integrity of the human personality, is Lewis Mumford. In the best American tradition, Mumford's thought is richly eclectic, drawing on many points of view, and developing out of the main currents of

twentieth-century cosmopolitan prophecy an exceptionally
broad and unified vision of world order. He is also one of
those few major American scholars who leave no doubt that
English is their native language. Since 1922 he has poured
out a stream of thoughtful, humane, elegant books on a wide
range of subjects: utopias, American literature, architecture,
technology, history, urban planning. His latest work, *The
City in History,* will no doubt stand as the definitive one-
volume history of urban civilization for a great many years.

He began exploring the larger designs of history much
under the spell of Toynbee; his history of Western civilization, *The Condition of Man,* first published in 1944, over-
flows with Toynbeean terms and concepts. More recently,
in *The Transformations of Man,* he has been in the debt of
Jaspers. Throughout, he speaks with the concern of a man
firmly attached to life and firmly persuaded that the ultimate source of all life is the "whole man," the person in
all his dimensions and powers, not multiplied into masses by
ruthless collectivization, or chopped into fragments by as-
sembly-line specialization. With Jaspers, he argues that the
twentieth-century world crisis is insoluble and the city of
man unattainable without an interior change in men. "The
very possibility of achieving a world order by other means
than totalitarian enslavement and automatism rests on the
plentiful creation of unified personalities," whole men of unusual creative vision precipitated by the world crisis but
themselves capable of precipitating a further transformation
in the rank and file of mankind. A handful of individuals or
even "a single human personality may overcome the apparently irresistible inertia of institutions," after the supreme
examples of Jesus and Mohammed. That such a "miracle"
will rescue man today is by no means sure. "On purely rational terms," Mumford is inclined to side with "the dying
judgment of H. G. Wells" that man is at the end of his tether;
but in any event there is no use looking for salvation outside

the self. All the important decisions are made there, and man's fate even now is locked in the hearts of living men.[47]

As a meta-historian, Mumford agrees with the cyclicalists that the pattern of the past presents itself in one sense as "the dynamic working out of the drama" of separate cultures. "In the drama of a culture, the nature of man defines itself and realizes itself in partial detachment from the world common to other living organisms. If nature is the theater of human life, the historic cultures provide the scenery against which men act their parts." [48] Each culture has tended to grow around "a dominant unifying theme" supplied by its religion. Then, "when a culture begins to disintegrate it does so, not because the seasons have changed, not because it is old and decrepit, not even because it has met an external injury or shock, but because its guiding theme, which bound all the parts of it together, political activities and economic affairs — and art and philosophy, too — has become exhausted. . . . The operative cause, which touches every institution simultaneously, is the collapse of meaning: the disintegration, not simply of this or that part, but of the overall pattern." [49]

But the historic cultures are not all of history. They can be studied separately, as Mumford has studied the Western cultures in *The Condition of Man*. Nonetheless, man taken as a whole has a history of his own, which transcends the drama of the cultures, and it is on this larger aspect of history that Mumford focuses in his recent book, *The Transformations of Man*.

Here he divides the history of mankind into six successive stages, not very different from Jaspers' four great turning points, beginning with the vital transition from animal to human in paleolithic times and leading through neolithic village life, the early civilizations, and Jaspers' "Axial Period," to the "New World Culture" of the last five centuries, which began in Renaissance Europe and has now spread to

most of the planet. This New World is literally new, an
entirely new type of civilization. In part, it is simply, as
Jaspers would argue, modern Western science and technology, the systematically regimented search for knowledge
and power. There is yet another aspect of New World
culture, however, which Mumford called the "romantic
ideology," a tumultuous cult of vitality never encountered
before in history. The romantic is a rebel against Old World
culture. He wants to "go back to nature" and explore the
wilderness. He is the passionate primitivist, lustful for love
and beauty. The two types, the romantic and the technician,
have flourished side by side in modern Western history
ever since the Renaissance, now working together, now at
odds, but transforming the world all the same, in their
common revolt against Old World culture. The romantic
furnishes the dreams, the heroism, the vitality, and the
wanderlust; the technician supplies the discipline, the tools,
and the organization.

This schizophrenic New World man has changed the face
of the earth in the last few centuries. The human race has
been thrown together into a single geographical community;
the inbred cyclical cultures of the Old World are all dead
or dying, although, paradoxically, their various nations
and empires still survive, intact and sovereign. A new confidence has been awakened in the unlimited potentialities
of man. Poverty, misery, and premature death have been
practically abolished, and not just for the favored elites of
the old order. The great majority of men in the most fully
developed parts of New World civilization enjoy economic
well-being and civil equality. At the same time, New World
culture has repudiated many of the essential insights of the
old, its sense of the timeless, its moral values, its methods of
truth-seeking. The merely useful, mechanical, and instru-
mental threaten to overwhelm the good, beautiful, and true,
even if Old World man was wrong in thinking he could

capture for eternity the good, beautiful, and true in the
phrases of a particular philosophy or sacred book. The order
of means and ends is often inverted, so that the person becomes the slave of the machine he built to serve him. Here
Mumford has reached independently the same conclusions
as Jaspers reached in *Man in the Modern World.*

Now Mumford sees contemporary man at a momentous
fork in the road of history. Because "the widening of the
base of human community" has been "one of the cumulative
results of human history," [50] and the world is now effectively
one single community, thanks to New World technics, man
must create a world polity and a world civilization. Unless
nuclear annihilation intervenes, all this is well-nigh inevitable. The choice at the fork, then, is not between world
order and world anarchy, but between two radically different kinds of world order. Choosing one route, man can
abandon history altogether to become what Roderick Seidenberg calls "post-historic man," in a book published under
that title in 1950. Pursuing to its ultimate limit the tendency
in modern civilization toward more and more machinelike
organization of life, toward the standardization of personality, and the ruthless elimination of freedom, we can turn
humanity into an anthill. History in that event would be
simply a dynamic interlude of conscious action between two
long dreamless sleeps, the slumber of animal instinct and the
slumber of brainwashed mechanical conformity.

Or, choosing the other route, we can create a vital "world
culture," and this, of course, is Mumford's personal option.
It would be a world organically unified by organically unified
personalities, preserving the intimate family and local ties
of archaic culture, the civilized arts and axial insights of Old
World culture, and the adventuresomeness and technology
of New World culture, but bringing them into a dynamic
synthesis in which nothing would remain unchanged, not
even the axial religions, which must "disavow their naïve

claims to special revelation or exclusive spiritual leadership"
in order to make a true world culture possible.[51] A world
government and a world economy geared to the needs of con-
sumers instead of producers will hold the world civilization
in dynamic equilibrium.

Meanwhile, we in the West cannot go on trying to per-
petuate our disintegrating provincial culture. To postpone
the transition to a world civilization any longer is to court a
nuclear holocaust that will end everything. The Western
drama is played out, and its "overall pattern of meaning"
has broken down. The forces of the Freudian id, once "held
in restraint by the very requirements of the drama, manifest
themselves in an upsurge of untrammeled lust and aggression, greed and senseless violence." Our sour-souled intellectuals and our neo-barbarian dictators alike revel in
nihilism. In a disintegrated society such as ours, the drama
turns itself inside out: "it begins with the murder of the
hero and successively multilates, tortures, or exterminates
every subordinate character. Boasting his decapitation, modern man parades, like a figure by Dali, in a blasted land-
scape, kicking his own head before him." [52] Out of this chaos
will come order, if we survive, and the choice lies clearly between a freely created organic world community and a
Brave New World of robots. "The kind of person called for
by the present situation," Mumford concludes, "is one capable of breaking through the boundaries of culture and history, which have so far limited human growth." [53] Here and
there, singular personalities must seize the initiative from
disaster and lead humanity to a new world order.

Needless to say, Hocking, Jaspers, and Mumford are not
the only prophet-historians of the last generation to focus
on man's history as a whole and envisage some kind of world
civilization as the next stage in human progress. Erich
Kahler, a refugee from Hitler's Third Reich and now an
American citizen, has written *Man the Measure,* conceived as

a biography of humanity, rather than a history of peoples or special fields of human activity, in which a social-democratic world commonwealth emerges as the only sane way out of the world crisis precipitated by Western machine culture. His vision of world order, further elaborated recently in *The Tower and the Abyss,* puts Kahler squarely in the camp of the prophets studied in the present work. His ethical philosophy, in particular, strongly suggests Mumford's. Another prophet of world integration is Oliver L. Reiser, of the University of Pittsburgh, who argues in his *Promise of Scientific Humanism* that the "curve of human evolution" runs from the pre-Aristotelian cultures of the East and Western antiquity through the Aristotelian civilization of the classical and Christian West to a post- or null-Aristotelian planetary society in which East and West must be dynamically fused by a multi-dimensional scientific humanism.[54] And there are many prophets of world integration, from F. S. C. Northrop at Yale University to Sir Sarvepalli Radhakrishnan, India's great philosopher-statesman, who have by and large eschewed the historical approach altogether, but have arrived by other routes at a vigorous philosophy of world order all the same, which will find its place in later chapters.

But for better or worse, these broad schemes of world history, cyclical or progressive or both, seem to meet a very real need in contemporary culture. They are all different, which is inevitable, but they are also very much alike, especially in their common intuition of a common destiny for mankind. They convert the writing of history into a vehicle for exhortation, prophecy, and a definition of human purpose. To see them only as studies of the pattern of the past is to miss their whole significance.

The Doctrinaires

BEFORE turning to a more detailed inquiry into the shape of things to come as viewed by contemporary prophets of world integration, a postscript is in order. All the thinking studied so far has been done by independent spirits, all of them highly educated men with time for leisured reflection, most of them unaffiliated with groups that would or could in any way stifle free expression of thought. That notable exception, Teilhard de Chardin, though one of the freest spirits of them all, did fail to secure permission to publish his work during his lifetime; but his church could not prevent its publication after his death.

There are other contemporary visions of world order founded on theories of history that do not originate in perfectly free reflection. In this case, the visionaries hail from organizations — churches or political parties — that found the Way, the Truth, and the Light before our century. Often they manage to inject many fresh ideas into their sources, but the result is always a body of sacred dogma or a set of views dependent on a body of sacred dogma. Because of the tangible power of some of the organizations involved, and the many intrinsic merits of their world-views, it would be unrealistic to ignore them altogether.

In two instances, the origins of the body of sacred dogma in question have already been explored in Chapter One.

The two greatest forces in what remains of religious life today are unquestionably the Roman Catholic Church and the world brotherhood of Islam. Each, as we have noticed, started out the instrument of a vision of world order. But each also demanded that the whole world submit to its particular idea of a theocratic world society, and even its particular theology, ritual, and law. Catholicism had the better organization, but Islam made up for its organizational defects by possessing a more unified body of sacred scripture. As time passed, despite and perhaps because of serious sectarian conflicts, each grew more dogmatic. In the case of Catholicism, the most severe blow fell in the sixteenth century, when the fanatically dogmatic Lutheran and Calvinist secessions from Roman Christendom forced the mother church to retaliate, at the Council of Trent, by crystallizing her own position in equally brittle phraseology.

In the twentieth century, both faiths still have devotees who dream of a world united under their sign, cross or crescent. Islam may profit from her extensive footholds in both Africa and Asia and her appeal to all colored peoples for whom Christianity is indelibly tainted with white imperialism. Already there are more than 400 million Muslims. A rejuvenated Islam astride half the world is no fantastic prospect, although Muslim hopes in Europe and North America ring hollow, except among the colored proletariat of the United States. As Dr. Khalifa Abdul Hakim of Lahore argues, Islam with its absence of racial prejudice, its unambiguous monotheism, and its organic view of man, society, and cosmos, may be well suited to "mediate between the East and the West." [55] But in its present variety of forms, Islam shares all the fatal weaknesses of the disintegrating civilizations in which it thrives, and the amount of rejuvenation needed to enable it single-handedly to win the world will probably not be forthcoming.

Although the incubus of Western unpopularity sits heavily on the Roman Catholic Church in the non-Western world, its rapid growth in northern Europe and the North American continent, its already vast power in the Latin world, and its superb *esprit de corps* make it perhaps the most formidable single institution working for world unity outside the Soviet sphere today. It remains astonishingly vital — above all where it is not the established church — in spite of the disintegration of Western culture as a whole. In most countries it has publishing houses, universities, parochial school systems, and loyal bands of lay and clerical intellectuals who do not shrink from sounding its praises.

There are Catholic nationalists in abundance — witness those two-fisted paragons of patriotism, G. K. Chesterton and Hilaire Belloc! But the Catholic thinker tends to be a cosmopolitan in spirit, because he is the self-conscious heir of the great cosmopolitan civilization of the Middle Ages. It is not surprising that Pope Pius XII sent his good wishes to the 1951 meetings in Rome of the World Movement for World Federal Government, or that distinguished Catholic intellectuals like Robert M. Hutchins should be active in the postwar propaganda for a world federal republic.

Like most Christians, the Catholic is also deeply aware of what the Christian faith has regarded as its historic mission since St. Paul and St. Augustine. Karl Löwith points out in *Meaning in History* that our whole modern Western sense of history really goes back to the Fathers of the early Church. The Christian is almost obsessed with history: his whole faith can be summed up in a list of dates, from the events in Genesis through the ministry of Jesus and the Resurrection to the Second Coming and the Last Trump. No pagan or Oriental religions are comparable in this respect.

The Roman Catholic Church today remains adamantly convinced that its world-historical mission since Jesus entrusted the Keys of the Kingdom to St. Peter nearly two thousand years ago is to act as the sole agency of God's

will, in Christ's place, on earth. It seeks to convert every
living soul and establish its spiritual empire over the entire
world, and in so doing it would undeniably create a world
civilization, which might or might not also entail a world
government. It regards schism as heresy and humanity as one.

Two different but not irreconcilable views of the prospects of man in the light of a Catholic philosophy of history
are offered to the present generation by Christopher Dawson
in Britain and Jacques Maritain in France. Both are eminent
Catholic laymen, whose books reach a wide audience all over
the West among Catholics and non-Catholics alike. Neither
speaks for the Church officially, but neither is ever likely
to find himself entombed in that sixth circle of Inferno
Dante reserved for heretics.

Dawson rejects as impossible any effort, à la Toynbee, to
do a systematic and thorough study of world history in its
totality, but, as John J. Mulloy urges, "There is implicit
throughout his work a conception of the development of
world history which . . . turns upon the major changes
which have taken place in man's view of reality as they have
found expression in the life of particular societies and cultures." [56] Mankind in its development has passed through
four ages: primitive culture, the archaic civilizations, the rise
of the world religions, and the period of world unification
now unfolding, inaugurated by Western science and technics.
Of the "world religions," however, only one succeeded in
fully reconciling the conflicting demands of the spiritual
and the material orders of life: Christianity. "The great
Oriental religions are no longer culturally active and . . .
have become divorced from social life and from contemporary culture." The dynamism of Christianity accounts in
large measure for the success of the West in recent centuries
and for the fact that Western civilization, and not some other,
has taken the lead in forging the world civilization of the
future. Dawson quotes with approval Cardinal Newman's

judgment of a century ago that Western Christian civilization is "distinctive . . . luminous . . . and utterly without a rival upon the face of the earth." [57] To the Catholic Church and to the Western tradition of science, scholarship, and literature "we must look for the creation of a new world civilization, which will unite the nations and the continents in an all-embracing spiritual community." [58]

But the Catholic Church, and its child, Western civilization, are not simply superior to all others, as one man might be taller or stronger than another. Christianity, as Father D'Arcy writes, is "dipped in immortality and therefore indefectible." [59] Again, to quote Dawson, the Catholic Church is not "subject to the limitations of human culture. For she is essentially a supernatural organism which transcends human cultures and transforms them to her own ends. As Newman insisted, the Church is not a creed or a philosophy but an imperial power." [60] The Church also "remains the guardian of the secret of history and the organ of the work of human redemption which goes on ceaselessly through the rise and fall of kingdoms and the revolutions of social systems." Hence, not even world integration will bring the work of the Church to a close. The struggle against evil will go on forever, since "in every age and among every people it is her mission to carry on the work of divine restoration and regeneration, which is the true end of history." [61]

Maritain, the leading spokesman in our century of the philosophy of St. Thomas Aquinas, shares Dawson's general view of church and history. The Catholic faith alone is the direct revelation of God to man. Maritain looks with pity on the nations of the East "situated on the frontiers of darkness, and lacking a divine revelation of truth." Moreover, the philosophy of Aristotle as revived and enriched with Christian wisdom by St. Thomas is "the only true philosophy." [62]

But as a good Aristotelian and also as a good liberal, Maritain is not enthusiastic, to say the least, about the idea

of a unitary world state. Medieval man attempted to create
a sacral civilization based on the worthy ideals of strength,
organic unity, and fortitude in the service of justice and
order, to the greater glory of God. Medieval civilization
"lived on the ideal of the Holy Empire (and died of it)." [63]
Today, Christian man has a new conception of service to God
on earth, equally valid, but different. In place of the medieval ideal of the unity of society is our ideal of the unity
of the person, a God-centered integral personalism not without deep roots in Christian teaching, but with a different
emphasis from the medieval social idea. The coming social
order must respect the dignity and freedom of the person,
church and state must be separate, and nations must be
self-governing. The Mother Church must continue her efforts to bring all humanity into her bosom, but without
use of force or abuse of the rights of conscience. At the same
time, the nations must voluntarily pool their sovereignties
in a federal world political community, retaining autonomy
and relinquishing to the community only the power necessary to keep order in the world.

But of all the positive religions on the contemporary
scene claiming divine authority, the only one unambiguously and almost single-mindedly consecrated to the job of
unifying mankind is the Bahai Faith. Its origins are recent,
its believers few, its ambitions breathtaking. It goes back
only as far as 1863, when a member of a heretic sect in
Persian Islam took the name of Bahaullah — "Splendor
of God" — and announced that he was the divinely appointed successor of Jesus and Mohammed for the modern
world. Bahaullah revealed the word of God for nearly
thirty years, most of them in detention under guard in a
private house in the Turkish prison city of Acre. On his
death in 1892, leadership passed to his son, Abdul Baha,
who was pronounced by his father the only infallible inter-
preter of the Faith; and when he died in 1921, leadership and

infallibility *ex cathedra* were duly conferred on his grandson, Shoghi Effendi. There are now several thousand Bahais
scattered all over the world; their sacred scriptures have
been translated into most languages; the chief centers of the
movement are Wilmette, a suburb of Chicago, the site of the
"Mother Temple of the West," and Haifa, in Israel.

Although in its early days the Bahai Faith seems to have
anticipated only the establishment of world peace through
collective security arrangements or, in Abdul Baha's time,
a league of nations, present-day Bahais are vigorous champions of the idea of a world government and a single world
civilization. In the Bahai philosophy of history, God has
three times specially intervened in the world, first to create
man, then to accelerate human evolution by instructing man
in the arts of civilization some six thousand years ago, and
most recently to make possible true human unity by inspiring
man to create modern science and technology. He also sends
Manifestations of Himself to earth from time to time, to give
man the spiritual wisdom necessary to live according to His
will. Bahais also believe that the founders of all the world's
great religions were Manifestations of God and hence that all
living religions are already one, although some have hewed
more closely to God's words than others. After the Bahai
texts, the Koran is nearest to the word of God, followed, in
descending order, by the Christian New Testament, the Jewish Old Testament, the Buddhist and Hindu scriptures, and
the sacred texts of the Chinese.* The present task before
man is to achieve the "seven candles" of unity: political
unity, unity of thought in world undertakings, unity in freedom, and unity of creeds, nations, races, and languages.

In the new world civilization, the Bahai Faith will become
the soul of humanity. It is the one true world religion,
says Shoghi Effendi, which fulfills all the others and is

---

* It would be impudent, perhaps, to point out that this is also the descending order of their historico-cultural connections with Bahaism.

"destined to attain, in the fullness of time, the status of a world-embracing Commonwealth." Domed and nine-sided Bahai temples will serve God and minister to man in every town and city, under the supreme jurisdiction of the Guardian of the Faith in Haifa. There will be a world language, such as Esperanto, in addition to the various mother tongues; a planned world economy; a uniform system of currency, weights, and measures; and a world metropolis acting as the "nerve center" of civilization. As Shoghi Effendi wrote to the Bahais of the world in 1936: "A world federal system, ruling the whole earth and exercising unchallenge-able authority over its unimaginably vast resources, blending and embodying the ideals of both the East and the West, liberated from the curse of war and its miseries, and bent on the exploitation of all the available sources of energy on the surface of the planet, a system in which Force is made the servant of Justice, whose life is sustained by its universal recognition of one God and by its allegiance to one common Revelation — such is the goal towards which humanity, impelled by the unifying forces of life, is moving." [64] Bahaism, then, is both a vision of cosmopolis founded on a historical faith and a dogmatically self-righteous program for the subjection of the human spirit to a particular historical creed.

In the last volume of *A Study of History* Toynbee traces this intolerant exclusiveness in all the Western monotheistic religions, and in such secular ideologies as Nazism, Russian messianism, and contemporary communism, to the "ancestral Judaic" myth of the Chosen People.[65] Toynbee is notoriously hard on things "Judaic," but for this very reason. The myth of the Chosen People, while it is not the only or the oldest such case of ethnocentrism in history, does run like a blood-red thread through all the creeds of Western man and his Islamic cousins. Even when a Western movement, like Baha-ism, does set out to reconcile the faiths of man, it falls prey

to the same pathetic disease. The Bahai World Faith is one
of the noblest in history, but it is also a lineal descendent of
Islam, and through Islam, of Christianity and the "Judaic"
ancestral myth. They are all ultimately immune to earthly
criticism. As the phrase now fashionable in neo-orthodox
Protestantism goes, "our" faith is not a mere "religion" like
all the others, because with "us" it is God seeking Man
instead of Man seeking God. Of course, as it turns out, "we"
are the only people who think so.

A final doctrinaire route to world integration, which Toynbee correctly links with the great Judaic myth, is Marxist-
Leninist world communism. At the present writing, world
communism has a marginal chance of imposing its particular
creed, mores, institutions, and symbols on the entire planet.
If this were a book of movements, rather than a book of
ideas, communism would deserve two or three weighty chapters. It has one third of the world's peoples militantly
enrolled in its cause, and the state treasuries of such formidable powers as the Soviet Union at its command. Where it
controls the government, it also controls all mass media,
education, and cultural organizations. It has a dynamic
philosophy of history which gives it the predestined authority to guide and inspire a world revolution that will destroy
all rival religions and philosophies, transfer all property
to public ownership, unite all peoples in a world system of
brotherly societies, and so end "history" as we know it.

What communism lacks is a systematic, clear-cut body of
dogma on the very world order it intends to build. Ever since
Marx himself, it has concentrated on a devastating critique
of nineteenth-century capitalism — it all but ignores contemporary capitalism — in the terms of a philosophy of
history that becomes positively cryptic on the subject of the
future. Marx was vague about the communist world order
perhaps because he despised the relatively easygoing utopian
socialism of his time, which specialized in glowing visions

of the future and overlooked the hard fight necessary to get there. In place of utopian pipe dreams, he supplied tough-minded economic analysis and cold-blooded programs for revolutionary action. Marxism is a "science." Then, too, no socialist has ever been primarily concerned with the problem of world unity, except a few odd types like Comte and Wells, who were barely socialists at all. Almost by definition, a socialist is a man preoccupied with socioeconomic problems.

Thus, some of Marx's critics maintain that he did not advocate a world state at all; but at least one, Elliot Goodman, in a recent study of communist thinking on world government, concludes from the admittedly fragmentary evidence that Marx "favored a highly centralized world dictatorship of the proletariat, modified by the federal principle only if necessary, and then only as a transitory measure to complete centralism." [66] One thing is clear, in any case. Marx did foresee a communist world civilization. He had no intention of limiting proletarian revolutions to Western Europe. The whole world would in good time turn to communism. And with the liquidation of all aristocratic and bourgeois elements from world society, the social philosophies, religions, and other systems of thought and culture generated by these elements as part of their way of life would also vanish. Even government itself would ultimately wither away, in favor of mere public administration.

The Marxist outline of history is too familiar to need another rehearsal here. Sufficient to say that the history of civilization since classical times falls into three epochs: the feudal age, in which a small elite of aristocrats holds the toiling peasant masses in bondage to the soil; the capitalist phase, in which power shifts to the bourgeoisie, who convert the toiling masses into wage slaves; and the coming stage of communism, when the proletarianized masses will overthrow their exploiters and establish a perfect society ending the exploitation of man by man and transferring

the ownership of all means of production to the workers.
All this is inevitable.

Unfortunately for Marx's reputation as a prophet, this
"inevitable" course of events failed to materialize after his
death. In the Western world, where Marx predicted the
first revolutions, a three-cornered alliance of capitalists,
workers, and governments has postponed revolution indefinitely by inventing that most pragmatic of all possible
societies, the democratic welfare state. In the relatively
unripe East, pseudoproletarian revolutions have occurred,
but under the aegis of militant, conspiratorial political
parties and huge national armies. As G. H. Sabine once
pointed out, Lenin, the real founder of modern communism,
"stood Marxism on its head." [67] Since Lenin's successful
seizure of power in Russia in 1917, communism has won
nearly all its victories by direct political and military action,
instead of waiting for purely economic conditions to create
and later topple the bourgeois state. In short, Lenin sub-
stituted for Marxist economic determinism his own messianic
political determinism.

Another peculiar effect of Lenin's mutilation of Marxism
is that the party line, since Lenin's time, has become sacrosanct and infallible. Marxism — or the current party interpretation of it — is now "a solid block of steel." Neither
Marx nor his colleague Engels had ever claimed infallibility,
although they stated their views with a characteristic firmness
that could easily be misinterpreted. Good communists today
are taught to suppress all doubts and skepticism. The truth
is known.

But the "truth" about the coming world civilization remains somewhat cloudy. Before the 1917 revolution in
Russia, the Russian Marxists most passionately committed
to the idea of total world revolution were A. L. Helfand, better known by his pen name of "Parvus," and Leon Trotsky.
Parvus' *idée fixe* was the obsolescence of the nation-state

system and the interdependence of all states and peoples in
the rapidly maturing world economy. He predicted revolution in Russia, and out of that, a world revolution. Parvus
greatly influenced Trotsky in his younger days, and the result was Trotsky's celebrated doctrine of "permanent revolution," which he persisted in holding after 1917, and which
eventually cost him banishment from Russia and assassination in Mexico. For Trotsky, the Stalinist idea of "socialism
in one country" was ludicrous. The world could not endure
part capitalist, and part communist. Because they were
deadly enemies, one or the other had to conquer once and
for all.

The more practical Lenin and his still more practical
successor Stalin did encourage the now defunct Comintern,
with its headquarters in Russia, to proclaim loudly the need
for an "International Republic of Soviets" in the desperate
years immediately after the Revolution. "The International
proletariat," in the words of the Manifesto of the Second
Comintern Congress in 1920, "will not sheath its sword until
Soviet Russia is incorporated as a link in the World Federation of Soviet Republics." [68]   After Lenin's death, Stalin
continued for several years to pay lip service on public
occasions to the idea of a world union of soviets. During the
thirties and forties, when Soviet communism was fighting for
its life against resistance from within and fascism from without, the theme of a world state and a world under communism almost disappeared from Soviet oratory; the Comintern
was abolished; and of course no private citizen dared speculate in print about matters so momentous.

Today, in the Khrushchev era, it is again perfectly clear
that world communism proposes to create a literally world-
wide civilization, and probably some kind of world state as
well. But the thorny problems involved in wooing the un-
committed countries, preventing a nuclear catastrophe that
could destroy Russia, and meeting rising consumer demands

within the Soviet sphere have forced the men in Moscow to speak rather softly, at least by comparison with the lions who roared in the Comintern congresses of forty years ago. Comrade Khrushchev believes in "peaceful co-existence" and at the same time, ultimate "victory in peaceful competition with capitalism" and the "disappearance of borders between states." His Chinese confrères seem more impatient, but they are not yet in a position to cast a deciding vote for world war, even if they wanted one. For the time being, world communism seems reasonably content to wait for the collapse of capitalism through its own "internal contradictions," which is a partial reversion to Marx's original ideas.

All this notwithstanding, no good communist can permit himself to doubt that the type of social system now prevailing in Soviet Russia will some day girdle the globe. Goodman is convinced from a careful study of the relevant published documents that the present leaders of the U.S.S.R. intend ultimately to establish a unitary world state, culturally Russified, and governed from Moscow as Rome once ruled the *orbis terrarum*. Perhaps this is a bit exaggerated. But as Marshall Shulman recently wrote in the *New York Times*, "The central conception of Soviet policy, and the distinctive source of its dynamism, is that the world is in a process of transition; that our social order is no longer effective in the changing environment, and is therefore in a process of disintegration and replacement." [69] World communism takes the narrowest possible view of man and history. Nonetheless, it takes a revolutionary view of what it does choose to see, and this gives it a tremendous advantage over the apathetic governments of the West which imagine that just because they have scored some remarkable successes in national social and economic integration, their whole civilization and its nation-state system are impregnable to radical change.

*   *   *

It is time now to take a closer look at the coming world civilization, not simply as the next stage in a scheme of history, but as a living organism, with an intellectual and spiritual life, a culture, an economy, and a political system. Contemporary prophets, especially the "independents" as opposed to the "doctrinaires," have devoted many chapters and volumes to this problem of exactly what may, can, or should replace the divided world of mid-twentieth century. Chapters Three and Four offer a panoramic summary of their speculations, arranged topically rather than by individual thinkers, to point up the very real areas of agreement that exist on many levels. No effort will be made to blur important differences. Also, no effort will be spared to bang heads together where differences seem genuinely trivial.

Three

The Concert of Cultures

The Organic Society

ONE GENERALIZATION holds good for nearly all recent attempts to anticipate the over-all structure of the world civilization proclaimed in meta-historical prophecy. Whether a prophet stresses the spiritual, the intellectual, the economic, or the political aspects of cosmopolis, he is likely to contend that healthy societies, and the civilizations that sustain them, are "organic"; hence the world civilization must also be "organic." The term is generally used loosely and analogically, rather than strictly and literally. Analogies to life may seem more apt than analogies to natural or man-made machinery if only because living organisms — somewhat like human societies — have unpredictable destinies, in which the whole and its parts work together for the same internally determined ends. The machine, on the other hand, is purposeless, futureless, inert, and un-self-willed; its parts have only an external, utilitarian relationship to the whole, and there is so little *esprit de corps* that the breakdown of the smallest part can send the whole machine grinding to a stop. An organic unity perseveres through thick and thin. The tendency, then, is to look on the coming world civilization as a kind of superorganism. But, of course, the question is, how much organicity? Must men become Man, the "Great Being" in Comte's phrase, a human coral reef of one blood, flesh, mind, and spirit? Or will something less titanic do?

Thinkers have compared societies to organisms since the earliest recorded essays in social philosophy. Ancient Indian, Greek, Roman, and medieval Christian thought bristles with organic analogies. During the Enlightenment, it became popular, following Hobbes and Locke, to think of societies and states more as mechanical contrivances created by individuals to serve their mutual interests than as organisms. This theory, the logical corollary of Enlightenment individualism, led to the dismantling of the *ancien régime* in France in 1789; but the passions generated by the French Revolution swept up the individuals involved and ironically fused them into a national organism, *la France,* which tried with limited success to reproduce on a smaller scale the organicity of medieval Christendom. Nevertheless, most liberal thought still adheres to the Enlightenment idea of society as an inorganic contractual arrangement, a machine built by individuals to serve their individual ends: life, liberty, and the pursuit of happiness. The United States is expressly founded on this mechanical principle. A hopeless contradiction yawns between Enlightenment liberalism and organic nationalism, which sometimes divides a man even against himself in modern Western countries. Witness the liberal patriot, forced to choose between the national interest and civil rights.

But organic theories have not been rare in the past century and a half. Comte and Spencer both used elaborate organic analogies in the nineteenth century, and Spencer at least was simultaneously a fervent individualist, which has puzzled his readers no end. Toward the close of the century, a number of professional sociologists especially on the Continent worked hard to rejuvenate organic theory. Most of them, like von Lilienfeld, Worms, Novicow, and Cooley, are now more or less forgotten. Even the great organic nationalists, like Treitschke and Barrès, seem remote in the Europe of NATO and the Common Market.

But the world crisis has forced a reopening of the whole question of whether cultures, societies, and civilizations must be, in some sense, organisms — in order to thrive and survive. Spengler looked on his cultures as organisms with life-histories. Most of the exponents of a world civilization, even those firmly attached to the liberal gospel of the existential uniqueness and freedom of the person, argue that the person cannot realize his potentialities except in a civilization that coheres organically, through the sharing of commonly agreed upon values, goals, symbols, and institutions. That is to say, fullness and wholeness of life in the person requires fullness and wholeness in the common life. Some prophets emphasize the need for synthesis in philosophy and science, others in religion and ethics, others in the arts, others in economic and political life; and there is a vast literature, in particular, on the ultimate question of East-West cultural synthesis. The common denominator throughout is the demand for organicity, in some measure, with formulas running all the way from loose-spun arrangements for cooperation and continuous dialogue to highly unitary schemes for a world brain and a world state. In all events, scarcely any thinker committed to the idea of world integration believes in a world simply of individuals each going his separate way like the golfers in a country club. The goal is a union of the liberal philosophy and the organic quality of nationalism in a durable, viable world order of free men freely united.

Recall, for example, Lewis Mumford's diagnosis of the disintegration of the historic cultures. They have all collapsed, he writes, because their guiding theme, the pattern of meaning in which they grew to maturity, wore threadbare and lost the power to attract creative genius to its message. Our task now is to conceive "a new drama, in which elements of the human personality that have been repressed or mutilated by older institutions will form the core of a new synthesis." The requirement is for "a deep organic transformation in every department of life. . . . The field for transformation is not this or that particular institution, but our whole society." [1]

Then, too, Sorokin's "cultural supersystems" by definition are characterized by "sociocultural integration." The personalities, cultural life, and social institutions of a thriving supersystem, including the new "ideational" or "integral" supersystem he sees on the horizon for mankind, must be meaningfully related and united in order to exist. Sorokin also anticipates that the coming world order will be built more on "familistic" than on "contractual" or on "coercive" relationships. Familistic systems are "permeated by mutual love, devotion, and sacrifice." What success the Soviet Union and other twentieth-century totalitarian societies achieve they owe to the familistic quality of some of their institutions, the creation of a "we" feeling that warms the soul and makes men willingly sacrifice personal gain for "higher" causes. "The new rising socio-cultural order," he concludes, "promises to give a spontaneous unification of religion, philosophy, science, ethics, and fine arts into one integrated system of supreme values of Truth, Goodness, and Beauty." [2]

Toynbee also embraces the organic theory. "A growing civilization," he points out, "can be defined as one in which the components of its culture . . . are in harmony with one another; and, on the same principle, a disintegrating civilization can be defined as one in which these same elements have fallen into discord." The unity of purpose and direction necessary to the spiritual health of a society is achieved by coordinating all the elements in its culture "in a harmony such as is maintained by the various instruments in an orchestra when the musicians are playing a symphony under the leadership of a conductor." An integrated culture is also like "a flint that has been compacted by the age-long pressure of enormous forces." [3]

For F. S. C. Northrop, a culture is the product of "a basic

philosophy in terms of which the economic doctrine, the political doctrine, the legal theory, the religious theory and the artistic forms of that culture are defined." [4] His hopes for the "meeting of East and West" and the "taming of the nations," to quote the titles of his two most important prophetic books, rest on the possibility that through a fundamental re-examination and organic synthesis of the ideological premises of all living cultures, a world civilization can gradually evolve, with a single integrated world ideology.

At least two prophets of world order seem to use even what might be called "organismic" analogies: they anticipate the emergence of a collective human organism, not simply with organic properties, but with a literal biological unity difficult to describe in ordinary prose. Teilhard de Chardin ingeniously combined, as we have seen earlier, a sincere personalism with a faith in the approaching development of a "hyper-person," "the birth of some single centre from the convergent beams of millions of elementary centres dispersed over the surface of the thinking earth," "an organic super-aggregation of souls," thinking and living as one being.[5] And Oliver Reiser writes of "the birthing of a Planetary Being . . . in very fact a biological-social entity" with a Wellsian World Brain uniting East and West.[6] But genuinely organismic concepts are always too ecstatic to reduce to plain language.

Chapter Three treats all those aspects of the organic world civilization which can be subsumed under the general heading of a "world mind" or a "world culture," leaving to Chapter Four the more practical problems of economic and political integration.

World Philosophical Synthesis

MOST contemporary prophets of world order agree that no lasting concert of nations, no true world commonwealth, is possible without a concert of cultures. The United Nations or an arms control commission acting under its supervision could conceivably hold back the deluge for some time, but men must think and feel as one, before they can make the leap to cosmopolis.

As Toynbee points out, in discussing contacts between civilizations, when a culture reaches the "radioactive" stage and begins penetrating another, its economic techniques move most rapidly and penetrate most deeply, whereas the systems of thought and faith at its core arrive last and take the longest time to sink in.[7] So, in the modern world, Asian countries influenced by Western civilization have adopted Western technological know-how most readily, Western political ideas and institutions with much difficulty, and Western philosophy and religion hardly at all, except in communist China, and there only by ruthless totalitarian tactics quite alien in their dogmatic thoroughness to Asian traditions. The West is similarly unsympathetic, on the whole, to Eastern thought, although it responds warmly to Eastern cuisine, dress, and *objets d'art*. As a result the world is growing together most rapidly on the level of technics and trade, and least rapidly on the more fundamental level of belief, outlook, and value. The failure of modern technics to give the world more than a superficial physical unity is precisely what we should expect. Technics pave the way for communication and exchange of ideas, but they cannot alone create a world culture or even a world state. The only permanently viable societies are founded, in the final analysis, on a common spiritual and intellectual culture, which in turn makes possible unity and fraternity in the sphere of practical politics.

The problem of world cultural synthesis may be attacked at several different levels, and although some prophets operate on all of them equally well, the more typical prophet of world integration in mid-century tends to focus on one and ignore the rest. Philosophy suggests one approach, theology and ethics another, science and education a third, and there are even speculations here and there on the role in cultural synthesis of the arts. If we adopt the undramatic but common-sense point of view that an organic world culture will hardly be able to get along without philosophy, religion, ethics, science, education, and art, all tending toward organic unity, there is not much point in trying to figure out which department of culture has "priority" over all the others. They all hang together.

In any event, one major approach to world integration favored by many prophets is the synthesis of the world's great cultures and civilizations through a unification of their basic habits of thought. Most often, this amounts to a proposal for world philosophical synthesis. The premise here is that "a man is what he believes," [8] that cultures are the products of their philosophies, and that only by a fusion of the philosophical underpinnings of cultures can the people in those cultures feel members of a common family of man. Japanese and Americans, for example, may both play baseball, both eat sukiyaki, and both build steamships, and still go to war and treat one another as vicious animals. Only

when Japanese and Americans, and all other peoples, look at
the totality of things from the same philosophical point of
view, or from points of view considered complementary, will
they create a true world civilization and enjoy lasting
peace. This is a thesis impossible to prove except by trying
it out in the real world. The relative philosophical homogeneity of the nations of Western Europe did not prevent
them from springing at one another's throats for centuries.
On the other hand, although ideological differences are
clearly not the only cause of war, harmony of thought and
culture is just as clearly a major asset to a people in process
of building a new civilization or even a single nation, as history suggests time and again. Even the great American
"melting pot" might have cracked and shattered generations
ago, if there had not been a hardy core of Protestant North
European settlers in possession of a distinctive American way
of life and willing and able to initiate immigrants into its
mysteries. The immigrants have made their contribution,
but within the framework of traditional American culture.

A genial, brilliant descendant of those same Protestant
North European settlers, F. S. C. Northrop—his ancestor
Joseph Northrop founded the town of Milford in Connec-
ticut in 1639 — has done more than any other single Western philosopher in recent years to advertise and elaborate
the idea of a concert of cultures through world philosophical
synthesis. He is that philosopher rarely encountered nowadays who still adheres to the classical textbook definition of
philosophy as "a reflective and reasoned attempt to infer the
character and content of the universe, taken in its entirety
and as a single whole, from an observation and study of the
data presented by all its aspects." [9] He moves about with
equal sureness of touch in metaphysics, epistemology, ethical
and legal theory, the philosophy of science, Oriental thought,
and political philosophy, and for many years until his retire-
ment in 1962 occupied a chair at Yale which straddled the de-

partment of philosophy and the school of law. The present writer remembers with much pleasure auditing a "seminar" of his in the Yale Law School with an enrollment of nearly a hundred students. The meeting place had to be changed twice, to accommodate the overflow.

Northrop's formula for world cultural integration begins with a flat statement he seems to take on faith. "The presuppositions of a culture determine its empirical manifestations and institutions." [10] A culture does not develop out of pure whim or chance: every part of it is organically related to its fundamental assumptions about nature, man, and ultimate reality. The first step to synthesis, then, is the purely scholarly job of determining exactly what are, in fact, the presuppositions of a given culture. This requires painstaking analysis. Glib generalizations based on styles of art, for example, or tour guide information, or positive law codes, or historical descriptions of "national character," will not get to the heart of the problem. A congenial desire to compromise is not good enough either. Philosophical analysis comes first. If analysis discloses that the basic assumptions of the cultures being studied are compatible and even complementary, then the total ideology on which they are founded can simply be enlarged to incorporate the new insights. Nothing need be lost. The total cultures of East and West are complementary in just this way, and Northrop's technique for East-West philosophical synthesis is described in some detail below.* If incompatible elements exist, as obviously do exist between, say, North American, Nazi German, and Soviet Russian culture, they must be tested against the only objective criterion available to man — nature herself. Quite often one or more of the incompatible elements will be found to derive from a false interpretation of naturally given facts, as, for example, the Nazi assertion that white Nordic Europeans constitute a biologically su-

* See pp. 142–45.

perior race. When natural science has corrected these er-
rors in the interpretation of nature, and when a new and
more catholic set of assumptions has been worked out true
to our best currently available scientific knowledge of man
and nature, all the elements of all cultures concerned can be
harmonized, and the cultures themselves will gradually unite.
Northrop looks forward to a world order "in which the diverse basic conceptions and resultant valuations" of East and
West will be "combined into a single world civilization, the
richer and better because it includes in complementary
harmony with balanced emphasis the most profound and ma-
ture insights of each." [11]

Not many prophets of world integration would agree with
Northrop on the role of Western natural science in the forming of a world culture; and of course Northrop himself would
not suggest that a conference of philosophers could assemble
and unify the world in one blow by sheer brain power. But
his fundamental argument seems solid. And his view of a
world culture as a balanced synthesis rather than a patch-
work quilt or a lopsided cultural imperialism reflecting the
basic assumptions of only one parochial culture, is quite
typical. Modern prophets of world order want unity and
diversity in dynamic equilibrium. "We should not aim,"
writes Sir Julian Huxley, "at the spread of one uniform type
of culture over the entire globe, but at what has been well
described as a world orchestration of cultures." [12] And in the
words of India's Aurobindo Ghose, written over forty years
ago, although "the unity of mankind is evidently a part of
Nature's eventual scheme and must come about," it must be
achieved "with safeguards which will keep the race intact in
the roots of its vitality, richly diverse in its oneness.[13]

Aurobindo worked much of his long life for a reconciliation of East and West, and for exponents of a world culture
this, of course, is the ultimate challenge. An integration
of Western civilization, with its centers in Europe and the

American hemisphere, and the Eastern civilizations of India and East Asia would bring most of the world's peoples together and prepare the way for an authentic world commonwealth.

As if following Northrop's advice, scores of Easterners and Westerners alike have been trying for many years to fathom, by philosophical and historical analysis, the basic, underlying ideational differences between Eastern and Western culture. Some have decided that the problem is insoluble because falsely stated. Sorokin, with his theory of cultural supersystems passing through all possible phases in endless succession, cannot accept the idea of a permanent, thorough-going distinction between East and West at all. A good many professional scholars of Eastern history and cultures also dismiss the whole concept of the "Orient" as antiquated, in view of the deep gulf between the cultures of India and East Asia: a gulf hardly noticed by earlier generations out of sheer ignorance. In a telling attack on Northrop's *Meeting of East and West,* for example, Arthur F. Wright maintains there is no such thing as a traditional culture of the whole Orient. Nor can either "Eastern" or "Western" cultures be taken in three-thousand-year doses, in the Northrop manner, missing all the immense changes in orientation through the centuries.[14] This is clearly only one more episode in the perennial struggle between the erudite specialist who sees nothing but trees and the high-flying generalist who prefers forests; neither is infallible. But "East" and "West" can and have been distinguished in general terms, even if each is less monolithic than each once supposed. Also, in recent centuries, Western technical progress has had the effect of neatly dividing the world economy in two, its Western half prosperous, its Eastern half poor. Under the circumstances, the Eastern peoples have drawn more closely together than ever before, not only because of reawakened interest in such ancient historic ties as Buddhism, but also for the practical reasons made very plain at the Bandung Conference in 1955. The immediate political and economic problems of the Asian nations are all painfully similar; they run a common race against time, in light of which the famous Cold War seems even more imbecile than it is.

Taking into due account the broad differences between the various parts of Western culture, and between India and East Asia, what marks off the "East" from the "West"? What basic attitudes will have to be harmonized in the ultimate synthesis? Each thinker who has accepted the problem as legitimate has solved it somewhat differently. The most ambitious collective efforts to uncover the "real difference" between East and West have been made at the three East-West Philosophers' Conferences held under the auspices of the University of Hawaii at ten-year intervals since 1939. Northrop's widely discussed book, *The Meeting of East and West,* published in 1946, grew out of a paper he presented at the first conference. Other important contributors have included Charles A. Moore, William Ernest Hocking, George P. Conger, E. A. Burtt, Charles Morris, and John Wild, all American philosophers; and such Oriental scholars as Chan Wing-tsit, Junjiro Takakusu, and Daisetz Suzuki.

Most of the papers read at the Hawaii conferences have agreed that significant basic contrasts can be drawn between Eastern and Western thought, and as a rule the scholars participating have also been able to reach agreement on the areas where East-West differences are most clear-cut. Eastern metaphysics, they argue, incline almost always to monism. For the Eastern cultures, the cosmos is a single, undivided, harmonious reality, whereas the Western religions and philosophies tend to carve the cosmos into two or three distinct realms of being, such as Descartes' mind, matter, and deity, or the conventional Judeo-Christian contrast between creation and creator. In habits of thought, the East prefers intuition, synthesis, the pointing out of similarities; the West prefers closely reasoned analysis, exhaustive fact-finding, the drawing of precise and minute distinctions. Eastern ethical philosophy stresses the search for inner peace and harmony with the cosmos; Western moralists stress the active and practical life.[15]

Most of these same contrasts reappear in recent prophetic literature on the prospects for world order. Erich Fromm, for example, sees the great differences between Eastern and Western thought in the Eastern preference for a logic of "paradox" and the Western for a logic of "identity." The Western mind classifies and organizes reality, whereas the Eastern mind rejects isolable, articulated, objective truths in favor of the ineffable Whole, of which all specific things are manifestations. "Various cultures have emphasized various aspects of the truth, and the more mankind becomes united culturally, the more will these various aspects become integrated into a total picture." [16] Denis de Rougemont, taking India as representative of the East, and Western Europe as representative of the West, finds that the Eastern way is "excarnation," absorption into the cosmos through concentrating on the spiritual dimension of reality, whereas the West seeks "incarnation," a this-worldly life centered in the person and marked by ceaseless adventure and anxiety. The Eastern idea of society is a magical body held together by ageless tradition and in harmony with the cosmos. The Western is of a society of persons forever seeking new meanings and new hazards.[17] Lancelot Law Whyte discovers in Western thought a perpetual dualism between mind and matter, intellect and instinct, which keeps Western man forever at war with himself. Eastern man, on the other hand, accepts intuitively the unitary nature of the world-process. In the coming world civilization, Asia will borrow the West's most distinctive achievements, but the West will also accept from Asia her "deeper aim of harmony as proper to all men. . . . A new type of man emerges combining the unity

of the East with the differentiation of the West. The separation of East and West is over." [18]

But, again, perhaps the most elaborate and careful analysis
of East-West differences comes from F. S. C. Northrop. His
formula for East-West philosophical and cultural integration
has attracted, in its field, the same kind of broad public interest as Toynbee's *Study of History,* even to the extent of an
article in *Life;*[19] and it explains, ingeniously, how the Western mind can be both dynamically this-worldly and yet
highly abstract and theoretical, whereas the Eastern mind
can focus simultaneously on concrete experience and undifferentiated ultimate reality. Northrop himself is a perfect
example of the Western penchant for abstract theorizing
and classifying. He helps prove his own theory, by the very
methods he uses to arrive at it.

Northrop's argument recalls in places Sorokin's entirely
independent theory of the phases of a cultural supersystem.[20]
His starting point is the distinction between what he calls
the "aesthetic" component of knowledge and the "theoretic"
component. Aesthetic knowledge is reached by immediate
experience, which includes what is commonly called intuition. Knowledge in the theoretic component is reached
through concepts by postulation, as when a Western scientist, studying the history of forms of life through the fossil
record, formulates the theory of evolution; or looking at
man and nature in general, suggests the theory of the divine
Logos. The Eastern philosophies, and all Eastern cultures
necessarily, are founded on a very high development of the
aesthetic component of knowledge. The Western specialty,
of course, is the concept by postulation, which runs through
our monotheistic religions, Greek philosophy, and all later
thought evolved from these Judeo-Hellenic starting points.
Western knowledge tends, therefore, to be abstract, determinate, dogmatic, and precise. Not surprisingly, our chief
system of logic, the Aristotelian, holds that each "kind" of

"thing" is separate and distinct from each other "kind." The concept by postulation, reached inductively by empirical observation and followed through all its logical consequences by rational deduction, is the secret of the West's amazing success in the natural sciences. It gives man a way to scrutinize nature objectively, with a minimum of interference from the investigator.

There is more to the aesthetic component of knowledge, however, than may meet the eye at first glance. Knowledge in the theoretic component is always highly determinate, which is to say, expressed in certain exact words and/or mathematical symbols, which tend to shut it off from other similar bits of knowledge and from reality as a whole. A concept by postulation, one might say, taking a few liberties with Northrop, mentally slices the cosmic pie and tears pieces out of their existential context. Still other concepts by postulation slice the pie other ways. The world is thus mentally slashed into an infinity of sometimes overlapping, sometimes entirely isolated tatters of knowledge. Moreover, such knowledge is always indirectly verified. A theory cannot be seen, touched, or tasted. It cannot be scanned existentially by the inner eye of intuition. It is, so far as the living mind goes, "abstract." Knowledge in the aesthetic component, on the other hand, is always vibrantly direct, and it ranges anywhere from the sensuous experience of sound, smell, and color common to all men everywhere, to the Eastern mystic's intuitive absorption in total reality. In explaining the latter, Northrop argues that even Western science, with the advent of field theory in physics, has come around to the recognition that the entire universe can be regarded as a single continuum. This total continuum can be studied through theoretical differentiations, as in Western science, or as in Eastern philosophy and religion, it can be felt in its entirety, undifferentiated and inexpressible in any kind of language: hence, Northrop's much debated

phrase, the "undifferentiated aesthetic continuum," symbolized by such Oriental terms as Brahman-Atman and Tao,
but knowable aesthetically only through the direct Eastern
experience not of communion but of actual self-equation
with the world continuum. In the Hindu formula, *tat tvam
asi:* "that thou art." The genius of the East lies in its profound, direct cultivation of this sense of the unity of all being.

Clearly, Western culture has much to offer the East, but
Eastern art, religion, and formal thought can also greatly enrich the West, which has been notably sluggish in developing
the potentialities of the aesthetic component of knowledge.
Northrop feels that both components are worth exploiting.
Each is irreducible into the other, but a set of basic assumptions can be devised more catholic than either, asserting the
validity of both. An integral knowledge of reality requires
the "epistemic correlation" of both components, which can
lead not only to a deeper sense of reality in East and West
alike, but also to the foundations of a world civilization
uniting them both in a higher synthesis. On the Indian subcontinent, for example, an acceptance of the complementarity of theoretic and aesthetic knowledge would make Muslims less fanatic and Hindus more scientific — the Muslims
with their dogmatic monotheism representing an eastward
migration of Western culture, the Hindus with their lack of
enthusiasm for the theoretical articulation of the aesthetic
continuum illustrating the lopsidedness of Eastern culture.
The result would be peace and prosperity for the whole
subcontinent. And India is, in this sense, the planet in microcosm.[21]

Northrop has not escaped severe and able criticism. Sorokin and Radhakrishnan object vigorously to the sharpness of
his contrast between Eastern and Western modes of thought.
As Northrop himself has always conceded, but never stressed,
the West has its mystics, its monists, its existentialists, its artists and musicians deeply skilled in plumbing and com-

municating purely aesthetic experience. The East has its logicians, its theorists, its concepts by postulation. "Almost all the main concepts of Indian thought," Radhakrishnan writes, "are more concepts by postulation than concepts by intuition." Not all Westerners are dogmatic, as the history of Western science and exploration shows plainly, whereas the East has had its share of quarrelsome pedants and furious fanatics. The difference is a matter of degree. "The truth," Radhakrishnan concludes, "which is somewhat exaggerated in Northrop's analysis, is that in the East there is greater preoccupation with the richer and less determinate facts of existence than with the abstract and determinate facts of essence." [22]

Exaggerated or not, Northrop's formulas for East-West synthesis have given wide publicity to the problem of East-West differences, and they contain more than a few grains of useful truth. The main thing, again, is a passionate conviction of the complementarity of cultures. The very act of synthesis will have to be a joint East-West project, if Northrop's analysis is at all sound: Western philosophers are best qualified by their traditional methods to analyze the problem, Eastern philosophers to supply the conviction of cosmic harmony without which no attempt at synthesis could expect organic results.

Of course the need for painstaking analysis of differences can itself be challenged by Eastern thinkers, leading to a more characteristically Oriental formula for synthesis. Radhakrishnan prefers to emphasize the broad areas of agreement between East and West. All cultures, he writes, ask much the same questions and search for much the same things, each in its own way. Western culture is no morass of materialism, nor is Eastern culture so profoundly spiritual as many of its modern apologists like to think. Enough links exist between the two worlds of thought to bring them into fruitful union. All that is needed is tolerance and mutual sympathy. And since "great spiritual revivals occur through the fusion of different traditions," he expects a mighty spiritual renaissance to emerge from the true meeting of Eastern and Western minds. "The separation of East and West is over. The history of the new world, the one world, has begun. It promises to be large in extent, varied in colour, rich in quality." Men must bend every effort to forge a "unitary world culture," which is "the only enduring basis for a world community." [23]

Along somewhat similar lines, Jaspers calls for free and limitless communication between East and West, suspecting that "we are on the road from the evening-glow of European philosophy to the dawn of world philosophy." [24] Denis de Rougemont even predicts that by the turn of the century the debate between communism and capitalism will be replaced by a great and sober dialogue between East and West. "And I mean a real dialogue, at the level of religions and philosophies; that is to say, at the level on which civilizations and cultures are created." Whether one will absorb the other, or a transcending principle will be discovered uniting both, he cannot say; but he hopes at least for the "sincere alliance" Minerva negotiated between Ulysses and his foes at Ithaca.[25]

Meanwhile, East and West go on meeting — and colliding. Through the United Nations and its affiliated agencies, through trade and tourism, through the exchange of students and films and books and art, through conferences such as the series in Honolulu, the conferences on Oriental-Western literary relations at Indiana University, the annual Eranos symposia on Lago Maggiore in Switzerland, the Salzburg congress on comparative civilizations, and many others, the two cultural hemispheres of the world slowly coalesce. Perhaps, as Toynbee suggests, the final synthesis will be, in outward appearance, a "Westernization" of the world accompanied by profound Easternizing counter-tendencies within the West proper. Eastern acceptance of Western

science and technology has gone a long way toward ho-
mogenizing the two sets of civilizations, if only because,
as Gandhi foresaw, it is hardly possible to industrialize an
Eastern country without also, in the long run, bringing in all
the rest of the Western way of life. The East throws off the
chains of Western imperialism, but "the formerly subject
non-Western peoples . . . are all using their newly won
power of self-determination to Westernize their social
structures and their cultural configurations of their own ac-
cord. In doing this, they are laying the foundations for a
single world-wide society and for a uniform world-wide
culture that will take its first shape within a Western-made
framework — though, no doubt, it will become less specifically Western in complexion as all the cultural heritages of
all the extant societies come to be the common possession
of the whole of mankind." Toynbee hopes with fervor that
"the ex-Western oecumenical civilization" will assimilate
"all that was best in all the heritages of all the civilizations
that . . . preceded it." [26]

Of course this over-all question of total East-West synthesis far from exhausts the problems involved in the concert of cultures. It is probably the gravest challenge before
us in the long run. If the two worlds do not permanently
fuse, an exasperated, hungry, overpopulated Orient armed
with nuclear and bacteriological weapons may turn on the
West some day and overwhelm it, counting its casualties
as blessings in disguise and eager to even the score with
its thriving ex-conquerors. This might be poor justice,
but the Occident would not go to its grave entirely guilt-
less. And there are other problems. Within the West proper,
the Latin American cultures clash with the North American way of life. The English-speaking world is not entirely
at harmony with Continental Europe, and perhaps the German question is not yet solved, in spite of two world wars.
The Islamic West remains at loggerheads with the Chris-

tian West, after thirteen hundred years of conflict. Within
the Orient proper, no one could imagine the cultures of such
disparate areas as India, Indonesia, China, and Japan in perfect harmony with one another, in spite of a certain vague
fellow feeling, and many ties of blood and outlook and history. Negro Africa must also be reckoned with: a whole continent neither Eastern nor Western in cultural origins.

Finally, there is the gargantuan issue of communism, a
Western cult now in possession of half of Europe and most of
East Asia. As the other Western social philosophies and
creeds become noticeably more flexible and tolerant, and
even anxious to win Oriental friendship, communism sets
out to conquer the world with genuine nineteenth-century
Western verve. But dressed as it is in Russian sheep's cloth-
ing, it can somehow detach itself from the "real West" and
appeal to the East as an almost Eastern creed.

Something has already been said of the world ambitions of
the communist movement.* In its growth and expansion,
communism has undeniably created a new kind of culture,
bringing the West proper into a strange new union with
traditional Russian Orthodox culture, and into an even
stranger alliance with traditional Chinese culture. The meeting of East and West, then, is by no means confined to the
encounters and collisions of the Euro-American West with
the non-communist East. For practical political and military reasons, it is clearly imperative to persuade the new
Eurasian communist cultures to enter into a serious and
frank dialogue with the rest of the world. Now that Moscow is no longer the unrivaled capital of world communism,
and there is a wider variety of contacts between East and
West, the prospects for such a dialogue are no doubt improved.

A number of plausible solutions can be imagined, if both
camps in the Cold War manage to avoid a suicidal global ex-

* See pp. 120–24.

change of intercontinental ballistic missiles. Except for the extremists on either side, the most hopeful possibility is a gradual growing together under the impact of technology: as the two systems become less different, their missionary ardor may wear off, and they may little by little join forces. It is also conceivable that both will go on indefinitely, distinct from one another, but able to cooperate in keeping the peace for practical reasons. Or communism may — to use a famous phrase — wither away altogether, as the Soviet people, at least, outgrow their need for it.

From the point of view of the new science of economic development, capitalism and communism are only two different ways of reaching much the same economic goal. As Robert L. Heilbroner notes, communism is a substitute for capitalism, accomplishing for stagnant and backward economies in countries without a tradition of vigorous free enterprise what capitalism did, more gradually, in the nineteenth century for the West.[27] Walt Rostow strongly suspects that when Soviet Russia enters the era of high mass-consumption already reached by the West, communism "is likely to wither" and Russia is likely to fall prey to that notorious but not necessarily fatal affliction of all families and nations once they have achieved prosperity and want to enjoy it in peace: like the Buddenbrooks in Thomas Mann's early novel, they no longer care for empire-building. Rostow is hopeful that "the Buddenbrooks' dynamics will operate in Russia, if given time and a strong Western policy that rules out as unrealistic Soviet policies of expansion." The new generation will demand a higher standard of living, more personal freedom, a richer cultural life, and no part of messianic communism.[28]

Of course capitalism is changing, too. The graduated income tax, public welfare programs, social insurance, government controls, public ownership in many sectors of the economy, collective bargaining, and the cooperative move-

ment have totally transformed the old laisser-faire capitalistic system of Marx's time. The individual entrepreneur
counts for much less, just as his Soviet counterpart already
counts for much more. Lewis Mumford hears the death
knell of Economic Man in the steady movement of capitalist countries toward the welfare state and of communist
countries toward many of the virtues of individual initiative. In the change from "a money economy based on power
and productivity to a life economy based on participation
and creativity," the long-drawn-out industrial crisis in civilization will finally be resolved, and "instead of maintaining
their ideological purity," capitalist and communist regimes
"will tend to take on more of the diversified attributes of
living systems." [29] Economics will give place, at last, to life
itself, and goods will be produced in accordance not with
economic laws, but with human desires and needs. William
Ernest Hocking insists that even now the dichotomy between
capitalism and communism is wholly fictitious. "All actual
economies of developed nations are *mixed economies.*" Capitalism, whether of the public or private variety, has turned
out to be the best way of mobilizing resources for maximum
production; the socialist or communist principle is everywhere applied to some extent for equitable distribution of the
goods so produced.[30]

But differences do and will persist between the total culture and ideology of the West and of Soviet Russia, even if
the economic issue no longer really divides them or will not
divide them in the near future. Northrop sees Soviet culture dogmatically committed to the Hegelian-Marxian concept of the individual as merely a part of a social organism
which fits into a vast historical process, and as having merely
set physiological needs, which can be satisfied by planned
production. Since all this goes along with a typically Western
conviction of absolute rightness, a familiar failing of ideas
in the theoretical component of knowledge, Soviet culture

is dynamically aggressive. It cannot be reconciled with the liberal democratic ideology of the West derived from Locke and Bentham unless its fundamental presuppositions, and those of the West, are enlarged and purged of the "nothing but" fallacy, so as to create a new ideology embracing the insights, compatible with each other and true to human nature, of both. Obviously both rest, for example, on pitifully thin psychological assumptions: Soviet culture on the idea that men are bodies, the liberal-democratic West on the idea that men are simply consciousnesses which seek pleasure and avoid pain, in the famous formula of Jeremy Bentham. The nature of man is much fuller and deeper than either capitalism or communism would have us believe. In China, Northrop similarly hopes that communism will be able to achieve a higher synthesis in union with the rich culture of Confucian-Buddhist-Taoist tradition. If such a synthesis proves impossible, then he sees no alternative but the total extirpation of one or the other, communism or Sinism, since the two cannot coexist peacefully. The Red regime's massacres of monks and destruction of family life are ominous strides in the direction of the de-Sinicization of China. But the whole communist bloc must be politically quarantined by the rest of the world, through collective military action, until a true meeting of minds can produce a true reconciliation of the deep ideological differences separating communist cultures from those in the so-called free world.

Jaspers is still less optimistic about the possible role of communism in the coming world civilization. He accepts the need for a measure of socialism and for democratic planning, but he sees no compromise possible between the Soviet idea of total planning and the Western idea of freedom. A world totally planned would be a world totally despiritualized, closed to transcendence, reduced to insecthood. "Either . . . we have confidence in the chances of the free interplay of forces, notwithstanding the frequency with which they give rise to absurdities . . . or we stand before the world planned in its totality by man, with its spiritual and human ruin." [31] Toynbee sees some possibility of partial reconciliation in a democratic socialism that accepts but constantly strives to minimize the inevitable tension between the equally essential values of personal liberty and social justice. He looks on the new West European welfare states with their mixed economies as the most promising sign for the future. But at the level of the purely human, he admits that freedom and equality are basically incompatible abstractions. Only spiritual forces greater than the forces of this world can make them work together: in the Christian symbols, the brotherhood of man and the fatherhood of God. [32]

Perhaps, in another hundred years, the Cold War between capitalism and communism will be a dead issue, as de Rougemont prophesies. Or, perhaps, of all the obstacles in the path of world cultural synthesis, communism will prove the highest. It is certainly a most formidably tough nut at the present writing. Charles Moore makes the point that the philosophical attitudes of the traditional Orient and the traditional Occident are in fundamental harmony, even though emphasizing different things, whereas communism, with its materialism, determinism, totalitarianism, economic obsessions, ethics of crass expediency, and rejection of all spiritual or divine power, is basically incompatible with both. [33] This may be a harsh and extreme judgment born of Cold War hysteria, but there are times when the most cheerful observer cannot help but agree with it.

Still, no man can predict what changes may overtake communism in succeeding decades. Its program has not remained strictly consistent even over the past forty-five years. In the case of both Russia and China, revolutionary messianism has already been displaced to a very marked degree by old-fashioned great-power chauvinism, which may be just as dangerous to world peace in the long run, but at any rate is not the same thing. Nothing absolutely rules out the possibility that the Eurasian communist cultures will some day take their place in a unified world civilization, if the will for harmony exists on both sides.

Even assuming that all living creatures will eventually and freely flow into the common stream of humanity, the prophets leave us somewhat in the dark, as they must, on the total ultimate shape of the world culture. It may be one uniform culture, an alloy blended from all the best in the contributing historic cultures. Or the separate regional cultures may continue to flourish on a reduced scale, as Welsh or Basque culture persists in Britain or Spain today, with the true world culture limited to a few authentic cosmopolitan centers located here and there around the planet, analogous to the role of Paris in modern France. Or each regional culture may become the nucleus of its own particular independent version of world-synthesis, making the world a confederation of "globalized" Brazils, Germanies, Indias, Chinas, and so forth. Or finally, it may be a world of mishmash.

This last prospect seems to bother a good many people. Anyone familiar with the mammoth critical literature on Toynbee will remember, for example, Hugh Trevor-Roper's maliciously witty lampoon of the Toynbeean world civilization. Toynbee himself will be its divinely inspired prophet, he says, and his *Study of History* its only sacred book. Western civilization will disappear and "all that is good in it, and in other civilizations" will be "preserved and pickled in the universal world-state with its universal world-religion of Mish-Mash." [34] This is the usual quarrel of critics fond of the status quo with the coming world civilization, and especially its concert of cultures. Their favorite epithets, after mishmash, are "syncretism," "eclecticism," and "hodgepodge." If the prophets of world integration may be believed, this is a pseudo problem. No world culture, unitary, federate, confederate, or what not, is going to hang together in tomorrow's world unless it is growing in the direction of organicity at a convincing speed. But this is only the historical process. Roman culture was outrageously syncretic, no doubt, in the second and third centuries A.D., but out of it flowered the medieval synthesis. Christianity itself is a fantastic potpourri, if broken down into its constituent bits. No one looking at the agony of fifth- or sixth-century China, overrun by barbarians and invaded by alien religions, might have anticipated the incredible syntheses of T'ang and Sung culture. Synthesis is never born fully formed out of the brain of Jove. It arrives by degrees, from hodgepodge and confusion; and if it comes to the whole world in the centuries ahead, it can only come the same way.

But the prophets of world integration have investigated some special features of a world culture in more detail, which deserve separate treatment. Two essential ingredients, for prime examples, are religion, which will link Eastern and Western insights, and science, which the world civilization will have to borrow principally from the West. In both instances, especially the first, integration at several levels is urgently needed, if World Man is to think, feel, and act in creative harmony. Many prophets would argue that religious and intellectual integration may even, to some extent, have to precede the sort of philosophical synthesis surveyed above, although all three are intimately interrelated.

Religion and the World Order

THE RELIGIOUS component of the total ideology of a culture determines what, in the final analysis, is good and what is worth doing. Nothing else matters so crucially to the organic wholeness of civilized life. When, as very generally happens today, established religion clashes violently with new upstart faiths and all the rest of culture, the result is disorientation and spiritual chaos. This is an old story in our more volatile Western civilization, and not unheard of in the East, but today it takes on unprecedented gravity. There can be no world civilization, as its prophets agree, without some kind of harmony among the religions, and between religion itself and culture. All this may even be essential to sheer survival.

So, William Barrett in his luminous study of existentialism, *Irrational Man,* looks on the decline of religion as "the central fact of modern history in the West." Religion had served for centuries as a "psychic container," surrounding and sanctifying all of life. "In losing religion, man lost the concrete connection with a transcendent realm of being; he was set free to deal with this world in all its brute objectivity. But he was bound to feel homeless in such a world, which no longer answered the needs of his spirit." [35] Paul Tillich feels that "the decisive event which underlies the search for meaning and the despair of it in the twentieth

century is the loss of God in the nineteenth century." [36]
Toynbee, Jung, Jaspers, Hocking, Sorokin, most existentialists, most Catholic and Hindu philosophers, and — if one
were really to begin counting — practically everybody who
has written recently on the subject of religion, for or against,
agree that the contemporary crisis in religion is radical,
painful, decisive, and tragic. The Victorian agnostic's pre-
sentiment that religion was "on the way out" no longer
warms the soul, not even the souls of twentieth-century ag-
nostics. A good index to our despair is the polyglot cast of
characters in Arthur Koestler's mid-century novel, *The Age
of Longing.* Not one has a religion, except Comrade Nikitin;
each looks, none finds, all are miserable in their unrequited
longing.

Definitions of religion vary, enough that the orthodox adherents of the great "revealed" Semitic religions — Judaism,
Christianity, Islam — fail to find themselves engaged in a
common undertaking with the Indian and Far Eastern faiths.
Both Western and Eastern positive religions, in turn, see no
true religion in Western atheistic humanism or the ethico-
religious aspects of Marxism-Leninism. But religion is man's
concern for ultimate value and meaning in life, whatever
creedal form such concern takes, and whatever institutions
grow up to give concrete expression to faith. Religion in
this broad sense saves man from the desolating limitations
of his mortality and finitude. The world civilization clearly
cannot survive without religion, nor can it be preserved
over the centuries if men set themselves to the achievement of incompatible goals or the valuing of incompatible
ideas of the good because of fundamental differences in religious faith. Harmonious cooperation among the world's
religious leaders, pointing toward ultimate religious unity is
the least, perhaps, that will do. Even this may fall short, if
two or more faiths with the same goods and goals insist on
driving one another from the field by force.

The major positive religions have been thrown together many times in the past, have fought, divided, amalgamated, and exchanged ideas for thousands of years, but never all at once in the single arena of a united planet. This total confrontation goes back only a few generations, into the nineteenth century, when the West temporarily had the whole world under its wing and Western scholars invented the discipline of "comparative religion" or "religious history." By the late nineteenth century skeptics and naturalists were describing all religions as "relative" products of "relative" cultures. Anthropology, led by Sir James Frazer, joined in the game. And latitudinarian spirits assembled at the Chicago Exposition of 1893 to hold a World's Parliament of Religions, at which fifty-nine delegates marched onto the platform representing all the major religions: Hindu Swamis and Buddhist missionaries joined forces with rabbis and archbishops in a bewildering demonstration of good will and friendly competition for souls.

What happened to the great German theologian Ernst Troeltsch gave fair warning of things to come, at least among liberal laymen and clergymen who could neither live without the insights of religion nor accept the claim to exclusive or supreme authority of any living creed. Troeltsch started out his theological career in the Germany of Wilhelm II as a thorough Christian, finding all faiths wanting in divine grace but Christianity. Further study and reflection brought him around, as it has brought Toynbee after him, to the realization that other religions are also unique, in their own ways. They are all patently inferior to Christianity in providing what Christianity specializes in providing, but Christianity is not omnicompetent. "The Divine Reason, or the Divine Life, within history, constantly manifests itself in always-new and always-peculiar individualizations." Christianity is "final and unconditional for us," but "this does not preclude the possibility that other racial groups, living under entirely different cultural conditions, may experience their contact with the Divine Life in quite a different way." [37]

Out of this basic discovery, be it true or false, all recent attempts to supply formulas for the harmonization of the positive religions naturally flow. With academic theology, by and large, going other ways since Troeltsch's time, the great initiative in recent years for religious synthesis has come from the prophets of a world civilization, who — in the West — are nearly all unattached humanists or Protestant laymen with only slight influence in bona fide theological circles.

William Ernest Hocking's Hibbert Lectures, published in 1940 as *Living Religions and a World Faith,* stand out as one of the real landmarks in this recent prophetic literature. Hocking had earlier served as chairman of a lay commission of appraisal appointed by seven Protestant groups to study at first hand the work of their missions in Asia; its report, *Re-Thinking Missions,* had drawn heavy fire from the orthodox camp. "The original objective of the mission might be stated as the conquest of the world by Christianity," the commission wrote, but now, without abandoning Christianity, the Christian missionary should "regard himself as a co-worker with the forces which are making for righteousness within every religious system." [38] The missionary should welcome signs of resurgence in the native Asian religions and associate himself with all that is best in them, eager to learn as well as teach. The real enemy of all religions is secularism, not fellow faiths.

If *Re-Thinking Missions* left anything unsaid, Hocking has made his position unmistakably clear in his Hibbert Lectures. The plurality of creeds is, he notes, a matter of historical accident. If history caused it, "history may undo it. And history appears to be undoing it. . . . To-day, through the penetrating power of commerce and science, something like a world culture begins to appear," and the coming world culture will no more be able to survive without religion than the local cultures of the past. He defines religion as "a passion for righteousness, and for the spread of righteousness, conceived as a cosmic demand." Religion is both universal and particular: universal because it arises from a universal human craving for an equally universal truth, particular because religious teachers must always communicate their findings in particular language to particular people, which forces a faith "to assume the burden of an infinitely extraneous specification." All would-be universal faiths throughout history have "fallen into a new particularity" almost from their inception, as Christianity became Helleno-Romanized and Islam Arabianized.[39]

There are three possible ways to a world faith, which Hocking examines in order. The first is "radical displacement," the method of Christian and Muslim missions in the past. It is founded on St. Paul's assumption that "natural religion" is a contradiction in terms, the assumption taken up in modern times by theologians like Karl Barth that Biblical Christianity, "a dated product of God's wisdom and goodness wholly unimaginable to man," alone can save souls. As Barth says, the Christian missionary must not accept the "fellowship of fallen faiths" or "howl with the wolves." The result, since Christianity is a Western faith, is to make pseudo Westerners out of Christian converts in non-Western lands, people cut off from the living traditions of their own heritage, which includes, above all, religion. "By a strange reversal of fates, the native Christian might conceivably become the international Jew of Asia."[40] The way of radical displacement would work only if all cultures could be wiped out except the culture of the religion which triumphantly displaced all the rest. This is clearly just another variation of old-fashioned imperialism.

Having dispatched radical displacement, Hocking turns to

the second way to a world faith, "the way of synthesis." By synthesis, he means the process by which living religions incorporate into themselves certain congenial elements from other religions, as Christianity borrowed from its rivals in its formative centuries, or Confucianism borrowed from Buddhism in medieval China. True synthesis requires organic development, which takes a long time. Any shortcut to religious unity through a mere artificial blending of creeds, as in nineteenth-century Theosophy, leads to sterile, inorganic aggregates, not true religions. But gradual organic synthesis does prepare the ground for what Hocking regards as the most fruitful way to union, the "way of reconception."

Reconception is somewhat suggestive of Northrop's epistemic correlations. The enrichment of the living religions by their absorption of congenial elements from rival faiths will not solve the basic issues which divide them. Synthesis broadens without deepening. The living religions must finally come to an awareness of their basic, culturally conditioned narrowness. "They are all wretched vessels. They are all wrapped in sanctimony, dusty-eyed with self-satisfaction, stiff-jointed with the rheum-rust of their creedal conceits, so timorous under the whips of conformity that only a few dare the perilous task of *thinking,* and the complacency-disturbing task of trying the spirit of other faiths." [41] What each must do is think down deeply into the bowels of its belief, discover its essence, and try to reconceive its fundamental option in such a way that it can accept the insights of other religions, even though those insights may contradict its original tenets. The way of reconception is not tolerance or charity, but a self-deepening, a digging out of new and deeper foundations, ample enough to support a more catholic structure of faith. Instead of religion A merely reaching out and helping itself to attractive morsels of religion B, religion A so alters its basic approach that it can, in its ampler proportions, include all it thinks valid in religion B without losing its organic identity, on the one hand, or remaining fundamentally unreconstructed, on the other.

Each religion professing universality has much to offer the rest. Christianity is unique in its intuition of ultimate reality as a personal, loving Father who suffered in human flesh on earth to save mankind from sin; its dynamic gospel of unconditional love gives it a readiness to apply itself to social betterment and the relief of human misery not so well developed in other religions; it has much skill and experience in doing battle with secularism, since secularism is a Western disease; and it reaches common folk easily because it is not a monkish or aristocratic faith, but a way of salvation for everyone. Islam uniquely emphasizes the unity of God, obscured by the subtleties of Christian theology, and the fraternity of all men regardless of race, a point on which Christians, bogged down by some of the secular conceits of their Western culture, sometimes equivocate. Hinduism and Buddhism excel in seeing the divine ground in its impersonal aspect, and they have more advanced techniques for the intuitive understanding of ultimate reality. They achieve more serenity of spirit. They are less tied to pseudo-historical myth, dogmatic literalness in interpretation of religious symbolism, and all the sins of pride which follow therefrom. The indigenous Chinese faiths supply more organic communion with the universe than other religions, a communion not only at the level of spirit, but at all the levels of human experience, which gives them a cosmic cheerfulness absolutely unique in the history of religions. Hence, no one faith is fully enough developed not to need insight from the others, which cannot be fully assimilated save by self-reconception.

In his Hibbert Lectures, Hocking is somewhat vague on the question of whether thoughtful reconception of each of the universal religions will be enough. Mankind in the coming age will need a world morale, he writes, made possible only by the sharing of religious faith, both in the realm of universal religious truth, and in the realm of concrete religious expression and symbolism. In his more recent book, *The Coming World Civilization,* he elaborates on this theme to urge that the living religions should not unite in one literally global religion, although they are all "already fused together, so to speak, at the top," through their sharing of certain universal spiritual truths. Each must retain its integral identity and emphasize what it emphasizes best, and the result will be a unity in diversity, to which the individual man will find himself heir *in toto.* "To every man, the West and the East alike will naturally contribute whatever is universal in their cultures, no longer as western or eastern, but as his own." The plurality of religions will, thus, be a kind of optical illusion. "Retaining the symbols of their historic pieties, the great faiths will grow in their awareness of a unity more significant than the remaining differences." And after reciting a Hindu tradition about the confluence of rivers, he closes with the cryptic question, "if Jumna and Ganges run together, shall the united lower stream be called Ganges or Jumna? Is it neither? Is it both? Or is that one whose symbol men freely find compacted with the sense of both, holding in a historic life and deed, for which there can be no repetition and no substitute, a prophetic answer to man's eternal need?" [42]

These are deep waters, indeed. Another intrepid explorer well launched on them is Arnold Toynbee, especially in volumes VII and XII of *A Study of History,* and in two sets of lectures, his 1952-53 Gifford Lectures at Edinburgh, published as *An Historian's Approach to Religion,* and his 1955 Hewitt Lectures at three American theological schools, published as *Christianity among the Religions of the World.*

Toynbee's attitude toward the higher religions has changed markedly through the years. In the earlier volumes of his *Study,* civilization was obviously to be saved by Chris-

tianity alone, the way of "transfiguration" and "palingene-
sia" revealed in history by the mission of Jesus Christ, and
by Him only. At this stage, Northrop not unreasonably
labeled him an exponent of religious imperialism.[43] In the
batch of volumes appearing in 1954, Toynbee elevated to
equal rank with Christianity a few other higher religions, not
concealing his preference for the Mahayana Buddhism of
China and Japan because of its doctrine of the bodhisattvas
who postpone their final translation to nirvana out of Christ-
like compassion for the souls of men. On the same Christo-
centric principle, he also rated Shi'ite Muslims with their
doctrine of the Promised One over the more orthodox Sun-
nite Muslims, accepted Hinduism without much enthusiasm, rejected the other main branch of Buddhism, the Hinayana, and omitted Judaism and all the indigenous Far
Eastern faiths. His latest tallies of the higher religions admit
Judaism, Zoroastrianism, and Hinayana Buddhism to the
select company discussed in 1954.

However many higher religions he finally decides upon,
Toynbee's present position is as far from Christian orthodoxy as possible. Each of the higher religions sees divinity
from its own special point of view, but all "establish and
maintain direct communion between human souls and absolute spiritual Reality." [44] All agree that man is not the
greatest spiritual presence in the universe, and needs contact and union with the higher spiritual reality behind the
phenomena of sense experience or physical theory. They
differ in their holy places, rituals, taboos, social conventions,
myths, and theological systems, but the openhearted be-
liever, by disengaging the nonessentials from the essentials
in mankind's religious heritage, can find a common core
of truth in all the positive religions.

The higher religions can be classified in several ways: by
their attitude to their rivals, by their emphasis on the personal or impersonal aspects of divinity, and by psychologi-

cal appeal. In Volume VII of *A Study of History,* Toynbee
experimented with a psychological classification, using
Jung's theory of the four basic personality types as his starting point. By this criterion, Christianity and Islam were
the extraverted members of the species, one emphasizing
"feeling," in its paramount doctrine of divine love, the other
"sensing," in its direct uncritical acceptance of a fixed rule of
belief and worship. The two Indic faiths, Hinduism and
Buddhism, were the introverts of the species, Hinduism corresponding to the Jungian personality type which stresses
"thinking" and Buddhism to the type which stresses "in-
tuiting." [45] It would be easy to make intellectual mincemeat
of Toynbee's particular choice of categories here, but his
main point certainly has merit: each of the higher religions
is not only the product of a particular culture but also appeals across cultural lines to one or more different varieties
of human personality.

The steps to world religious integration, then, to draw on
all Toynbee's recent thinking, are three. First, a mutual
confrontation of higher religions impelling devotees to examine their creeds and disengage the essence of each from the
nonessential cultural baggage which each has accumulated
over the years. This will lay bare the basic harmony of all
the higher religions, and also their essential differences.
Second, out of this confrontation must develop a spirit of
friendly cooperation and mutual respect. "The divers
higher religions must resign themselves to playing limited
parts, and must school themselves to playing these parts in
harmony, in order, between them, to fulfill their common
purpose of enabling every human being of every psychological type to enter into communion with God the Ultimate
Reality." [46] Authentic adult freedom of choice of creed may
become common, as the world grows more closely together.
A Frenchman for whom Buddhism will unlock the cosmos
better than Christianity will become a Buddhist. A Bur-

mese whose psychological make-up inclines him toward a more extraverted faith than local tradition allows, may choose Christianity. This is already happening on a very small scale, all over the world. "All religions, while retaining their historic identities, will become more and more open-minded, and (what is more important) open-hearted, towards one another as the World's different cultural and spiritual heritages become, in increasing measure, the common possession of all Mankind." [47]

Finally, Toynbee even hints at an eventual world religion. He does not "expect to see mankind converted to a 'syncretistic' religion, constructed artificially out of elements taken from all the existing religions." Nevertheless, one of the major faiths may prove sufficiently broad and full to "win the allegiance of the whole human race." But "the winning religion, whichever it may be, will not eliminate the other religions that it replaces. Even if it does replace them, it will achieve this by absorbing into itself what is best in them." [48]

Some years before Toynbee's experiment with Jungian personality types, the American philosopher Charles Morris, in *Paths of Life: Preface to a World Religion,* did much the same thing on a larger scale, using William H. Sheldon's three basic "somatotypes" — endormorph, mesomorph, and ectomorph, or, very roughly, fat, muscular, and thin — as his springboard for a typology of systems of religious value and orientation. Through history, all religions and religious philosophies have taken one of six possible "paths of life," each developing from a different combination of endomorphic, mesomorphic, and ectomorphic tendencies in the personality of the founders. All six are lopsided, containing three parts of one tendency, two of another, and one of a third.

But there is a seventh possible path, neatly assembled from two parts of each component, which Morris calls the "Maitreyan path of generalized detached-attachment," after

Maitreya, the bodhisattva venerated by Buddhists as the next Buddha scheduled to appear to mankind. "The essential characteristic of the Maitreyan," he points out, "lies in his need to accept and to integrate all of the features of the human self which in various ways are given unequal supremacy in the other types of personality." [49] This seventh path may become a genuine world religion in the coming planetary society; it is a path which Morris, on the basis of extensive research, feels is already winning steadily wider acceptance among young people in mid-century.[50] Not every world citizen will find the Maitreyan path suited to his personality, but the presence of a broad stratum of fully integrated Maitreyan types in the world's population will exert a potent force for peace, harmony, and toleration of diversity in the coming world civilization. The "Maitreyan" world religion strongly suggests Sorokin's hopes for a new "Integral" cultural supersystem, with a threefold "Integral" theory of knowledge. Still another proposal along similar lines is Gerald Heard's concept of a three-ply world religion ministering to man's three great religious needs, only one of which is well served by any single positive faith: rites of identity with nature, a revealed code of law, and spiritual exercises for the integration of the self.[51]

Other prophets studied earlier for their thoughts on the larger problem of total cultural integration run true to form on the question of religion. At one end of the spectrum, Jaspers, with his emphasis on freedom and historical concreteness, argues that a world order preserving human personality can exist "only when the multiple contents of a faith remain free in their historical communication, without the unity of an objective, universally valid doctrinal content." [52] A single fixed world creed would cripple human reason and enslave the soul; but he is also categorically opposed to all dogmas and claims to exclusive or final truth in the historic religions. He would agree with Radhakrishnan's goal of "an altogetherness in which we walk together creatively and to which we all contribute," a universal church established not through fusion, but through fellowship.[53]

Northrop, on the other hand, prefers a literally world religion. In a carefully reasoned essay in *The Logic of the Sciences and the Humanities,* he applies his "philosophical anthropology" to the problem of East-West religious differences, and emerges with a plea for "a truly global, as opposed to a provincially Eastern or a provincially Western, morality and religion." [54] The Western religions, Judaism, Christianity, and Islam, all begin by postulating a determinate transcendent God, who generally speaks through inspired prophets or saviours, since He is postulated, rather than directly experienced, and therefore inaccessible to ordinary mortals. Most Western religions also preach the immortality of individual souls, which are determinate, theoretical entities like God Himself, and they verbalize their faith in allegedly inerrant, precise dogma. In short, Western religious knowledge is in the "theoretic" component, whereas Eastern religious knowledge, with its non-theistic, indeterminate, mystical, and directly experienced truths, operates in the "aesthetic" component. The two must be brought together in a higher synthesis through what Hocking would call reconception. The coming world civilization will have a single, all-embracing religion, just as it will need a federal world government and an integrated world economy.

Another possible path to world religious unity that would also arrive at a single world faith is taken by those humanistic prophets who reject the positive religions altogether. The humanists are rebelling against the authoritarian, dogmatic, inhumane streak in the Western monotheistic religions, rather than against religious faith itself; they are often intensely religious men, and the net result of their rebellion is the vision of a more thoroughgoing unity in the

spiritual life of man than most schemes for an integration of
the positive religions would require.

So the German humanist Gerhard Szczesny, for example,
sees Christianity as a desert people's creed, basically incompatible in its dualistic world-view with philosophy and science, and a brake on their progress for two thousand years;
he calls for a secularization of "all national and cultural 'holy
things,' " as the prelude to the emergence of a world civilization with a world ideology grounded in the monism of modern science.[55] Erich Fromm looks forward to the appearance
of "a new religion" within the "next few hundred years, a
religion which corresponds to the development of the human race; the most important feature of such a religion
would be its universalistic character, corresponding to the
unification of mankind which is taking place in this epoch;
it would embrace the humanistic teachings common to all
great religions of the East and the West." It would be a rational, ethical, practical faith, in harmony with science and
enabling man at last to live in harmony with himself and the
cosmos, the first "fully human" religion in history.[56] Sir
Julian Huxley preaches a world scientific humanism, a "naturalistic belief-system" drawing its basic inspiration from
evolutionary biology; and similar "scientific" or "organic"
humanisms are advocated by Erich Kahler, Lewis Mumford,
Hugh Miller, Oliver Reiser, and many others. The common
denominator in all of them is the conviction that man has out-
grown the provincial creeds of the historic civilizations and
now needs a universal religion based on the modern world-
picture and committed to unconditional faith in the unity
of mankind.

These two approaches to religious unity, the conservative
program of integrating or harmonizing the living religions
and the radical program of creating a humanistic world religion more or less from scratch, may not be dialectical op-

posites, but here, very plainly, is an area of profound disagreement in the contemporary prophetic literature on world
order.

The spiritual leaders of the positive religions themselves
are also split in a number of directions on the question of
what attitude to take toward rival creeds. Liberal churchmen tend to be shyly cordial. The more orthodox leaders
have turned inward in recent decades, an attitude which
breeds infinite misunderstanding. Most of the best minds in
Protestant theology since the first World War, for example,
have been trying to clarify the spiritual identity of the Protestant tradition by getting a new grip on the essential insights of their sixteenth-century Reformation, with the help
of Kierkegaard and existentialist analysis. Catholic theologians are doing the same sort of thing with Aquinas, and
similar movements to redefine and revive the traditional
faith are at work in Islam and the Eastern religions. Most of
these campaigns of revival do not simply retreat into the
past; the insights of modern philosophy are freely used;
fresh truth is discovered; and, indeed, no religion can hope
to take its proper place in the world orchestra of religions
without a distinct idea of its own history, essence, and peculiar genius.

But this preoccupation with the distinctiveness of one's
own creed leads inevitably to neglect and even distrust of
other creeds, if carried too far. There is still much monstrous
arrogance abroad in the historic faiths, comparable to the
chauvinism of the surviving Great Powers. Even contemporary Hinduism, commonly thought of as the most tolerant
and catholic of all living religions, succumbs to provincialism by insisting on embracing all other faiths in its own
motherly *paramavidya,* or "higher truth," which, in effect,
relegates the insights of other religions to the rank of "relative truths" and asserts the supremacy of the specifically
Hindu outlook.[57] Meanwhile, in the West, the Swiss Prot-

estant theologian Emil Brunner warns that any effort to combine non-Christian insights "even in the most modest way with the Christian idea must lead to failure"; and Father Martin D'Arcy concludes that a world culture "which will contain the best of the past and be open to further extension" can be created by Roman Catholic Christianity alone.[58] With less arrogance, but to much the same final effect, the Dutch theologian Hendrik Kraemer admits that there will and should be a frank exchange of ideas among the great positive religions. But brushing aside proposals for world religious synthesis as "thought-poems," he insists that in the coming dialogue Christianity must stick to her exclusiveness with an iron will, since her missionaries have something unique and precious to offer the non-Christian world: the word of God. The Eastern religions are all systems of self-salvation, elaborate, subtle, and refined, but nonetheless works of men, based on the "cosmic naturalism" common to all primitive peoples. Only Christianity is directly from God.[59] *

There are signs also of a more cosmopolitan spirit in the Christian churches. The ecumenical movement, launched at the great conferences in Stockholm and Lausanne in 1925-27, promises to promote more friendly — dare one write "more Christian"? — relations among the three main branches of Christianity, and even to encourage the integration of some of the major Protestant denominations. Under Pope John XXIII the Roman Catholic hierarchy is showing renewed interest in the problem of Christian unity. An ecumenical movement of sorts is also under way in Buddhism. Difficult but profound attempts have been made to harmonize philosophy and religion, such as the well known theology of Paul

* Of course Kraemer overlooks the crucial point that when the true self — as in the Indian religions — is regarded as ultimately identical with the impersonal divine ground of all being, it is no longer the "self" of Western psychological theory at all, and hence Hindu or Buddhist "self-salvation" is something inconceivably different from what such a term would mean in Western mouths.

Tillich, which is a synthesis of practically all the major trends in Western thought, uniting mysticism, Platonism, idealism, existentialism, and Biblical Christianity in a subtle system that might satisfy even many Asian thinkers.[60]

On the other hand, many religiously inclined laymen, especially, are unhappy with the isolationism of their traditional faiths in this rapidly coalescing world. At best the faiths take only a few faltering steps toward unity; the lay prophets of world religious order, men of the stature of Toynbee and Hocking, may have a great deal more influence on the future of religion than the spiritual leaders of the religions themselves. The prophets of world integration are, in fact, helping to create what F. L. Baumer calls a "Layman's Religion," a faith growing up alongside the neo-orthodox theologies, which finds that no one culture or tradition enjoys a monopoly of spiritual truth, and stresses the transcendent value of existential religious experience, articulated in the language of myth and symbol, rather than in the brittle catechisms of dogma.[61] Given the failure of the orthodox to escape the confines of their separate traditions, the only question that remains is whether this lay religion, the way of communion, will become the faith of the world culture, or whether something much more radical, some metaphysically ambitious variety of humanism, can be brought to organic life by the sorcery of time and circumstance.

This much, at least, is clear. If we descend from the mountain peaks of theology to the plateau of ethics, all the formulas for the spiritual unification of man converge in perfect harmony. The prophets of world order seldom try to anticipate the ethical content of the world faith, but in the whole body of their writings, most of them do take personal stands on the great moral issues, and they almost invariably uphold the same supreme values. They all affirm and reverence life; they all believe in the freedom and integrity of the person; they all urge the existential self to seek self-transcendence in organic union with mankind and with the mystical or divine ground of the cosmos; and they all discover the spiritual resources for human effort in the power of unconditional love. About these four final values — life, personality, transcendence, and love — there is no disagreement whatever in nearly the whole range of contemporary prophetic literature. This unanimity is all the more encouraging because each prophet has his own quite different method for discovering the good: Northrop draws on the "natural law" of modern physical theory, Huxley the "laws" of biological evolution, Toynbee the Helleno-Christian tradition in moral philosophy, Jaspers his own philosophy of nature and existence, and so forth.[62] If a dozen or more thinkers each approaching the problems of ethics from a different metaphysical or theological position can independently adopt the same system of values, the world civilization, too, may be able to reach a common conception of the good.

But whether One World Man will subscribe to the same moral code as his twentieth-century ancestors cannot possibly be foreseen and may not even matter. All that can be said with conviction is that, like the prophets of world order, he will have a deep sense of value. For him, the universe will not be silent. He will avoid the fragile certainties of dogma, but he will find indications of a higher lawfulness in the cosmos above the conscious desires of individual men. And if he succeeds in duplicating the agreement on ultimate values of the modern prophets of world integration, harmony in ethics may inspire further harmony in other fields of religious thought, clearing the way for an all-encompassing world faith.

The Integration of Knowledge

THE HARMONIZING of rival cultures at the decisive level of philosophy and religion will help lead to a world culture, but not, according to some thinkers, unless giant steps are also taken to unify the specialized knowledge-seeking disciplines in each culture. The need for intellectual synthesis has become especially acute in Western civilization, and to the extent that we all live in Toynbee's "Westernizing world," this peculiarly Western problem touches all mankind. The world organism will be as helpless without well-coordinated sense organs and a well-organized memory, as without the power to reason, judge, and value.

In at least the natural sciences, the integration of knowledge is much nearer at hand than the integration of philosophy and religion. In the progress of modern science, Teilhard de Chardin sees "the first lineaments of a common consciousness," the emergence of a world mind. The scientists' "synthesis of the laws of Matter and Life . . . is nothing else but a collective act of perception." Sir Julian Huxley finds men throughout the world already unified intellectually by the triumphs of modern science: it only remains for man to "unify and universalize his religion." [63] Up to a point all this is true. The methods of science supply techniques of studying the natural world which now enjoy universal acceptance. Western natural science is a way, not of discovering absolute truth, but of getting people of all cultures, hues, creeds, ideologies, temperaments, and sexes to agree on procedures and results within, though not beyond, the limits science imposes on itself. This is something new in history. Since man's idea of the natural world conditions his whole outlook toward ethics, metaphysics, and the meaning of life, science may be doing more than anything else to lay the foundations for a true world culture. Clearly, science and technology in their interaction have begun to create a common material culture for all humanity: the culture of airplanes and automobiles, hospitals and printing presses, electric power and big cities.

But the prophets of world order are not all as optimistic about the integration of human knowledge as Teilhard and Huxley. Some, like the British scientist Lancelot Law Whyte and the American philosopher Oliver L. Reiser, cast science in the role of a savior of mankind, but deplore its fragmentation in mid-century into thousands of virtually self-contained separate disciplines. As they see it, the crisis of our age is primarily the disunity of science and, in a larger sense, the total failure of all the knowledge-seeking disciplines, the human sciences even more than the natural, to produce a single, unified picture of the phenomenal world. Like the pieces of a jigsaw puzzle scattered in confusion over a table-top, the separate sciences do not make a coherent whole, although, with effort, they *could*. The result is that no one mind has anything like a connected picture of the world, much knowledge goes to waste, many fruitful interrelationships are never explored, and we are faced with conceptual chaos. At the same time, older prescientific approaches to knowledge also persist in attenuated or decadent forms. "We must stop this descent from conceptual, to ethical, to social confusion," Reiser warns, "before it moves to irretrievable economic, political, and finally military exhaustion." [64]

The problems are legion. The physical and life sciences

have recorded solid achievements over the past few hundred years, but in the behavioral and social sciences, the unanimity possible in natural science has never been reached. In these sciences of man, there are only frontiers, no conquered and settled provinces. Disciplines overlap and fail to mesh. Knowledge is produced at a rate far exceeding presently devised methods of assimilating and transmitting it. Each major country now churns out from twelve to twenty thousand new books each year, vast numbers of them technical monographs from several dozen major university presses. Over a million articles appear each year in the world's 50,000 periodicals devoted to the natural sciences alone, according to a recent Unesco survey. "Informed sources have it," says the *New York Times,* "that between 1900 and 1960 man learned more than in all the centuries that preceded our own." [65] To this staggering glut of knowledge must be added the super-problem of how to fit the knowledge we have into a metaphysical framework big enough to hold it. Here, chaos is even more universal; the methods of modern science offer no help; many philosophers have long ago abandoned the search for frameworks altogether.

Fully aware of the magnitude of their job, the prophets of world order most interested in the problem discuss intellectual integration at three levels: the metaphysical framework itself, ways of knowing, and interdisciplinary contacts. At each level they have worked out similar general answers, which do not so much solve problems as suggest lines of attack. In any event, their goal is not unity for the sheer sake of unity, but a unified science and a unified world-picture that can help give shape and substance to a unified world culture.

The metaphysical starting point in each case is a conviction of the organic coherence of the cosmos. Nearly all the prophets, whether they are especially concerned with in-

tellectual integration or not, take this same basic position on
faith. They are all monists: for them, the universe, all
reality, all being, is ultimately one. If monism cannot be
demonstrated in any final way, now or ever, still it is almost
inevitable that prophets of world order should be monists,
and above all prophets of order and unity of knowledge. A
fractured, lawless, jumbled universe would necessarily rule
out both a unified science and a unified world-picture.

This overarching monism, which could also become the
first article of faith in a unified world religion if the prophets
prevail, is loudly rejected by a certain common type of twentieth-century intellectual; but it has a long history in East
and West alike. Most prophets of an ecumenical society as far back as classical times have embraced monism in
some form. Monism is the dominant assumption of all leading Oriental philosophies, and monism or a relative pluralism pointing to an absolute monism has always had its place
in Western thought. The struggle in theoretical physics today between the heirs of Einstein and the quantum physicists
is fundamentally a conflict between Einstein's monist faith
in the order and harmony of the cosmos and a skeptical
countertendency which grows out of the discovery of apparently insoluble technical problems in the study of sub-
atomic particles. If Einstein, himself a great supporter of
world government in late life, was on the right scent, the
unified field theory which was his last and never finished
project will some day close the gap between macrocosm and
microcosm, serving twentieth-century science as Newton
served the science of his own era, nearly three hundred years
ago. "The whole complex of the universe," writes Lincoln
Barnett, "will resolve into a homogeneous fabric in which
matter and energy are indistinguishable and all forms of
motion from the slow wheeling of the galaxies to the wild
flight of electrons become simply changes in the structure
and concentration of the primordial field." [66]

Whether Einstein's work is ever finished or not, the prophets of world order are already fully satisfied that man lives in a coherent universe. Sir Julian Huxley believes "in the unity of mind and matter in the one ultimate world-substance" and in the total evolving continuity of nature, in which there is not one phenomenon that stands entirely alone, unconnected and uninvolved. For Mumford, "From one end of creation to another . . . a unifying process . . . underlies all variety and diversity," evolving by purposeful strides toward man and mind. Northrop's key concept is the "undifferentiated aesthetic continuum," the universal field perceived as a whole only through intuition; Sorokin's is the "Infinite Manifold," Reiser's the "Cosmic Field," Teilhard's the "Totum." "No doubt all thinking," Toynbee writes, "is a mental fission of a unitary Reality." The truth sought by science and religion in their separate ways must ultimately be reducible to unity, although unity may lie beyond man's finite power to grasp. Gerhard Szczesny deplores the Judeo-Christian habit of seeing reality double, human and divine, natural and supernatural. In the world-view of a unified planetary civilization, there will be no bifurcation of reality, but only a "relative dualism of the knowable and unknowable." The "comprehensive world-scheme" of the future "will impress unity on the many partial forms of knowledge" and relate meaningfully to what man does know "the sphere of all that lies beyond human experience and knowledge." [67]

Monism, then, is the ultimate metaphysical commitment of the prophets, although most of them would not go so far as Szczesny in rejecting pointblank the Judeo-Christian symbolism of a "wholly other" creator or divine ground. As Toynbee suggests, Westerners cannot help but sense a profound gulf between themselves and God, even though they may also see, on another plane, the absolute unity of being. As a peculiar sharpness of vision or focus within a larger monist framework, Judeo-Christian dualism has its own spe-

cial spiritual value and should not be left out of the final
synthesis, just as the sciences cannot survive without specialization. A unified science will be no more a single great
undifferentiated block of knowledge carved from a monolithic monism than the world culture itself will require every
man and region on earth to adhere to exactly the same uniform style of dress or art or worship.

At another level, at the level of ways of knowing, the
prophets of intellectual integration generally agree that all
methods of seeking truth must be exploited to the utmost
limits, methods stressed in the Eastern and premodern
Western civilizations as well as those worked out by modern
natural science. Some of the most fully developed arguments
here have already been noticed in the pages on world
philosophical synthesis above. Especially important is Sorokin's "integral cognition," the thesis that a complete science,
like the ideal cultural supersystem, must use the full resources of the human mind and take every true avenue to
truth, from sensory cognition at one end of the scale through
reason to direct intuition. Not even traditional Western science has, in practice, been able to escape exploiting all
three: empirical observation, as in laboratory experiments;
rational hypothesis and analysis, as in the formulation of
theories; and intuitive insight, as in the superconscious flash
solution of a mathematical problem. A unified science will
have to make extensive use of all three in correlated harmony, especially of intuition, which has been neglected and
misunderstood by most schools of modern Western thought.
The same basic idea is involved in Northrop's "epistemic
correlation" of the aesthetic and theoretic components of
knowledge; Toynbee on "imagination" and "intellect"; Mumford on the synthesis of "subjective" and "objective" truth;
and Reiser's "cortico-thalamic integration." [68]

As Mumford points out, the narrow cultivation of only one
method of truth-seeking has divided man, as well as his cultures and sciences. "Neither the loose subjective wholeness

achieved by primitive man nor, at the other extreme, the accurate, piecemeal objectivity now sought by science could do justice to every dimension of human experience." The purely subjective and intuitive approach has led to capriciousness, the purely objective and rational to a damming of the free flow of inspiration. "Living in half-worlds, it is hardly strange that we have produced only half-men, or creatures even more distorted than these homunculi, 'inverted cripples,' magnified ears, eyes, bellies, or brains, whose other parts have shrunk away." Man needs "a sounder diet . . . than any self-enclosed historic culture has supplied him." [69]

This characteristic demand for an organic wholeness in methods of acquiring knowledge is coupled with a deep concern, which amounts in some to a consuming passion, for the harmonization of the knowledge man already has. It is at this level, the level of interdisciplinary contacts, that by far most of the more careful and detailed thinking has been done by prophets of world order interested in the problem of intellectual integration.

One of the great pioneers in the literature of disciplinary synthesis, best known in the United States for his studies of history and his activity in the world government movement, is Erich Kahler. He was already deeply involved in the problem of intellectual integration when he first appeared on the German intellectual scene in 1920 with a polemic aimed at Max Weber, *Der Beruf der Wissenschaft,* "The Scientific Profession," a reply to Weber's *Wissenschaft als Beruf.* In that early book, Kahler was already conscious of a civilization-wide intellectual crisis, caused in large measure by the scientist's passion for specialization, analysis, and moral neutralism. He sketched the outlines of a "new science," quite different from the kind so well represented by Weber, in which the principle of organic unity made possible a new way of looking at man and nature.

A good deal of *Der Beruf der Wissenschaft* survives into

his latest work in English, *The Tower and the Abyss*. Our spiritual and intellecual anarchy, he still thinks, "derives ultimately from the state of our learning." Neutral on questions of value, doggedly limited to the "facts," modern scientists have generated a welter of uncoordinated theories; with infinite modesty, each scientist scrupulously avoids intruding on the hunting grounds of colleagues working with other "facts" in other "disciplines." Also, as the number of facts multiplies, so does the number of specialized fields. "The result of this combination: democracy of views and shrinking of the scope of research, is a loss of distinction between essential and non-essential, a loss of the criterion of essence, a bewilderingly increasing accumulation of unconnected facts and theories and methods, and, finally, pluralism, an outspoken disbelief in coherence, in a unified structure of our world." Dadaism, existentialism, and many other twentieth-century movements spring directly from "the impossibility of drawing any meaning from the mass of material and reasoning assembled in our age." [70]

The solution is not easily found, since knowledge constantly grows and changes and specialization is indispensable for obvious reasons. But Kahler asks that we "try to correct the evil effects of boundless analysis . . . by a methodical effort toward synthesis. Analysis is humanly productive, that is, meaningful for human life only as it is held in check by synthesis." New discoveries must be "constantly integrated in a unified picture of our world, which alone can furnish us the orientation needed for the conduct of human affairs." Since most specialists are wholly absorbed in their teaching and research, professional synthesists must be trained to do the job. Kahler suggests a program of scholarships for studies in intellectual integration and a network of institutes "in which synthesis studies may be carried on by methodical teamwork." His proposed "Institute for the Integration of Studies" would clarify and coordinate the basic

concepts used by the various sciences, study the converg-
ences and correspondences in the findings of different disciplines, and evaluate the work of each separate discipline
with an eye to all its possible implications for other fields.
Research would also be guided, with the Institute's help,
along "strategic" lines, "to restore to the sciences the criterion of essentiality." The mere existence "of a rallying
place, of an organized effort to achieve coherence" would
encourage scientists to concentrate on problems of basic importance to mankind, rather than waste their energy in the
"aimless automatism" of research engaged in solely for the
sake of research. The Institute "would act as a constant re-
minder of the common aim: a unified picture of our world,
which is the indispensable prerequisite to the formation of a
human community." [71]

Toynbee sees signs of a breakthrough in the fruitful cooperation of such fields as psychology and biology, which,
by advancing from opposite quarters, "are bridging the
traditional gulf between soul and body, spirit and matter, organic and inorganic, animate and inanimate." In time, he
suspects, all psychosomatic phenomena will be studied by a
single science. "In fact, a day is now in sight at which the
minimum 'intelligible field of study' will be nothing less
than the whole of the phenomenal world in all its aspects." [72]
But meanwhile the disciplines, just like the parochial nation-states in the political world, feud outrageously: witness the large literature on the question of whether Toynbee
himself is an historian, a sociologist, a religious philosopher,
or something else again. He calls for a single unified science
of man, as a start in the direction of still larger syntheses.
What is needed now "is a ruthless demolition squad, armed
with the intellectual equivalent of atomic artillery, to batter
the traditional interdisciplinary walls down to the ground.
This would restore the natural unity of the field that has
been cut up, for so long, by these encroaching enclosures.

No doubt, at all times and in all intellectual situations, the huge field of human studies needs to be parcelled out for operational purposes. But the partitions should be provisional only, and they should be demarcated by transferable hurdles, not by embedded stone walls." [73]

But even institutes for intellectual integration and Toynbee's plea for the "ruthless demolition" of interdisciplinary boundaries seem like feeble half measures by contrast with the ideas of Lancelot Law Whyte and Oliver Reiser.

Whyte preaches what some humanistic prophets would probably reject as a kind of biophysical imperialism. Civilization can only be saved, he insists, "through the discovery of a universal method of thought providing the basis of a unified humane science," which in turn will create a world civilization uniting East and West. The solution is to find a basic principle integrating physics, biology, and psychology, on the conviction "that nature is simple, that a universal order awaits discovery. . . . All processes are to be represented as variants of one universal process." [74] The unifying principle must be universally applicable, intuitively as well as theoretically verifiable, and both consistent and simple.

Whyte thinks he has located such a principle in his intuition of "a universal formative process in nature and man." Physics and biology reveal the gradual emergence of symmetry and form from asymmetry and formlessness in the cosmos. It is this tendency toward the development of form through the continuous reduction of asymmetry, from inanimate matter up the scale of being to man himself, that gives the cosmos meaning and makes possible a new unitary thought transcending Western science and Eastern intuition altogether. The aim of unitary science "is a logical circle representing man and his ideas as part of unitary nature, and unitary nature as a valid idea emerging to clarity in man. Man will then understand the laws of nature, and the laws of nature will interpret man to himself." [75] Whyte urges the adoption of a set of basic conceptual instruments, a unitary scientific language, so comprehensive that it will embrace all the levels of reality and facilitate the translation of the ideas of any special field into the ideas of any other. His own efforts, in *The Unitary Principle in Physics and Biology,* to work out a unitary vocabulary for physics, biology, and psychology have not apparently solved the problem for his fellow scientists, but they are worth more attention than they have so far managed to attract.

He also weaves into his concept of "unitary thought" the point, familiar from the work of Mumford and others, that Western European man's great epistemological sin is his inveterate dualism, his "dissociation" of reason and instinct, of object and subject, which results in warfare between the two halves of man's nature, the distortion of knowledge and personality through the exaggerated cultivation of one half or the other, and, especially in the West, a science that fails to grasp the vital harmony of the cosmos. Unitary thought will end this imbalance, bring all facts into intimate interrelationship, and fuse science and religion in a new "universalism." This new subjective-objective way of thinking will be focused not on truth for truth's sake, nor on the inner life of faith and instinct, but on the development of life through ever-increasing approximation to truth.[76]

Reiser's ideas, offered in a long series of books beginning in 1940 with *The Promise of Scientific Humanism* and summed up in his recent study, *The Integration of Human Knowledge,* carry still further than Whyte's, if possible, the project of a unified science as the keystone of a unified world. Infelicities of style and organization have cost him many readers; of all the really prolific prophets of world order he is far and away the least known, even in his own country. But he has independently, and in his own naïvely enthusiastic way, arrived at a philosophy of world order very much like that of some of his more fashionable contemporaries.

He is basically a philosopher of science. Speculations on future developments in science are his stock in trade, so that his work verges at times on the brighter sort of science-fiction. But like all the prophets, he sees the world of today in a process of transition from one pattern of life and thought to another. The Aristotelian orientation of Western man has resulted in the fragmentation of thought, in minute classification and specialization of intellectual labor, and ultimately in mental chaos. "After the present age of specialization in science has passed," he writes, "or has been supplemented by an era of co-ordination and synthesis of knowledge, we shall attain an understanding of the interconnectedness of things which will resemble primitive man's sense of 'participation.' " The old maxim of "divide and conquer," as applied to methods of truth-seeking, will be replaced by the new maxim of "unify and understand." Reason and emotion will be restored to their natural unity, and a social philosophy grounded in "cosmic" or "scientific" or "planetary" humanism "will provide us with concerted plans giving unity and direction to the social process." [77]

The process of intellectual integration must begin with a bold acceptance of the monistic implications of the master-ideas in modern science, especially field theory in physics and evolutionary theory in biology.[78] From this monistic starting point, Reiser goes on to recommend a number of projects for translating into concrete reality the unity of knowledge which already exists in his metaphysics. His most modest idea is a "department of integrative studies" in each university, offering courses in the search for "trans-departmental" truths. Every effort must be made, in particular, to unify the sciences and the humanities — courses must be devised in a program of "integrated education which would cultivate a rapport between both fields." But this will not be enough. All specialized knowledge must ultimately be integrated into a single coherent world philosophy, and for this task no individual brain is adequate. "We must assemble the best minds of the world, put them in an academy where they will have the leisure, the facilities, and the social obligation of turning out a world philosophy." Each discipline must be fitted into a comprehensive scheme uniting them all; the fruits of each must be joined in a synthesis embracing the physical and social sciences and all the humanities in a higher world philosophy. The world academy will summarize its work in a world encyclopedia of the type suggested by H. G. Wells in his *World Brain,* issued periodically and kept up to date by constant editorial review. There will also be a unified symbolism to represent the unity of being and knowledge, a universal technical language which Reiser dubs "Wholingua," not unlike Whyte's unitary language. It will be a language able to express clearly and simply all kinds of knowledge, from a point of view so catholic that all parochialisms of concept and method will be transcended.[79]

Such a world philosophy cannot be compared to anything now in existence. It will replace modern science, philosophy, religion, and even some of the functions of government. It will become a great World Brain, acting through the world government, the world academy, and all surviving national institutions of learning, to guide the human race in its future evolution toward unimaginable destinies. It will somehow integrate reason and emotion, epistemology and ethics, science and religion. Like Wells, who has clearly influenced Reiser's thinking at several points, he ends in a concept of human synthesis so vast it eludes precise definition. Characteristically, he resorts to long chains of dubious organismic analogies, teeming with neologisms, less vivid but of the same species as Teilhard de Chardin's. Another suggestive comparison might be drawn with the "Bead Game" in Hermann Hesse's Utopian novel, *Magister Ludi.*

At this point our whole system of classification threatens

to break down. Studying theories of world integration from the angle of view of the "philosophy of history" or of the synthesis of "religion" or "knowledge" may be convenient, but the aim of the prophets in most instances is to transcend all categories and think on a new level of abstraction altogether. Each has his particular point of departure, growing out of the discipline most familiar to him; but each prophet also does his best, consciously or unconsciously, to hurdle professional boundaries and gain a total view of things. Hence, "history" in the hands of a Toynbee, "sociology" in the hands of a Sorokin, "philosophy" in the hands of a Northrop, and "science" in the hands of a Reiser or Huxley become all-encompassing *Weltanschauungen,* total philosophies of life. Unlike similar efforts by Hegel, Comte, and Spencer in the nineteenth century, these twentieth-century philosophies do often manage to get well above the usual limitations of their starting points. They all aim, perhaps, at what Mumford calls a "doctrine of the whole," a doctrine fiercely resolved to leave out nothing valid or valuable.

But insofar as the problem of intellectual integration can be isolated and distinguished from other aspects of the total problem of world synthesis, it is a major concern of many twentieth-century thinkers, some of them not interested in these other aspects at all. One of the most persistent themes in modern literature is the thinly veiled and entirely mutual antagonism of the sciences and the humanities, illuminated brilliantly by C. P. Snow in his little book, *The Two Cultures and the Scientific Revolution.* The Conferences on Science, Philosophy and Religion held annually in New York for many years, the Pugwash Conferences in Nova Scotia, and the Star Island Conferences held off the Maine coast in recent summers represent typical efforts to get the scientific disciplines into fruitful contact with the rest of culture.

Working from another direction, one substantial branch

of the logical positivist movement, once centered in Vienna, and later in Chicago, has been trying for many years to work out a conceptual framework for the unification of the sciences, or at least for a philosophy of unified science: men of the caliber of Otto Neurath, Philipp Frank, Charles Morris, and Herbert Feigl spring to mind. An *International Encyclopedia of Unified Science* began appearing in serial parts under the editorship of the late Otto Neurath at the University of Chicago in 1938; its goal of a "logico-empirical integration of all the sciences" has never been achieved, and it remains unfinished, a collection of preliminary monographs. Several international Congresses for the Unity of Science held in the late 1930's, the Institute for the Unity of Science directed by Frank, and the Minnesota Center for Philosophy of Science directed by Feigl have helped keep the idea of a formal integration of the sciences alive. The contribution of logical empiricism and linguistic analysis to any final resolution of the enormously complex technical problems involved in fully integrating even the natural sciences cannot be overestimated. It will take more than high hopes and large thinking to do the job.

The prophets' search for intellectual synthesis is also paralleled in the work of such small but persevering organizations as the Centre international de Synthèse in Paris, founded by the French historian Henri Berr in 1924, and in New York the Foundation for Integrative Education, headed by F. L. Kunz. The New York Foundation's official publication, *Main Currents in Modern Thought,* calls itself "a cooperative journal to promote the free association of those working toward the integration of all knowledge through the study of the whole of things, Nature, Man, and Society, assuming the universe to be one, dependable, intelligible, harmonious." The Foundation seeks "to remedy . . . the conceptual and hence the ethical, social, economic, and political breakdown of our times, looking to a peaceful world order." Reiser has long been an active participant in its work; here, and in Berr's center in Paris, are at least faint anticipatory gleams of the kind of "institute for the integration of studies" proposed by Erich Kahler.

But no one doubts that knowledge, like human population, is increasing at a rate far exceeding the capacity of all current efforts to reduce it to organic order. Again, as in every other field, there is no shortcut to a world civilization.

The Arts in Cosmopolis

NOT MANY thinkers interested in the prospects of a world culture have had much to say about the function of the arts, from belles-lettres and music to the graphic and plastic arts. Perhaps prophets of world order should remain discreetly silent about the "role" of the artist, since the true artist is beyond coercion, persuasion, or prediction. Any attempt to find a clearly defined place for him in a total cultural "plan" attacks his integrity. No aspect of Soviet culture is more pitiful than its stunted, enslaved, lifeless, and reactionary art, literature, and music. The "new Soviet man" enjoys in some ways a level of life more rich in brotherhood, purposefulness, and moral health than his counterpart in the West; but except for a few unusual personalities who reached full maturity in the 1920's, men like Pasternak and Prokofiev, and except for standards in the performing arts, carried over from Tsarist days, Soviet art is all but a contradiction in terms. A lesson of signal importance can be learned from this fantastic experimental new order, which its apologists see as the model for the coming world civilization. On the other hand, some prophets of world integration have been tempted to peer into the future of the arts, and what they have to say is worth summarizing. This much is clear: unless man changes beyond all recognition, there will be art in the world culture. The arts mediate experiences otherwise incommunicable, and convey in symbolic terms what would be flat, uncompelling, and even meaningless in its own terms. A world without art, spontaneous and genuine, would be a world without humanity.

As A. L. Kroeber has shown in his *Configurations of Culture Growth,* creative activity in the arts is not continuous, but comes in waves or bursts or clusters of unusually vital work, followed by seasons of routine repetition and lull, and, eventually, by a final collapse of the whole cultural pattern, its values, styles, themes, and forms all together. He suspects that we, in the twentieth century, have reached this point of utter collapse. A whole new tradition may emerge to take the place of the bankrupt culture of the modern West.

Kroeber is sparing in details, but from the perspective of the 1960's, the artistic movements of the twentieth century do begin to take on the appearance of a stupendously destructive explosion, which at the same time has been more lively and more perversely creative than the student of cultural history would have any good reason to expect. Stretching Kroeber's terms to fit the facts, we can see the outlines of a phenomenal and unique "culture-burst" in all the arts, produced by men born between 1870 and 1895 and reaching their peak years between 1910 and 1935: a generation of iconoclastic modernism, in which traditional forms have been weighed and found wanting; a generation of vital, hectic experimentalism unlike anything before in history. It has brought the Western tradition to a stunning and pyrotechnic finish, but a finish all the same.

Most of the prophets of world order who have something to say about the arts see in the nervous iconoclasm of twentieth-century artistic movements only what they would expect. The arts faithfully reflect the times. In a period of transition between different orders of thought, faith, and social organization, when new patterns have not yet crystallized and old patterns have lost their inner meaning; in a period, above all, when civilizational breakdown expresses itself in colossal total wars and dehumanizing total states, the sensitive artist cannot help screaming, or fleeing, or going berserk.

Mumford finds in modern art and literature a bewildering complex of clashing tendencies: romantic rebellion against the machine age, blank despair and self-contempt, a frenetic and dehumanizing worship of technics, all permeated with the spirit of revolt and disillusionment. "Plainly our writers have at least discovered, in man's own lower depths, the forces that have brought on the series of catastrophes that have marked out time." But they have succumbed to the very diseases they portray in their work, and contaminated the younger generation with despair and disgust. Writers and artists must "become something more than merely mirrors of . . . violence and disintegration; they, through their own efforts, will have to regain the initiative for the human person and the forces of life, chaining up the demons we have allowed to run loose, and releasing the angels and ministers of grace we have shamefacedly — and shamefully — incarcerated." Mumford sees signs of a renascence of personalism and life-affirmation in the arts in recent years, but he names no names. "We are moving . . . from twentieth-century multiplicity, with its specialisms, its divisions, its distortions, toward post-twentieth-century unity; and in our arts, as they receive these fresh currents of energy and hope, all of man's nature will be fully represented and utilized." The lopsided, disfiguring fashions of the early twentieth century, from cubism to surrealism, will be replaced by an art of organic wholeness.[80]

Sorokin looks forward by preference to an "idealistic" art in which the styles of materialistic, sensual modern art will be fused with the symbolic and transcendent art of the early Middle Ages to produce a dynamic synthesis akin to the art of Pericles' Athens and Renaissance Italy. For Northrop the arts have two functions: the communication of purely esthetic experience, in which the Eastern cultures have specialized; and the symbolic representation of the basic theological, philosophical, and scientific postulates of a culture. Illustrated by Dante's poetic synthesis of medieval cosmology and by Pope's of Newtonian physics, art in its second function is now completely demoralized because Western civilization has shed its traditional faiths and philosophies, leaving the creative artist with little to communicate except his own inner feelings. In the coming world culture, as a new *Weltanschauung* crystallizes, art in its second function will again flourish brilliantly; and art in its first function, especially as Eastern poetry and fine arts become increasingly familiar in the West, will enrich life as never before. In its turn, the East will learn from the West how to use the arts as media for the symbolic expression of concepts in the "theoretic" component of knowledge.[81]

Many professional critics and historians of art are beginning to think along the same lines as the prophets. Ernest Mundt views the responsible artist as a man uniquely qualified by his training to interpret and unify human experience. In the "new synthesis" on the horizon for mankind, the artist will play the indispensable role of giving organic form to the new world order by expressing its values in design and symbol. The new art will harmoniously integrate senses, feelings, intuition, and reason, as Mundt finds it has in all traditional cultures of the past. In a richly perceptive study of the dehumanization of art since the Enlightenment, Hans Sedlmayr foresees the possibility of a great renewal in the arts, in an emergent world civilization which has "its foundations in a true culture of the soul, in a re-integration of man and in a return to his true center." The new art can flower only in the "soil of knowledge, the knowledge that we are creatures of God." Its time is yet to come.[82]

But any attempt to forecast the forms and styles of the new

world art is bound to fail. It will be new in ways we cannot imagine, and it may also reach back into the past for inspiration and a sense of continuity. It will be responsible in the fullest sense: in a sane world order, the artist will no longer play the anxious fugitive from chaos; he will give dynamic expression to the deepest insights of science, philosophy, and religion; but he will also be true to his own artistic instincts, and to himself. Somewhere between the idiotically buoyant social art of Soviet civilization and the neurotic individual art of modern Western culture, a creative meeting point will be found.

Meanwhile, hardly a breath of fresh air stirs. Since the iconoclastic generation passed its peak in the 1930's, the arts have languished in a stupor that smells of death. There are no poets, novelists, symphonists, or painters of world integration. The prophets cock their ears and peel their eyes in vain. We must all wait a little longer.

Four

The World Commonwealth

Culture, Community, Commonwealth

"ALL THAT man seeks on earth," says Dostoyevsky's Grand Inquisitor, is "some one to worship, some one to keep his conscience, and some means of uniting all in one unanimous and harmonious ant-heap, for the craving for universal unity is the third and last anguish of men. Mankind as a whole has always striven to organise a universal state." This most quotable of Dostoyevskian villains — and there is also Shigalov, the mad theorist of another world ant heap in *The Possessed* — foreshadows brilliantly the demonic rulers of all the totalitarian cosmo-polities of contemporary counter-Utopian fiction, from Big Brother in *1984* and the oily psychocrats of *Brave New World* to the Devil himself, running the show from behind the scenes in C. S. Lewis' *That Hideous Strength*. Modern Western man fears falling into the clutches of a world despotism, fears the loss of his freedom as much as war and anarchy. His counter-Utopias mirror his anxiety. They also mirror the great flesh-and-blood caesars of our own time: Lenin and Mussolini, Stalin and Hitler. Even the Grand Inquisitor pales next to the Führer. And surely the Führer intended nothing less, in the long run, than a Germanized world order.

Most of the twentieth-century prophets of world integration side with Dostoyevsky against his Grand Inquisitor, although they will have no part of Dostoyevsky's mystical Slavophilism. They rebel as much against the prospect of a soul-destroying juggernaut state as Aldous Huxley or George Orwell, even when they favor policies that might unintentionally lead to despotism. They rarely plead for a world commonwealth at any price, out of sheer physical terror. They would rather see mankind in ashes than a mankind degraded to insecthood by its own stupid cunning. Nor do they look on a world state as a panacea that can erase war overnight, except for the most extreme partisans of the organized world government movement. "As part of a vast ensemble of social and cultural changes necessary for the elimination of war," says Sorokin, "some sort of world government is indispensable." [1] But the "ensemble" is enormous, and Sorokin can spare only a page or two in all his voluminous output for political and economic questions. If others have spared more, they agree with his basic approach.

All the same, a world civilization will have to be a thriving concern. It will minister to the bodies, as well as to the souls and minds, of men. It will serve fallible human beings, even if its moral idealism, its world faith and its world philosophy are ten times as efficacious as the faiths and philosophies of the past, which seems hardly credible. Like all historic civilizations, it will need a political and economic order of things, as much as a unified culture. This politico-economic order may not amount to a full-fledged world government or world economy, at the outset anyway, but binding order there must be. A common culture did not save Western Europe from war in 1914, and a world culture may not save humanity from catastrophe in the centuries ahead. Spiritual unity must be embodied in material unity.

To survey the recent prophetic literature on these more down-to-earth aspects of the coming world civilization, we have to make a radical shift in the dimension of our discourse. Aerial reconnaissance gives way to scouting on foot. Some of the prophets who figured most often in earlier chapters will have little or nothing to say; and there will be several new names. We descend from the intangible into the tangible, from the province primarily of the philosopher-prophet into the province primarily of the prophetic social scientist, although some of the most versatile philosophers, like F. S. C. Northrop, will survive the transition fairly well.

A stubborn minority of the philosopher-prophets, including Jaspers and Hocking, who were already near middle age before the débâcle of modern nationalism in 1914-18, and the Indian philosophers Aurobindo and Radhakrishnan, who spent most of their lives in an India struggling to wrest her freedom from an alien raj, have been positively hostile to the idea of a bona fide world commonwealth. They feel it can be nothing else but a Dostoyevskian ant heap, no matter what the intentions of its founding fathers. Although they oppose totalitarian nationalism, they revere historic nationality, and in the world order of their prophetic vision the nation-state will remain substantially intact, cooperating with her sister nations to keep the peace, but not welded into a larger polity. Hocking argues that "a world civilization must be an organism, not an endless homogeneity." Since "for any epoch, there is such a thing as national personality, and therewith national mission," and in these national experiments are "the sacred begettings of culture," he assumes that a true world government would be a disaster.[2] Jaspers, his memory of twelve years of Nazi *Gleichschaltung* still fresh, cannot imagine any world central authority, in control of all armed forces, able to resist the temptation to resort, sooner or later, to terroristic dictatorship.[3]

But most of the prophets studied in earlier chapters take for granted some kind of world government, preferably a federation freely formed by general agreement, with due safeguards for local autonomy and local mores, and an integrated world economy. They tend to see the world commonwealth as a logical outgrowth of the emergent world culture, necessary but less important than the meeting of minds which alone can make it viable. They reject all the more virulent forms of nationalism: for Mumford and Toynbee, nationalism is a kind of "idolatry," for Fromm "incest," for de Rougemont a Western "disease," and so forth. At the same time, they accept in principle the need for a continuation of national or local self-government into the new world order. Combining both emphases, Northrop anticipates a world government achieved in two stages: a world security system pledged to defend the integrity and independence of all its national members, and later on, a true world government, made possible by the creative fusion of the "living law norms" which underlie the positive law of each nation.*

There are also a good many thinkers, but fewer every year, in the world government movement in Europe and America, who propose the creation of a federal world government here and now. The movement has been moribund since the Korean War, but it attracted many excellent minds in its hey-day. Its fatal weakness has always been a relative indiffer-ence to precisely the problems raised in Chapter Three above. Reinhold Niebuhr summarized the classical objection to these clarion calls for immediate world federal govern-ment many years ago by insisting that there can be no world commonwealth until and unless a genuine world community grows into full self-consciousness, a world neighborhood in which men feel close enough through ties of common culture and common living to dare to make the leap to political union. The world community cannot be integrated "purely by artifact and conscious contrivance," by a world con-stitution, or a world police force, or any of the merely mechanical schemes favored by world government zealots. "If we are patient enough," he adds, "we could cultivate the gradually growing organic factors of world community and

---

* For the ideas of Northrop and others on world government *per se,* see below, pp. 229–34.

perfect them at opportune moments by the constitutional contrivances which always express and perfect what the forces of life and togetherness have established." [4] But the only alternative to this continuing organic growth is a super-state imposed by *force majeure*.

The leaders of the world government movement always returned Niebuhr's fire by pointing out that states also help fulfill and concretize communities. "Community and state," as G. A. Borgese put it, "peas and pod, are not separate entities, are born and grow in function of each other." History tells us "that a government, a state, meets halfway the needs of a fledgling community, arises at the critical stage when a community in the making demands a pattern, a mold of law, for its further maturation to take shape." [5] A world community already exists, spatially through the modern technics of communication and transportation, spiritually through the unanimous craving of intellectuals and masses alike for world peace and world order. Only the will to federate, especially among politicians, seems lacking; to ignite that will and keep it burning brightly is the task, said Borgese, of the world government movement. And so the argument went, at the level of assertion and counter-assertion, for a few years. But in the so-called placid fifties, the same kind of student and intellectual who had campaigned for world government in the previous decade now either lost interest in the global crisis altogether, or chased that far more fabulous, will-o'-the-wisp, "universal disarmament."

At the same time, and even earlier, social scientists, especially in the United States, set out to disentangle and study objectively the concrete problem — at issue between Niebuhr and Borgese — of just how much "community" was necessary, how many things had to be held in common, from the profoundest depths of philosophy and faith to the most superficial links of trade and technics, before the world or any appreciable part of it could federate politically. In general, the work of the social scientists has tended to support Niebuhr rather than Borgese, although not exclusively. The crucial factors in political integration are found to be "cultural" or "psychological" or "spiritual" forces, rather than economic ties or geography or technology. Material factors may expedite union, but union itself is a product of true inner community in the essentials of higher culture. On the other hand, it need hardly be added that cultural bonds themselves are also not enough; the will and the need for integration must be present, and no precise mathematical formula can be devised to tell when enough cultural unity exists to make heavy investments of willpower timely. The world situation was not ripe in the late 1940's; when it will be, no man knows.

Thus, for Crane Brinton, the world commonwealth cannot come into being without a cosmopolitan governing elite spiritually uprooted from the separate national societies, broad popular enthusiasm for world law, and the disappearance of all groups bent on one another's liquidation, such as doctrinaire capitalists and communists. F. L. Schuman in his study of world government, *The Commonwealth of Man*, warns that world federal union cannot become a real possibility until the great "myth of human unity" reaches down into the hearts and souls of millions of men all over the world, transmuting patriotism into true humanism. The indispensable prerequisite of world government for Gerard Mangone is "psychological-cultural integration" through "world patriotism," and for Werner Levi, common purposes, common principles of behavior based on universally shared values, common activities at all levels of culture, and rites of collective identity. Levi is especially interested, as are Margaret Mead, Harold Lasswell, and others, in the need for a highly developed symbolism of world unity, for world heroes, world insignia, world art, world songs. Throughout, the emphasis is on the spiritual rather than the concrete, on ideas rather than facts.[6]

In many ways the most interesting and ambitious attempt to explore the necessary preconditions for political synthesis has emerged out of the work of the Center for Research on World Political Institutions, founded in 1950 at Princeton University. In 1957, Karl Deutsch, R. W. van Wagenen, and a team of six historians published a study of the "elimination of war" from the historical experiences of several countries in the North Atlantic area, on the practical assumption that data of this sort might provide guidance for planners of a North Atlantic federal government. Their findings may have an even broader application.

The historical examples studied most thoroughly include the formation of the American federal republic in the eighteenth century, the relations since medieval times of the component states of the United Kingdom, the rise and fall of the Hapsburg Empire, the unification of Germany and Italy in the nineteenth century, the relations between Norway and Sweden since the Congress of Vienna, and the federal experiment in Switzerland. In each case, what the writers were trying to isolate and examine is the "security-community," the community of peoples in which enough integration has occurred that the members of the community resolve their common problems without resort to large-scale violence. This may lead, as in Switzerland, to actual political amalgamation; or, as in modern Scandinavia, peace may be preserved without any surrender of local sovereignty, and this arrangement is labeled a "pluralistic security-community."

The results as analyzed and correlated by Deutsch contain some surprises. In at least the North Atlantic experience, he thinks it fair to conclude that pluralistic security-communities hold up better than politically amalgamated communities. Canada and the United States, for instance, have been more successful in keeping the peace between them than the Northern and Southern states in the U.S.; and many amalgamated communities, such as the Anglo-Irish union and the Austro-Hungarian empire, have failed altogether. On the other hand, really successful amalgamations can be just as durable as pluralistic security-communities, and of course far more powerful in their pooled strength than countries relying only on treaties and alliances.

Contrary to what one might expect, the background conditions essential for the establishment of politically amalgamated security-communities do not include common language or racial ties, strong economic links, or common military enemies, but do include four other elements of crucial significance. First, the peoples amalgamating must share major ethical goals and values relevant to policy-making; this does not necessarily mean identical religions or common values in all respects, but simply harmony in all areas where common policies must be hammered out. They must trust one another to be able to do the "decent thing." Also, expectations of joint and mutual rewards from union must be widespread and present on all sides. Second, the societies concerned must be relatively mobile, have a high economic growth rate, show a rising capacity for handling large-scale administrative work efficiently, be developing unbroken links of social communication between especially the politically strategic social strata within each, and be actively recruiting fresh blood into the elite groups from the lower classes. Static, hidebound societies lack the momentum and drive to integrate. Next, there must be plenty of mobility of persons from one country to another, although not necessarily of goods, since the findings do not indicate that economic factors in this sense have much to do with the formation of security-communities. Men may fight one another for economic reasons, but they *abstain* from fighting most often for political and psychological reasons. Fourth, there must be a multiple range of common functions and services, as in scientific, literary, and professional life; and, moreover, all members of the integrating community must be able to contribute something vital to the whole: symbols, ruling houses, heroes, legends, high cultural achievement, and so forth. The United Kingdom, for example, survives as well as it does because Scotland and Wales have been able to contribute much of the paraphernalia of Scottishness and Welshness to the total "British" way of life.

Of these prerequisites, not all proved to be essential for a pluralistic security-community. Not as many contacts, not as much mobility, not as much cultural exchange were needed. But — and here is the principal discovery perhaps of the whole project — groups could not dispense with war as an instrument of policy in their relations with one another, federated or not, unless they shared the same basic values relevant to policy-making and mutually experienced a spontaneous, genuine feeling of "we-ness." "The kind of sense of community that is relevant for integration . . . turned out to be . . . a matter of mutual sympathy and loyalties; of 'we-ness,' trust, and mutual consideration; of partial identification in terms of self-images and interests; of mutually successful predictions of behavior, and of cooperative action in accordance with it — in short, a matter of a perpetual dynamic process of mutual attention, communication, perception of needs, and responsiveness in the process of decision-making." [7] Against this yardstick, Deutsch and his colleagues find the North Atlantic community nearly ready for the transition to a pluralistic security-community, after many centuries of war, but political amalgamation is still out of reach. The great need is not so much for increased economic or military integration, as for more willingness on the part of leaders and peoples to consult one another, undertake more ventures together in the cultural field, promote a higher rate of international mobility of persons, and strive for maximum mutual responsiveness to one another's needs and desires. Respect and not fear is the greatest force working for integration, at least from past experience.

Deutsch and his co-workers are aware of the risks they run

in relying so heavily on historical data. Patterns do not necessarily recur indefinitely; factors present in every case of successful integration studied may not be the causal factors at all; many factors that do not appear in each case may still have been most decisive in their own specific cases. Also, conditions have changed enormously in the world since most of the historical experiences studied took place. In particular, a growing North Atlantic solidarity, achieved at the expense of friendly relations with Asia, Africa, and Latin America, may lead Western man into a disastrous blind alley at just a time when all nations are exposed to a common and ultimate peril. Finally, advocating a policy of "mutual responsiveness," as the Princeton group does, or education for "world loyalty," or the promulgation of a "myth of humanity," or any of the other slogans adopted by social scientists looking for ways of integrating the world community, only begs the supreme question: how do we make the people who must make other people see the light, see the light themselves? Where does the whole process begin?

The answer, perhaps, is that human affairs are too complex to reduce to a simple staged sequence of cause and effect relationships leading up a logical ladder to final ends. But those who have explored the problem of what makes communities integrate, and how states form, and applied their findings to the problem of the world community in midcentury, break vital ground. Even if they are all wrong, every sort of informed speculation about the prospects of world integration at any level helps by encouraging thought, by bringing the idea of human unity out of the inarticulate obscurity in which it usually lurks, by stirring imaginations and making new values familiar. As the Princeton group points out, the integration of communities seems to occur in two totally different stages, a long preparatory stage in which only a few intellectuals, statesmen, and pressure groups have the idea, and then, at the point of ignition or "take-off," the movement suddenly becomes rapid, universal, and irresistible.[8] The same is true of all revolutionary movements of all kinds: the dreaming and the speculating come first, and take longest; change itself, once in motion, may occur almost abruptly.

At any rate, the road to a world commonwealth, or even to the world "pluralistic security-community" preferred by Jaspers and Hocking, promises to be just as steep as the road to a world culture. Since a world culture at some reasonably advanced stage of evolution may be an essential prerequisite of further integration, the two roads may for long stretches be one and the same.

Distant as world political integration seems to the prophet in mid-century, most have grasped very well the importance of trying also to visualize the ultimate economic and political objectives in view, for which men are asked to sacrifice present comforts and shed settled opinions. In the next section, recent thinking on the question of a world economy is canvassed; and in the last section, the structure and powers of a world government.

World Economic Integration

THE ECONOMIC dimension of world order fails much more even than the political dimension to interest deeply most of its prophets and apologists. The trend in recent years in history and the social sciences has been strongly away from economic determinism, in the direction of cultural, psychological, and political determinism. The Christian thesis that man does not live by bread alone is often encountered nowadays as the thesis that man does not live by bread at all. The prophets of world order bend with the prevailing winds. The findings of the Princeton research team headed by R. W. van Wagenen and Karl Deutsch, summarized above, typify the trend: they rate economic ties among the "non-essential" background conditions for the formation of a security-community in the experience of the North Atlantic countries. Other researchers are similarly unimpressed by the positive role of economic factors in community integration.

But as Mumford, Toynbee, Huxley, and many economist-prophets have argued, the economic dimension of world order remains crucial for two unassailable reasons. It is crucial because without an integrated world economy, world order will be sabotaged from within by the tensions and resentments growing out of gross disparities in the wealth of the member societies of the world community. Poor men and rich men cannot live happily together forever after, under modern social conditions, nor can poor countries coexist forever with rich countries, in an age of total war, universal literacy, and modern communications systems. An integrated world economy is also intrinsically worth while, because it will ensure a maximally high world standard of living. Even if prosperity does not lead, in and of itself, to brotherly love or world peace, the liberation of mankind from the marginal existence and the dawn-to-dusk toil of all preindustrial societies, and also from most of the drudgery of modern industrialism, has a self-sufficient value in the eyes of nearly all prophets of world integration. Not one would turn the clock back. Most would agree with Lewis Mumford, in *The Transformations of Man,* that the world civilization must be an open society, with freedom of personal movement, freedom of trade, an economy of high mass-consumption geared to human needs and wants rather than the convenience of profiteering entrepreneurs or political commissars, and an equalization of wealth through an adequate program of world economic development, financed in part by nations with available surplus capital.[9]

World economic integration involves at least two distinct goals: an integration of economic systems and a fusion of national economies into a genuine world economy. Neither can be achieved to any extent without some progress in the other, but of the two, only the first seems to be taking reasonably good care of itself. Capitalism, socialism, communism, and all the popular mixtures thereof are advancing toward one another, strictly from the economist's point of view, at a terrific velocity. No nation is wholly cut off from any other because of differences in its economic system, and most up-to-date economic systems have largely eliminated class warfare and are in process of eliminating backward regions in their own national economies.

But the second problem, the problem of the "developed" versus the "underdeveloped" countries, is a much more serious business. From the developed areas of the world, it demands a readiness to part freely and unconditionally with surplus funds that could probably be invested in the home market, and to compete commercially with countries where production costs are much lower. From the underdeveloped parts of the world, it demands extraordinary self-discipline and belt-tightening, saintly patience, birth control measures, and the constant risk of political absorption into the Western or Soviet power blocs, with loss of self-determination. The time lag between full realization of what must be done — acquired in the past twenty years — and its earliest possible final accomplishment, is a century or more in most underdeveloped areas. Men must be willing to sacrifice present comforts for the sake of their great-grandsons, which puts an unconscionable strain on their paternal instincts.

In short, the price of a true world economy will be high. Although the present disparity between rich and poor countries must be drastically reduced, as Toynbee points out, "the cost of this will be enormous, if we aim at the goal of bringing within the reach of every family in the World the material facilities and spiritual opportunities that a Western middle-class family already enjoys." The problem of birth control also involves an intangible cost in habits and outlook that many economically backward peoples may refuse to pay, although Western-style prosperity without birth control is clearly impossible.[10]

What makes world economic integration particularly difficult under twentieth-century conditions is the absence of a true world economic community, even to the limited extent that one did exist before 1914. The argument that the world's peoples are so economically interdependent that a world economy is already in good running order, needing only a world government to impose the finishing touches by law, is obsolete. In a wide-ranging survey of the forces tending toward world synthesis published in 1930, J. H. Randall, Sr.,

could still write that the world was economically an "organism," because manufacturing in every country depended on
thousands of products imported from abroad, every consumer used thousands of imported consumer goods, and
many firms in many countries owned gigantic overseas investments.[11] Today, as Karl Deutsch, Werner Levi, Gunnar
Myrdal, and others have shown very clearly, the nation-state
has largely exchanged nineteenth-century laisser-faire, free
trade policies for rigid economic controls which attempt to
insulate it from world business trends, especially deflationary
and depressive trends. The modern welfare state or regional
common market strives for self-sufficiency and concentrates
on maximum internal integration, doing irreparable damage,
above all in the case of the wealthy Western economies, to the
health of the world economic community. As the authors of
Political Community and the North Atlantic Area report,
"Most countries in the world today devote a larger part of
their resources to their domestic economies, and a smaller
part to their foreign trade, than they did a half-century
ago." Discrepancies between average income levels from
country to country have widened; higher tariffs, trade and
immigration quotas, border formalities, and iron curtains
have ended the once almost free movement of goods and
peoples across national frontiers; there has even been "a
considerable decline in the share of foreign mail among the
total volume of letters written." [12] With most of the world
politically unstable and national economic planning or controls so successful in most advanced countries, it is only inevitable, as Gunnar Myrdal observes, that national economic
policies should tend toward autarky. Given a state of international chaos, only national supply and demand relationships
are predictable and controllable; the nation naturally cleaves
unto itself.[13]

But men are not saints. It would be absurd to expect nations, rich and poor alike, to knock down all trade and

immigration walls and enter into unlimited commercial competition with other nations where prices and wages are entirely different, disrupting national economic planning and
throwing millions of people temporarily out of work, just
for the sake of a hypothetically higher standard of living
twenty-five or fifty years hence. Free trade in a world of full
employment, full industrialization, and mutual confidence is
one thing; free trade in the mid-century world is another.
On the other hand, the picture is not entirely hopeless. Most
progressive economists who favor ultimate world economic
integration, and a good many prophets of world government
and a world civilization, attach great importance to the role
which the governments of the economically advanced nations can play in helping underdeveloped countries make the
awkward transition to economic maturity.

The program most often suggested would set up what
Stringfellow Barr calls an "international development authority" to furnish all the investment capital and technical
assistance to the underdeveloped countries they can usefully
absorb. Estimates vary as to how much a program of this
sort, conscientiously administered, would cost. Grenville
Clark and Louis B. Sohn, in their scheme for the transformation of the United Nations into a world government, speak
of a "World Development Authority" which would spend
twenty-five billion dollars annually. Harrison Brown estimates that to get the poor countries of the world up to the
standard of living now enjoyed in Japan would require a
total investment of some 500 billion dollars over a span of
fifty years, half of which would have to come from the developed countries. The American contribution would probably
run to nearly four billion per year, at least during the first
decade. This is less than the total foreign aid bill now being
met by the American taxpayer, but of course much current
foreign aid goes to military assistance. C. P. Snow also points
out that the underdeveloped countries will need the full-

time services of as many as twenty thousand engineers from the developed countries, a sacrifice which might hurt them more than the loss of capital, given a continued shortage of engineers in the developed areas of the world. But he feels it is "technically possible to carry out the scientific revolution in India, Africa, South-east Asia, Latin America, the Middle East, within fifty years." C. Wright Mills suggests an international fund for development to which the United States should contribute a sum equal to 20 percent of its current military budget. Walt Rostow, before he joined President Kennedy's brain trust in Washington, proposed an international program of economic assistance to cost from twelve to fifteen billion dollars during the first five-year period, administered by existing agencies but with new machinery created "to co-ordinate information, set the ground rules, and secure acceptance of the criteria for the investment program." In his most recent book, he estimates that the entire underdeveloped half of the world could begin regular growth, without waste, if an increase of something in the vicinity of four billion dollars were made available annually by the developed countries. Larger amounts could not be efficiently utilized.[14]

These are not incredibly huge sums. Clark and Sohn estimate that the world now spends one hundred billion dollars, eight percent of its gross annual product, on the arms race each year.[15] Much more than this is spent for sophisticated luxuries each year by the middle and upper classes of the wealthy countries. The capital is there: only the will is lacking. As every writer on the subject has said many times over, and as almost every major news story from the underdeveloped areas of the world bears out, the instability of the poor countries during these agonizing decades of transition to industrial maturity is a major and continuing threat to world peace. Since the poor countries cannot, until they have reached what Rostow labels the "take-off point" in their economic growth, save enough capital themselves, they must either turn to the West for help or accept communism, a tried and true method for countries that want to lift themselves by their own bootstraps, which comes at the high price of transforming men into robots with a collective persecution complex: witness China. The lesson is clear.

One of the most penetrating, sober, and humane recent analyses of the world economic situation may be studied in two recent books by the Swedish economist Gunnar Myrdal, who is also in his own way a prophet of world integration. His idea of an integrated world economy joins persuasively the classical ideal of free movement with the modern concern for public welfare. It will be a world in which all individuals everywhere choose freely their conditions of work and life, and enjoy equal remuneration for productive labor regardless of race or culture. It will be a world in which capital, labor, and goods move freely from place to place in response to world needs, and in which all areas of the world and all individuals enjoy equality of opportunity. Such a world economy did exist for the advanced Western peoples before 1914, within certain limits, and at the expense of the working classes and the economically backward continents. Since the first world war, the world economic community has steadily disintegrated, under the impact of war, business depressions, political instability, and the national self-centeredness of the modern welfare state. Now that the underdeveloped countries are mostly independent, and the Western states have achieved a high degree of national integration, the stage is set for a resumption, Myrdal hopes, of the growth toward an integrated world economy.

The most crucial problem in the building of a world economy is the elimination of the enormous gap between the developed and underdeveloped countries, which has only widened in the last fifty years. There can be no world economy so long as the world exists half rich, half poor. But

Myrdal points out that the gap cannot be closed by trying, prematurely, to establish a free world market. The poor countries could not compete, and they would remain unindustrialized and exposed to every fluctuation in the marketplace, any one of which, at the wrong time and in the wrong place, could have a fatal effect. The first and most urgent requirement is national economic integration, preferably on the Western rather than the Soviet model. This means, in effect, that the route to a world economy lies through an intensification of economic nationalism in the poor countries, especially in their dealings with the West. Until and unless the underdeveloped countries set their own houses in order, as most are desperately trying to do, they will have nothing to bring to the emergent world order but their misery, poverty, and envy. Myrdal's program for the governments of underdeveloped countries includes the reduction of consumption levels to a bare minimum for all strata of the population; the stabilization of savings at a high annual average, to squeeze out of the economy every possible investment dollar; the diversification of production and export trade, with the use of foreign exchange acquired in trade to buy capital goods; rigid state control of trade to protect domestic industrial development; the achievement of national social solidarity by taxing or confiscating out of existence the still immense socioeconomic inequalities that linger on in many semi-feudal areas; and extensive cooperation with other underdeveloped areas to pool ideas and set up common markets, eliminating tariffs within the market but retaining high protective tariffs against the outside world. All of these ideas are thoroughly familiar to the governments of underdeveloped countries, and most are being tried. But never with the vigor and enthusiasm necessary for maximum progress, except perhaps under communism.

The Western countries can do a great deal to help themselves and the underdeveloped areas, most of which they are not currently doing, or even thinking of doing. Specifically with respect to the poor countries, they should encourage or certainly not discourage regional economic cooperation among the underdeveloped nations, even though such cooperation would no doubt hurt them financially. Current Latin American experiments in regional free trading, for example, may temporarily work to the disadvantage of North America, but they could contribute materially to the maturation of the Latin American economy. The rich countries should import goods from the poor countries at fair prices to the limit of their capacity and patience, and allow the sale only of the most essential goods to poor economies, and then only at the lowest possible prices. As of now, towering tariff walls keep out many imports and poor countries are often talked into buying goods they do not need, or forced to pay exorbitant prices for goods they must have, because of the vagaries of the international "market." Measures should also be taken to stabilize the prices of primary products, such as oil, coffee, cotton, and tin, since violent fluctuations in the price levels of these goods can all but ruin poor countries dependent on the export of one or two such primary products for their continued growth. There should be international regulation of industrial and shipping cartels, to prevent extortion not controllable by national governments. The international market in private capital, virtually in a state of collapse since the early 1930's, should be rebuilt, even if it takes government-backed financial inducements to private investors to do the job. Every effort should be made to encourage private investment in underdeveloped areas, as an alternative to outright government grants.

But in an age when domestic prospects are so tempting and world conditions so unsettled, private investment will never be enough. Myrdal favors a joint effort by all the advanced countries, working through international agencies, to supply the underdeveloped areas with whatever capital and technical assistance they need and cannot procure for themselves in other ways. His plan for a world development fund differs from those cited above in its heavy emphasis on the need for substantial contributions from advanced countries other than the United States. American taxpayers might be induced to part with the funds needed, in light of their generosity thus far, but even if they did, Myrdal argues that unilateral American aid is basically immoral and cannot be anything else. The national state is not a philanthropic foundation, and every government receiving aid directly from another government cannot but feel that the aid is being given for purely selfish reasons. Since the state is an institution for exercising power, and power always demoralizes charity, unilateral aid makes the recipient ungrateful, cynical, and ultimately irresponsible, and arouses in the benefactor a feeling of self-righteous superiority or self-pity. "The world," says Myrdal, "cannot be run as a company town." [16] The only way to convert international economic assistance into a humane program for the good of all mankind, with no political strings attached, is to internationalize it in the fullest sense, which means that all countries who can afford to contribute must get together with the underdeveloped countries and work out a joint scheme administered unpolitically by international experts. In such a scheme, the wealthy countries of the world would all contribute in proportion to their national incomes, and the man in Stockholm, Geneva, or Brussels would pay as much as the man in the same income bracket in Columbus, Detroit, or Denver. All national governments have been unwilling so far to make more than token use of such existing international machinery as the International Bank and the United Nations Fund for Economic Development, pleading their desire to keep closer tabs on appropriations and expenditures, but since nations cannot individually exert much influence on the internal policies of other free nations, the result has been a far greater misuse of funds allocated than would have been likely under international administration.

Finally, Myrdal believes that the Western countries can begin taking important steps toward the ultimate objective of an international economy by engaging in more far-reaching experiments in international economic planning than they have to date. A lot could be done, he suspects, even without stepping on toes or injuring vested interests, left undone thus far out of sheer inertia and lethargy. If the welfare state is here to stay, the only plausible substitute for it is a "welfare world." World planning, as in a program of coordinated economic assistance to the underdeveloped countries, can step by step replace national planning, by *including* national planning. In addition to the help given poor countries, Myrdal challenges the Western nations to enter into continuous negotiation among themselves on tariffs, dumping, agricultural price supports, possible increases in trade and movements of labor and capital across frontiers, and the like, to arrest the steady drift in recent years toward autarky, which is always inefficient and cannot help but retard economic growth in the long run. The aim would not be classical free trade, with each area specializing in what it can produce best and selling it on the open market according to the laws of supply and demand, but simply a few tentative steps toward integration, to reverse recent trends and restore an atmosphere of confidence to the Western community. It remains to be seen whether the new European Economic Community created by France, Germany, Italy, and the Benelux powers will turn out to be a stumbling block or a steppingstone on the road to total Western integration.[17] In any event, Myrdal is confident that the underdeveloped nations, too, would benefit from the closer integration of the rich countries, since this would get the latter in the habit of working out their problems, including their relations with the former, rationally and cooperatively.

But the final aim, for Myrdal, is always an integrated world economy, with East and West on a footing of equality and all working together harmoniously for the good of all. He hopes ultimately that the nations would even be able to formalize their cooperation by establishing a world federal government, although for the immediate future, world government is only a pipe dream. "Clearly, the complete realization of our ideals would create a world without boundaries and without national discrimination, a world where all men are free to move around as they wish and to pursue on equal terms their own happiness. Politically, the implication would be a world state, democratically ruled by the will of all peoples. Somewhere in the religious compartment of our souls we all harbor . . . this vision of a world in perfect integration, the *Urbs Dei* or *Civitas Mundi.*" [18]

The other major variety of economic integration, the synthesis of economic systems, is not dealt with by Myrdal at any length. We have suggested that it may be taking care of itself. The two extreme positions currently fashionable are the unplanned, uncontrolled free economy where individuals ruthlessly and amorally compete in the market place for unlimited private gain, which apparently works well during the early stages of industrialization in a country managed by an aggressive and sizable middle class with long traditions of effective self-government — a rare combination in history; and, second, the totally planned collectivist economy where the state indulges in ruthless and amoral exploitation of all its resources for the sake of unlimited national gain, at the expense of human dignity and at the risk of world war. Individualistic capitalism, of course, wants the world safe for "freedom," by which it means unlimited cutthroat capitalism; communism wants to see the world under "socialism," by which it means a world Sovietized and administered, at least to some extent, from Moscow. "Speaking of the future," says Khrushchev, "it seems to me that the further development of the socialist countries will in all probability proceed along the lines of the consolidation of a single world socialist economic system. . . . The common economic foundation of world socialism will grow stronger, eventually rendering pointless the question of borders." [19]

Most of the prophets of world integration, being neither doctrinaire capitalists nor communists, reject both extremes, and favor the emergence of a mixed system of private and public enterprise, adjusted to local mores and needs, which might leave much of both the American and Soviet systems unchanged.* Socialist prophets, like Erich Fromm and Erich Kahler, would prefer to see the world converted to the spirit of the communitarian movement in postwar France, pioneered by Marcel Barbu's "Community of Work" at Boimondau, and described at length in Claire Huchet Bishop's book, *All Things Common.*[20] On a morally less exalted plane, but with considerable practical success, several whole Western European countries seem to be moving in the direction of a sane compromise between freedom and planning: notably Myrdal's Sweden. Yugoslavia may be approaching a similarly sane compromise from the opposite direction.

Western Europe also, in the six-power Common Market which opened for business on January 1, 1958, provides a small foretaste, perhaps, of the coming integrated world economy. The relatively rapid progress toward integration of this European Economic Community is the economic phase of a movement that in its political dimension may even foreshadow a federal world government: which raises at last — to use Toynbeean capitals — the ultimate Question confronting Mankind.

* For the problem of the harmonization of the two ideologies, see pp. 148–53.

World Government

IF IT IS the "ultimate question" before mankind, world government is also the most thoroughly explored aspect of the nascent world civilization in recent books on world problems. Predicting or proposing a world constitution was for several years during and after the second World War a major national pastime of especially the English-speaking intelligentsia. In the late 1940's, the world government movement fathered about seventy organized groups around the world which enrolled hundreds of thousands of members. Nearly one quarter of the members of the American Congress and the British Parliament gave continuing support for years to resolutions favoring, in principle, a world federal government. Herbert J. Muller, at the close of his best-selling book *The Uses of the Past,* published in 1952, could reach "the commonplace conclusion" that man's best hope lay in "some kind of world federation on a democratic basis." H. Stuart Hughes in his *Essay for Our Times* spoke of "the solid and now familiar conviction that every nation must transfer the essentials of its sovereignty to a world authority." For Norman Couisns, world government was simply "coming." It was "inevitable. No arguments for it or against it can change that fact." [21] Prominent elder statesmen, scientists as famous as Albert Einstein, philosophers as famous as Bertrand Russell, churchmen, civic leaders, school children: the chorus grew until it seemed, for a brief deceptive moment, irresistible.

Plans for world government, usually in the form of constitutions, are relatively easy to concoct. Unlike schemes for a world religion or a world philosophy, they can be drafted in precise and convincing detail, replete with organization charts and tax tables. They were already popular among the "internationalists" of the nineteenth century, from William Ladd, whose *Essay on a Congress of Nations* won the American Peace Society contest in 1840 and was later vigorously advertised in Europe by Ladd's disciple Elihu Burritt, to the Scottish jurist James Lorimer and the Quaker world federalist Benjamin Franklin Trueblood. The Hague Peace Conferences of 1899 and 1907, the League of Nations movement, and the League itself with all its affililiated agencies gave fresh impetus earlier in this century to far-ranging speculation on the anatomy and physiology of a possible world government. By the mid-1950's, enough documents, papers, and books had been published by, for, and about the League, the United Nations, the many functional world service organizations, the European Union movement, and the postwar world government movement to fill several life times of serious reading. But the solemn lunacies of the Cold War and the apparent failure of existing international organizations to curb the aggressive instincts of the Great Powers make it difficult for thinking people in recent years to find schemes for world government exciting. The United Nations, or rather the more than one hundred sovereign states who kick, starve, and humiliate the United Nations, have won the well-earned contempt of rational men everywhere. Only Western European federalism seems to have the slightest breath of life in it at this writing.

The current collapse of interest, whether it be temporary or permanent, does nothing, of course, to refute the classical case for world government, nor does it wipe out the long history of world government activism. To follow F. L. Schuman's typology, five major routes to world political integration, involving five different concepts of world order, have been widely discussed, or even tried, in the twentieth century. Two — world conquest and mutual security alliances — have figured in the foreign policies of many modern states, failed infamously, and interested few thinkers. The one envisages a world empire ruled by a conquering superpower; the other a world of nations linked by treaties which prescribe common action against an aggressor. A third route to world order is "peace by treason," any scheme that subverts or attempts to bypass existing political authority, which includes Garry Davis' campaign after World War II to compile a registry of "world citizens" in Paris, the World Citizenship Movement in Britain, and Robert Sarrazac's "Mundialization" movement, which won the support of hundreds of local governments in France and other parts of Europe in the early postwar years. In "peace by treason," an individual or a community simply cuts loose from his or its national moorings and joins the commonwealth of Man, not otherwise defined. Still a fourth way to world political integration is the "functionalist" approach, most closely identified in recent years with David Mitrany and his book, first published in 1943, *A Working Peace System*. For the functionalist, the best hope for world order is through the proliferation and gradual interlocking of non-political regional and international agencies like the Universal Postal Union and the International Labor Organization. Like "peace by treason," functionalism is ultimately a plan for getting around and superseding the national state, an idea that always fascinated H. G. Wells. As Wells foresaw the new world order, it would not be a "state" at all, but something more like a world technocracy, managed by nonpolitical experts. Mitrany and most other recent functionalists, while not going this far in their depreciation of politics and government, tend in a distinctly Wellsian direction.

But it is Schuman's fifth route to world political integra-

tion that has appealed to the overwhelming majority of thinkers and prophets of world order during the past quarter
century: "peace by contract," or world federation. The federalist school, in turn, has divided into at least four distinct
factions. The "maximalists" advocate a complete, thorough-
going world federal government. The "minimalists" are willing to settle for just enough world government to keep the
peace, for the time being. The Atlantic Union movement,
organized in 1939 by Clarence K. Streit, urges immediate
federal union of the North Atlantic democracies, as the first
step toward ultimate world government, to be established
whenever the rest of the world "qualifies" for admission.
Finally, the European Union movement, launched immediately after World War II, but with many prewar roots, aims
at a United States of Europe and has blossomed out in such
divers forms as the Council of Europe and the abortive European Defense Community, struck down at the eleventh hour
by the French National Assembly in 1954, after the other five
signatory powers had ratified the treaty bringing it into
existence.

Only the maximalist and minimalist wings of the movement, then, seriously propose immediate world federation.
And these two positions have often cropped up in the same
organization, since they differ on tactics alone, not on ultimate goals. The great classic of maximalism is perhaps Emery
Reves' book, *The Anatomy of Peace,* which first appeared in
1945, a forceful, dynamic, sledge-hammer analysis of nationalism applauded on its dust jacket by people as various as Sen-
ators Fulbright, Pepper, and Thomas, Bishop Tucker, Albert
Einstein, Mark and Carl Van Doren, and Walter Wanger.
Its publication by Penguin Books in 1947 gave it such popularity in England that Alan de Rusett, in a study of world
government movements for the Royal Institute of International Affairs, could dub Reves the "Mazzini of world unity"
and the chief "philosopher" of world federalism in mid-cen-

ury.[22] Reves advocated immediate world federal government with tremendous *élan,* even to the extent of proposing
that if world union could not be achieved by reasonable
democratic methods, we — Americans? — should "precipitate
unification by conquest" rather than "prolong the agony of a
decaying, dying system of society." But he purposely said little
about the structure of the world government, on the thesis
that devising constitutions "would only hinder progress" by
leading to furious criticism and debate of individual clauses.
The immediate need was for agreement on general principles
and a vast campaign of public education through the mass
media.[23]

This did not prevent an able group of thinkers at the University of Chicago from forming, in 1945, a Committee to
Frame a World Constitution, headed by Chancellor R. M.
Hutchins and the Italian scholar G. A. Borgese, which produced in 1948 an eloquent draft world constitution along
maximalist lines. Other members of the committee included
Mortimer J. Adler, Erich Kahler, Stringfellow Barr, and Albert Guérard. Since its draft world constitution is the most
thoughtful and detailed exposition of the maximalist philosophy of government ever attempted, a summary is very much
in order here.

The framers of this so-called Preliminary Draft begin by
representing their work as a respectful proposal to history,
not a sacred document. Its purpose is to stimulate, and not
foreclose, discussion. In the first section a Declaration of
Duties and Rights safeguards the world citizen from despotism. He must take it as his civic duty to "serve with word
and deed, and with productive labor according to his ability,
the spiritual and physical advancement of the living and of
those to come," to obey the Golden Rule, and abstain from
unlawful violence. The "Law of Nature" reinforced by the
prescription of positive law will guarantee him the right to
material well-being according to his merit and needs, freedom

of peaceful assembly, protection against tyranny, "and any other such freedoms and franchises as are inherent in man's inalienable claims to life, liberty, and the dignity of the human person." Since "earth, water, air, energy" are the "common property of the human race," their use or ownership is subject always to the common welfare, a formula which admits the possibility of world socialism, without requiring it.

In the next section, the framers list the nineteen powers specifically delegated to the world government, from the settlement of all disputes by peaceful means if possible and by the federal armed forces if necessary, to the levying and collecting of taxes, the issue and control of a world currency, the control of local boundaries, and the regulation of transportation and communication. The world government is to be appointed by a federal convention, elected directly by the people, and subdivided into nine electoral colleges, one for each of "the nine Societies of kindred nations and cultures, or Regions wherefrom its members derive their powers." The nine regions are "Europa," with or without the U.K.; "Atlantis," the United States and whatever parts of the British Commonwealth decide to join with it; "Eurasia," the Soviet Union and all East European states deciding to associate with it; "Afrasia," the Near and Middle East, with or without Pakistan; "Africa," south of the Sahara; "India," with Pakistan if the latter chooses; "Asia Major," consisting of China, Korea, and Japan; "Austrasia," the Southeast Asian powers; and "Columbia," the entire Western hemisphere south of the Rio Grande. The world government proper would include a world president, elected by the convention for a six-year term, who in turn would appoint a chancellor, who in his turn would appoint the cabinet with the president's approval; and, as the major legislative body, a world council, chosen by the federal convention. The president would also appoint, subject to conciliar veto, sixty justices to sit on the grand tribunal, the supreme court of the world republic; and the council would elect a chamber of guardians, presided over by the president, to control the federal armed forces. An elaborate set of checks and balances in the best traditions of American constitutionalism is built into the scheme, to guard against delusions of grandeur on the part of any official or institution. The federal convention even elects a "tribune of the people," to act as spokesman for minority groups: the winner is the candidate who receives the second largest vote, not the largest, among those eligible. There will also be a federal capital, an official federal language, a federal calendar, and a federal system of measures. "The structure of the projected world government," as Schuman comments, "while perhaps unduly cumbersome and complex, is clearly a synthesis of European parliamentary practices and the 'Presidential' system of the U.S.A." [24]

Maximalism also flourished for some years in the Crusade for World Government, initiated in Britain by Henry Usborne, M.P., and in the People's World Convention, a movement linking the British Crusade with several other groups of similar persuasions. The P.W.C. managed to hold, with much confusion and wrangling, a "world convention" in Geneva in December and January of 1950-51. Its original plan had been to assemble at Geneva popularly elected delegates from the whole world, at the ratio of one delegate per million of population, and then to frame a world constitution, for submission to the U.N. and all sovereign governments. As it turned out, only two of the five hundred delegates at Geneva had been democratically elected at public polls — both from the state of Tennessee, whose embarrassed legislature hastened in 1951 to repeal the special law which had authorized their election. The movement dissolved in bitter factional conflict.

Minimalist federalism has typically taken the form of proposals to convert the United Nations into a limited world federal government by revision of the U. N. Charter, an idea more durable, together with the organizations sponsoring it, than any of the various maximalist schemes. In the United States, the chief organ for minimalist propaganda is the United World Federalists, still 15,000 members strong, whose first president, Cord Meyer, Jr., contributed still another "classic" to the modern literature of federalism, *Peace or Anarchy*, in 1947. The most elaborate recent plan for a thoroughgoing revision of the U. N. Charter may be studied in *World Peace through World Law*, by Grenville Clark and Louis B. Sohn. The authors spare no pains to show how, article by article, and clause by clause, the Charter can be amended to transform the United Nations from the hapless Petrouchka of the carnival of nations into a federal world government. They propose staged world disarmament over a period of thirteen years, with a fool-proof inspection system. The armies of the world will be replaced by a U.N. police force with 200,000 to 600,000 professional troops and up to 1,200,000 reservists. A popularly elected General Assembly, with each nation's voting strength determined by its population, will become a genuine legislature with full power to enact all laws necessary for the maintenance of world peace. The Security Council will be reorganized as an executive council, similar to the British cabinet, in which all major powers will enjoy permanent representation but no right of veto. The International Court of Justice will have compulsory jurisdiction, at last, over cases that can be decided by law; a World Equity Tribunal will handle cases between nations to which no laws apply, and there will also be regional U.N. courts. A world development authority will dispose of twenty-five billion dollars annually to industrialize the underdeveloped countries, whose plight generates "instability and conflict" in today's world. In full harmony with the minimalist thesis, the authors insist that the powers of the federal world government must be strictly limited "to matters directly related to the maintenance of peace. All other powers should be reserved to the nations and their peoples." [25]

Also worth mentioning from recent years are the minimalist proposals of the all-party Parliamentary Group for World Government, headed by I. J. Pitman and Arthur Henderson, which has the support of 150 peers and commoners in the British Parliament, and urges the complete transfer of troops and arms to a world security authority and a world court with compulsory jurisdiction; and the work of the new World Rule of Law Center at Duke University. Its first publication, Wallace McClure's *World Legal Order,* 1960, argues the familiar case for supremacy of treaties over national statutes, strengthening the present framework of international law, and referral of all disputes endangering world peace to the World Court for compulsory arbitration.[26]

The prophets of world integration studied in Chapters Two and Three above are not given, as a rule, to constitution-writing, although one — Erich Kahler — served on the Chicago Committee to Frame a World Constitution. But most of them, including Lewis Mumford, Sir Julian Huxley, Arnold Toynbee, Pitirim Sorokin, F. S. C. Northrop, and Oliver L. Reiser, have come out publicly in favor of some kind of federal world government. Mumford in 1948, for one example, proposed an immediate "armistice" to suspend the Cold War and a world conference with joint Soviet-American initiative to transform "the dummy model of the United Nations, which is a disguise for a feeble confederation of independent sovereign states, into an effective working machine: a complete system of world government." [27]

Toynbee has been ardently supporting world government for many years. At the height of the world government campaign in the late 1940's, he perhaps dismayed some of his more Augustinian admirers by suggesting that of the three steps most desperately needed to save mankind from de-

struction — world government, working compromises between free enterprise and socialism, and an inward spiritual
transformation — the building of "a constitutional co-operative system of world government" was the "most urgent of
all." In 1954 he predicted that a universal state achieved by
federation and not by the usual method of conquest would
be a tremendous breakthrough in history, bringing the pattern of the first 6000 years of history to a triumphant end.[28]
In his 1961 "Reconsiderations" he is still wholly dedicated to
the cause of a world state. He now thinks it possible that
such a state might grow out of international arrangements
for "an effective world-wide control over the use of atomic
energy." In any event, the historic universal states were
only "so many preparatory exercises for the eventual establishment of a literal universal state." When it comes, it will
follow the good example of the Roman and Han empires
and grant a liberal measure of local autonomy. "Our paramount loyalty must be transferred from our local nation to
mankind as a whole," but "local administration, in a hierarchy of different geographical scales, will continue to be
necessary." Nations will function as American states or British counties do today — Toynbee seems to skim obliviously
over the political scientist's time-worn distinction between
federal and unitary states — and national feeling will persist
in such innocent fields as literature, art, and sport. Elsewhere
in the same abundant volume, he foresees in the still more
remote future a drift away from units based on physical
neighborhood to "diasporas" united, like the Jewish dias-
pora today, by "a community of beliefs, ideas, aspirations,
interests, or activities." The crucial factor will be the consolidation of much of the habitable world into a single continuous urban mass broken only by seas and wastes. "This
transformation of the World into a cosmopolis favours social organization on a non-local basis." Just as people in large
cities today draw their friends from "kindred spirits scat-

tered all over the metropolitan area," so, now that the world "is becoming one city, we may expect to see associations based on neighbourhood come to be overshadowed by others based on spiritual affinity." [29]

Northrop weaves together the regionalist, minimalist, and maximalist approaches to world government in *The Taming of the Nations,* a book which unfortunately appeared too late, 1952, to be of much help in reconciling the various contending factions in the world government movement. It faithfully translates Northrop's formula for world cultural integration into legal and political terms. Again, it proceeds from the thesis that national cultures, like all cultures, grow fairly consistently out of their fundamental philosophical assumptions. Those assumptions which give rise to standards of individual and social conduct he terms the "living law norms" of the nation. They prescribe liberal democracy in the United States, one-party dictatorship in the Soviet Union. Positive law is easily enforced and willingly obeyed when it corresponds to these living law norms, hard to enforce and strongly resisted when it does not. But in today's world, Northrop sees a powerful trend away from merely national cultures to larger allegiances, based on common religious and philosophical traditions, and this new ideological orientation he calls "culturalism," rather than "nationalism." Roman Catholic Western Europe, for example, is gradually coalescing into a single economic and political unit. This it can readily do because although each of the several major powers in Western Europe developed its own national ideology between the seventeenth and nineteenth centuries, they also have a vital common denominator which can act to unify them, in their common heritage of Catholicism and Roman law. Northrop sees parallel trends in the Muslim world of North Africa and the Near East, in Negro Africa, in the Far East, in the Soviet sphere, and in the Americas. If and when each of these super national groupings achieves political integration, it will bring world government that much nearer, by substituting a handful of states for the hundreds now in existence.

Meanwhile, there is an urgent need for all the peace-loving nations of the world, all those nations whose ideologies allow them to live in peace and friendship with other nations, to form a world federation for their common defense against maverick aggressor states, such as Soviet Russia. Such a world organization must frankly admit the existence of "living law pluralism" in the world today, and act to protect it. In Northrop's minimalist stage of world government, the world community of peace-loving nations will guarantee to each member the unhampered operation of the living law norms of its people within its territorial limits. Each member nation, to be on the safe side, will spell out "its specific ideology and living law norms" in the world constitution. Any attempt by another state to interfere with either the cultural or political integrity of a member power will then constitute grounds for federal intervention, by armed force if need be. With this guarantee each member state will turn over to the world organization the power to regulate that part of its life which is international in character, and without right of veto. Each member will come to the immediate aid of any other whose politico-cultural integrity is endangered by aggression. No other type of action need be taken by the world organization. There will be no wrangling over ideologies, or what is right and wrong by the standards of any one of them: all common action will be taken solely on the basis of a discovery that the principle of living law pluralism has been violated. "Such a simple basis for decision makes the decision clean cut, unconfused by the appeals by different statesmen to their respective national ideologies." [30]

But as the growth of supernational federations begins to reduce the number of member nations, the path to true cosmopolis will open up. Here, Northrop applies his method

for the fusion of cultures in higher integrates.* Living law
pluralism will gradually change into living law monism, as
all living law norms are put to the test of the natural sciences
and all methods of knowing come to be accepted as equally
valid. In time there will be a world ideology, making possible
the true world state of the most devout maximalist. At the
end of the long road is "Cosmopolis, that single earthly
polity whose model is the unity of the Asians' intuition and
the Occidentals' constitutional image of the universal City
of God." [31]

Of course Northrop is banking on the political sanity of
the newer "culturalism," a hope not warranted by the record
of its forerunner, "nationalism." Gerard Mangone makes the
useful point that an equilibrium based on regional amalgamations might not last as long as "a world with a few dozen
relatively independent states." [32] A united Europe or a
united Atlantic bloc, like the communist bloc already more
or less in existence in Eastern Europe and Soviet Russia,
could easily have the immediate effect of heightening the
tension between East and West, or even precipitating a world
war. Certainly the Soviets have been consistent in their para-
noid denunciation of all moves toward regional federation
emanating from the West — for that matter, all Western
schemes for world government. Streit's proposal of an Atlantic Union in 1939 was assailed as a plan for a super-empire
to save capitalism from its iniquities; Soviet scientists characterized federalist Albert Einstein as a dupe of the ambitions
of "world capitalism"; *Pravda* tarred and feathered Frederick
L. Schuman as an "apologist for imperialism" in reviewing
his *Commonwealth of Man*; Cord Meyer, Jr., was a "cosmopolitan gangster," Emery Reves a "fascist degenerate," and
the Chicago Committee's Preliminary Draft a plan for establishing Anglo-Saxon world domination. Proponents of European federal union are "purveyors of the bourgeois ideology

* See above, pp. 137–38.

of an 'imperialist' union of the world." [33] It all goes back, of course, to Soviet fears, at least half legitimate a generation ago, of "capitalist encirclement." The Soviet Union has even thwarted all efforts by its East European dependencies to form regional federations among themselves; without Soviet intervention, a Balkan federal republic might very well have been created shortly after the second World War.

On the other hand, many advocates of regionalism, especially Western European federation, see in their plans the first legitimate stage in the evolution of a world state. They sincerely hope that Europe's good example will touch off similar fusions elsewhere, leading to eventual world union. As one of their number, Denis de Rougemont, states the case, "Everything . . . singles Europe out to foment *the antibodies* that will render mankind immune to some of the viruses Europe was alone in propagating. In saving itself by federation (an arrangement far older than its nationalism), it can offer the world the recipe and the model of a fruitful transcendence of the national framework." [34] The danger of war, comparable to the national struggles of the past, among titanic "culturalist" federations, or the risk of Soviet wrath in the face of what might seem in Soviet eyes an exceptionally menacing case of capitalist conspiracy and encirclement, never deters the dedicated federalist.

Much more could be said about the world commonwealth, as it emerges from the visions of contemporary social prophets. Its form of government will obviously be democratic, although it may in its earlier stages be able to include among its member nations some that do not practice democracy in their own internal political life. It will guarantee to all its citizens full civil equality. Several prophets also stress the importance of democratically recruited "elite" groups, with high standards of professional and humane responsibility, who will not allow the world commonwealth to degenerate into a mobocracy pandering to the tastes of the mass-man; how this will work out remains far from clear.

But the outlines of the world polity foreseen by contemporary prophets are clear enough from what has been said already. If the amount of real agreement on tactics and strategy is negligible, still most mid-century Western thinking men in favor of a world commonwealth share the same ultimate goal. From the political and economic point of view, cosmopolis will be at least as good a place to live in as the United States or the United Kingdom or Switzerland today. The radical renovations and enlargements of mind necessary to form the world culture will not be needed, to the same degree certainly, in building the world commonwealth, except insofar as cultural integration is itself a prerequisite of political integration. But it will be a state in sheer geographical magnitude beyond anything man has ever known, and many deeply planted political loyalties will have to be uprooted and destroyed, before it can strike roots of its own. Well established interests will have to be pruned to give stunted and shadowed growths a place in the sun. To change the jungle-world of the twentieth century into a world-garden for all mankind to enjoy in peace and freedom calls for more than good intentions. It demands the total engagement of coming generations in its cause. It demands sacrifice of habits and powers unprecedented in recent times.

Do we dare to reach so high? Whether the absolute certainty of almost total obliteration if we fail to create a world commonwealth is enough to move the collective will of mankind to decisive action before time runs out, remains the great heart-stopping enigma of our century.

Five

Who Will
Integrate the Integrators?

Who Will
Integrate the Integrators?

THE IDEA of world order has haunted mankind for centuries, says Lawrence Frank. "But each proposal has demanded acceptance of the particular religion, philosophy,
political organization, or military power of the proponent.
. . . However lofty the aspirations, proposals for world order have been conceived primarily in terms of a single dom-
inating power, authority, creed or belief, or an exclusive
scheme of political and economic institutions to be imposed
on all peoples." [1] Over thirty years ago the great Czech
novelist Karel Capek gave the same theme an ingenious twist
in *The Absolute at Large*. An inventor named Marek devises
an atomic furnace which completely disintegrates matter,
converting it into pure energy easily harnessed for industrial
use; but at the same time, in the same process, the furnace
liberates a certain quantity of invisible, intangible, imma-
terial God-stuff, Spinoza's Absolute, which causes people who
get a whiff of it to see visions, hear voices, perform miracles,
and generally avail themselves of "that good old-time religion." Since Marek's furnace provides a cheap and inexhaust-
ible supply of energy, it is soon in use all over the planet, but
the result is world madness. Intoxicated by the Absolute,
mankind divides into thousands of fanatical religious sects,
each claiming infallibility, each determined to annex the
world. In the end, a gigantic war breaks out, lasting nine

years, in which 198 million men are killed, and most of civilization is destroyed. The industrialist who first manufactured Marek's furnaces reflects on man's plight. God, he says, is too big for man. " 'He is infinite. That's just where the trouble lies. You see, everyone measures off a certain amount of Him and then thinks it is the entire God. Each one appropriates a little fringe or fragment of Him and then thinks he possesses the whole of Him.' " We cannot bear to admit even to ourselves that we have " 'only a few wretched metres or gallons or sackloads of divine truth.' " [2]

This has been the pattern through most of man's past. But with the sole significant exception of the Soviet sphere, where doubt has become a crime against the omniscient state, modern man is in full revolt against the spirit of dogma. He is engaged in a wholesale process of de-absolutization, so that the mental climate will soon be completely free of those awesome jinn let loose by Capek's mad scientist. Rather the danger now is that we tend to believe nothing at all. Even if we wanted to conquer the world on behalf of some one true God, the new total weapons would hold us in check. There is no argument against megaton missiles and continent-blighting plagues. So long as ruling circles on both sides of the Iron Curtain keep a firm grip on their sanity — for which we have no guarantee — the integration of humanity cannot advance along the old historic route of conquest. The last safe chance to impose order on the planet by force was lost in the late 1940's by the United States, and such a chance may never come again.

The prophets studied in the present work see as the alternative to conquest a gradual and unfolding process of world cultural integration and political federation. The particular prophets heard here agree more often than they disagree, but they seldom realize it. Few know or say much about their contemporaries. Where disagreements do irrefutably exist, they can be bitter and even fundamental. Meanwhile, the great majority of contemporary thinkers either positively prefer not to have an "integrated" world or refuse to speculate. In refusing, they contribute enormously to our moral and spiritual paralysis, but they have good reasons for keeping silent.

For this is rapidly becoming a world without Truth. Not without practical truths, handy for solving immediate, everyday problems. What mid-century man lacks is utter Truth, and as far as he can see into the future, he will always lack utter Truth. The whole avant-garde in theology, philosophy, and science assures him that if he thinks he sees the utter Truth, he sees only a mirage. As Capek would say, the truth is infinite, man is finite, and all a finite creature can hope to enjoy of infinity is a few "sackloads." We stand condemned to ignorance. Each mind strikes out on its own, carves up reality to please itself, and there the matter usually rests. Even these far-ranging protagonists of world synthesis, with their staggering erudition and breadth of mind, each give us just one specialized, personalized glimpse of the Truth, too fuzzy and incomplete ever to be represented as the Real Thing. If mankind must "integrate," on what plan, and with what orientation, and in what direction? The prophets of integration try to lead the way, but who will integrate the integrators?

The intellectual confusion of modern man has many sources, some quite unrelated to the life of the mind itself. The present world political crisis, following so closely two dehumanizing world wars, cannot but challenge the sensitive thinking man to reconsider his values and his heritage. The intimate exposure of Western and Eastern cultures to one another leads to puzzlement, exotic syncretisms, and searching self-examination. But in the West, at least, the chief and continuing and only irremovable source of confusion is the revolution at the topmost level of man's thought: in philosophy, theology, science, and history. For hundreds of years

Western man has subtly but surely chiseled away at the underpinnings of his world-view. He has discovered that "truth" is relative to the observer and relative to the mental climate of the observer's historical epoch. Western thought, which grew by an overwhelming inner logic from the Socratic proposition that the good is the true and the true can be known, has in this way annihilated its own past and exchanged foundations of rock for foundations of shifting sand. The philosophic faith of reason, the theological faith of revelation, and the scientific faith of experience, all collapse together. The sequence of mental events which led to this *dénouement* is sketched briefly above.* But to recapitulate in two sentences: beginning in earnest with the critical philosophies of Hume and Kant at the end of the Enlightenment, Western man has moved in the last two centuries from a long era in which he rarely doubted his ability to know the Truth, to the present era, in which he knows he *cannot* know it. His perennial faith in the correspondence of his own ideas with external reality has almost suddenly collapsed, leaving him stranded in a cosmos he does not, at bottom, understand.

For the philosopher this means, in Northrop's terminology, that concepts by intuition or direct experience cannot be reduced to concepts by postulation, or vice versa. In other words, there is no way of equating sensory data with statements of theory.[3] The theoretical wavelength for "blue" cannot be translated into the sensation of "blue." Our experience of the sun's rising and the moon's phases goes on independently of our calendars and our astrophysics. We can get the two into a fair amount of practical harmony perhaps, but they never really fuse. And the problem of correlating wavelengths with colors or predicting solar appearances and lunar phases shrinks to the proportions of a nursery game next to such problems as the existence of God,

* See pp. 55–58.

the nature of man, the moral significance of war, and the integration of the world.

No philosopher has grasped the significance of this revolution in thought more fully than Jaspers. We have become able to see things "as they really are," he writes, "and that is why the foundations of life quake beneath our feet; for, now that the identity of thought and being (hitherto unchallenged) has ceased to exist for us, we see only, on the one hand, life, and, on the other, our own and our companions' awareness of that life. . . . Behind every apparent unity of life and the consciousness of life there looms the distinction between the real world and the world as we know it." This echoes, of course, Kant's distinction between the thing-as-we-see-it and the thing-as-it-is: but Jaspers goes beyond Kant to deny man any avenue whatever to final knowledge of things-as-they-are. We do not even all share the same illusions, since every "truth" is a personal truth, a product of our own unique perspective and innermost being, if we value and exercise our freedom. "No one," he says, "possesses the one truth valid for all. No one occupies a vantage point from which he can survey all truths, from outside, as it were, to compare and evaluate them. Rather, each of us is in the thick of it." In the final analysis, "we have no firm ground under us, no principle to hold on to, but a suspension of thought in infinite space — without shelter in conceptual systems, without refuge in firm knowledge or faith. And even this suspended, floating structure of thought is only one metaphor of Being among others." [4]

But practically all the newer trends in serious thought come to the same conclusion, in one way or another. In theology, the rather less radical equivalent of Jaspers' point of view is the argument that although "Christianity" must be absolutely true, since it represents the Word of God spoken to man, no man and no book can possibly capture it whole and undefiled in human language. "Revelation," says

Rudolf Bultmann, "is truth only in the event," not in the formulation.[5] The creeds and symbols and metaphors of the Christian faith flow from the minds and lips of finite men: they are man's way of describing his encounter with God; they are man's own devices. As Hocking warns, in discussing Christianity, "We have perpetually to distinguish between *its* certainties and finalities, and the tentative, partial character of our own achievements, insights, expressions." [6]

All modern science labors under the same crushing sense of man's finitude. In spite of its triumphs, science can no more reach final Truth about nature than the philosopher or theologian can reach ethical and metaphysical Truth. His kind of knowledge is far more objective, having nothing or little to do with man's inner being, but it is always partial, always subject to revision. Just as the arrow charted in its flight by Zeno had an infinite number of stations, since one can always halve and halve again *ad infinitum* the total distance an arrow must travel, so the scientist can approach reality from an infinite number of angles. Every theory is a way of parcelling the universe, and no human sensory apparatus or analyzing brain can or will ever see it whole or from every possible perspective. Scientific knowledge almost by definition is part-knowing, the isolation of a phenomenon or "class" of phenomena in order to study it more closely than it could be studied undetached from the cosmic whole. Worse yet, all the "laws" of science, which predict and explain similar sequences of similar physical events, cannot by any amount of logical manipulation be proved binding on the cosmos. Cause and effect relationships, as Hume saw many years ago, cannot be observed: they are all in our minds, devices we invent to explain regularities in the cosmos to ourselves. We take samples, devise systems of classification, try out different geometries, represent our findings in words and symbols, theorize, analyze, and sometimes synthesize, but we always fall short. There is nothing absolute in science, writes Ernest H. Hutten in a recent study of theoretical physics. And he adds: "Scientific method itself is not absolute, and it changes with science." [7] Nothing remains untouchable; nothing is sacrosanct, not even the methods by which we discover that nothing is sacrosanct.

So, says John Bowle, we have to give up the faded ideal of "dogmatic and final truth, of metaphysical total explanation." [8] Not every educated man and woman even today fully grasps the significance of de-absolutization in human thought, and quite a few still cling to absolutes and dogmas in spite of everything. But their numbers dwindle, this side of the Iron Curtain. And inexorably, little by little, the discoveries of the best brains filter down through the thinking population, like rust eating through iron. Uncertainty at the top cannot help but reach everyone, in the long run, from statesmen and editors, through teachers, clergymen, and second lieutenants, down to the rank and file in every walk of life. Perhaps the most common reaction is a suspension of belief, or a world-weary indifferentism to the ultimate questions. As a Yale senior, in one of twenty letters addressed in 1961 to the Yale student body of A.D. 2261, describes his generation, it questions everything, it hears all points of view, and then it takes no sides and no action. He commiserates with the students of three hundred years hence if "you are in the same state of suspension that we find ourselves in." [9]

Should de-absolutization turn out to be an irreversible process, three hundred years might make little difference; and yet mankind has some chance of steering a middle course between cocksure dogmatism and relativistic indifferentism. We cannot end the present study without affirming that such a middle course is possible. In spite of all the forces in modern life conspiring to make us shipwreck on the Scylla of dogma or the Charybdis of despair, we can avoid both. Most succinctly the middle course can be defined as the responsible use of freedom to pool our finite truths in a world mind, a racial will, a policy for Man. At the heart of the matter lies an indispensable revolution in attitude: call it simply a "will to agree."

From this perspective, as it unfolds on the pages that follow, the human enterprise will divide naturally into three great life-phases. In the childhood of the race, men lived secure in their possession of ultimate wisdom and utter Truth, except in eras like late Western antiquity, when different cultures with different Truths were hurled together by the vicissitudes of empire, and had to achieve some higher synthesis. In our adolescence, here and now, we shift uneasily between frantic dogmatism and the opposite assumption, based on sound analysis, that man is wholly blind and all values wholly relative. In the coming age of man's spiritual maturity, beyond dogma and beyond skepticism, he will somehow learn to live with perpetual uncertainty, and at the same time work in concert with his fellows to determine, in the light of all current knowledge and belief, what is the closest approximation to Truth possible at each successive stage in his development. If man cannot ever know the infinite Truth, still he can always strive to reach a common definition of what finite truths, subject to unlimited revision, seem cogent to him in the vital present. In a given epoch, at a given level of scientific knowledge, from a given perspective, the world will always appear to have much the same meaning to most men of intelligence and good will. And as we approach the epoch of One World, and a unified world science, and a world perspective in philosophy and religion, something remotely akin to what Teilhard de Chardin calls "Unanimity" may be possible for free minds working with passion and sincerity to reach tentative agreement on values, goals, and knowledge.[10]

Perhaps the agreement of men is a poor substitute for the possession of Truth, and perhaps one seems just as distant today as the other, but this is not necessarily so. Much of our present disagreement and unresolved uncertainty and unwillingness even to take hypothetical plunges into the Infinite stems from attitudes that can be changed freely, and not from the inherent nature of the problem of Truth. To create an integrated world civilization, and to integrate the integrators who will lead the way thither, requires not Truth but Will: *a new approach to thought based on the will to agree.*

At this point, the liberal reader will begin to smell a rat. "Agreement" is something of a bad word among intellectuals: their historic pose is "dissent." Charles Frankel takes Maritain, Toynbee, and others to task in his brilliant polemic, *The Case for Modern Man,* for asserting that a civilization, to cohere, must be built on certain fundamental shared beliefs and values, and his argument is too typical of many thinkers in mid-century to be overlooked. Integration, he says, is necessary: but "social integration in a liberal society does not come from integrating ultimate values. It comes from organizing secular institutions in such a way that men's 'ultimate' values — their consciences, their sense of the meaning of life, their personal dignity — do not become elements of public conflict." [11] In brief, society exists only to preserve freedom, and do whatever its individuals acting together decide is necessary to make that freedom as full and real as possible. Society leaves the individual free to believe anything and everything, and it will not crumble just because they each choose to believe entirely different things about God, nature, life, and man. Similarly, for Karl Popper, the ideal society is the Open Society of individuals making decisions for themselves, and not the organic Closed Society of tribal ritual or modern collectivism. Life and history, he says, have no meaning, although we may choose to give them meaning.[12] In the same vein, Aldous Huxley's novels are crowded with unpleasant caricatures of the technocratic behavioral engineer who wants to convert all men into obedient followers of a prescribed Truth: the reptilian rationalist Scogan in *Crome Yellow,* the dictators of *Brave New World,* the world integrator De Vries in *Time Must Have a Stop,* and so on.

All this is immeasurably useful in reminding us that the totalitarian approach to world unity destroys the integrity of the person. But let us not make the mistake of destroying the integrity of the human race, or preventing it from achieving full self-realization of its integrity. The person out of touch with the racial adventure is no person at all, and a civilization composed of more or less isolated individuals bottled up in the vacuum of an empty freedom never used, will sooner or later die, cut off from the individual minds and spirits from which it draws its vitality. And further: to assert that agreement on fundamentals does not matter, is to assert that fundamentals do not matter. It is to argue that a civilization without goals or values can spin aimlessly through the endless oceans of existence without making its passengers mortally sick. Some countries, like the United States, have managed in modern times to dispense with thought-controlling totalitarian states and churches, but only because nearly everyone in them did tend to share a common heritage of fundamental values spontaneously; and even these fortunate countries are finding it hard to weather the winds of change now sweeping across the face of the earth, especially as that common heritage of fundamental values itself shatters under the impact of revolutions in thought.

Even Aldous Huxley, in *Time Must Have a Stop,* puts next to the unsympathetic figure of De Vries a typical latter-day Huxleyan hero, Sebastian Barnack, who is converted to Huxley's own variety of mysticism and then spells out a "minimum working hypothesis" for the spiritual integration of mankind. The fact remains, says Sebastian, "that a shared

theology is one of the indispensable conditions of peace.
. . . Peace can't exist except where there's a metaphysic
which all accept and a few actually succeed in realizing." [13]
Even more astonishing than Huxley's pilgrimage to mysticism is the great existentialist Sartre's recent *démarche* in
the direction of a Stalinesque Marxism, on the sound theory
that the free man who does not use his freedom to find
solidarity with his fellows, might as well not have it.[14]

No: there will be no world civilization without a substantial measure of tentative agreement among its intellectual
leaders, on ultimate values as well as on the details of practical policy. Most contemporary prophets of world order envisage an "organic" society, and so it must be, held together
by the concerted minds of men.* But this still leaves unan-
swered the question of how much the "will to agree" specifically demands of its practitioners, and how agreement can be
fashioned out of disagreement, in an age of confusion, without resort to force or brainwashing. The prophets themselves, let it be said frankly, seldom set a good example. They
tend to work very much alone. They have scarcely made any
effort at all to hammer out agreements among themselves.
Each one prefers his own particular formula of response to
the world crisis, and each one goes on repeating that formula
down through the years, in book after book.

Now this is the traditional pattern in intellectual life, and
it is a pattern that will soon have to change. We cannot conduct an interminable debate on the ideal form of a hypothetical world civilization, a debate that could last for thousands of years given unlimited time; the world crisis may
not even allow us to live out the twentieth century. A whole
new attitude must typify the next generation of integrators,
animated by a whole new fanaticism: the fanaticism of the
will to agree. It can by no means climax in total agreement
or rule out further open-ended debate after mankind gets be-

* See pp. 129–33.

yond the present impasse of total peril: but it must make a considerable change in the climate of future thought, at every level and in every field.

In a society of free men, which is the only situation where there is any need for will, the will to agree begins as the will to communicate. "Truth," says Jaspers, "must be communicable. . . . We are what we are only through the community of mutually conscious understandings." [15] The sheer act of listening to other minds in a receptive mood, of speaking one's own mind clearly and honestly, not with the intent to dazzle, but with the intent to communicate, can make all the difference between "agreement" and "dissent." One of the great shortcomings of the keenest minds is their almost ineradicable fondness for paradox, hyperbole, logic-chopping, and every other kind of rhetorical fireworks. Their idea of high adventure is an intellectual wrestling match with no holds barred, a chance to crush opponents by some stunning flash of wit. The better the mind, the more it likes to prove itself — under modern conditions at least — in furious controversy. What H. R. Mackintosh once said of the German mind is true generally of the highest-powered intellectualism of all Western countries in recent times: it is "prone to advance in a zigzag manner, tacking from one extreme to another, enveloping all in a fierce spirit of party, equipping each new school with the penetrating power of a one-sided fervour." [16] But this brand of intellectualism, with its rapid oscillations from one extreme to another, is characteristic chiefly of the prima donna intellectuals of only the last few centuries, the product of a raddled and restless age. Under the sobering exigencies of the world crisis, it is not too much to hope that communication will replace controversy as the central aim of thinking people. The rule of thumb to follow is astonishingly simple: speak so as to be understood and to further understanding; listen to understand, by putting one's own mind in the mind of the other, and trying to reason as he reasons, from his perspective. The mental habits of the college debating team must be shelved, at least for the duration of the present world crisis.

Apropos of communication, it goes almost without saying that the greatest obstacle to a settlement of the issues at stake in the Cold War, apart from a real will to conquest on either side, is the near impossibility of communication on the deepest levels between thinking people in the opposing camps. Hysterical fear of communism often blocks contact from the Western side, but the Soviet policy of rigid censorship and restrictions on foreign travel raises an immeasurably higher barrier to communication. There is little chance to exchange views in an atmosphere of friendship and a spirit of open-mindedness. Soviet and Western minds meet as antagonists; each have their stock questions and answers, their prearranged strategies of defense and offense; and so the minds never really meet at all. If Soviet spokesmen sometimes seem to come off rather better, it is only because they plan and train better.

But if lines of communication can be opened up, the next step perhaps is to have enough love and respect for other minds to assume, on principle, that other minds have something to say. If they are not entirely right, neither are they all wrong. What major school of thought, be it Marxism or Zionism, naturalism or mysticism, existentialism or technocracy, Zen or Thomism, followed with fervor by many brilliant minds through many years, could possibly fail to have enunciated, in the finite manner of all things human, some especially cogent and elegant truth, and probably quite a few? To quote Leibniz, that greatest diplomat among philosophers, "I find that most systems are right in a good share of that which they advance, but not so much in what they deny." [17] And in this event, how can we be satisfied, in seeking a new and more comprehensive world-view for the coming world civilization, if we do not winnow from every grain its kernel of truth? In times of reconstruction, every school of thought, every discipline must be laid under contribution.

This was basically the approach to knowledge of the late Karl Mannheim. As a sociologist, and one of the modern founders of *Wissensoziologie,* the "sociology of knowledge," what most interested Mannheim in ideas was the extent to which they are all "situationally conditioned," or influenced by the class affiliations of the thinker. On the basis of studies in the religious, political, and socioeconomic thought of Europe, especially Germany, since the Reformation, he reached the conclusion that practically all types of knowledge are, in fact, socially conditioned. But this did not mean, for Mannheim, that all knowledge was merely relative to narrow class interests and hence all equally invalid or non-objective. In place of this meaningless relativism, he proposed in his concept of "relationism" a theory of knowledge which argued that knowledge approaches a steadily higher degree of validity as it becomes more comprehensive, uniting more and more perspectives in a single all-embracing perspective as free as possible from situational conditioning. The "free-floating intellectual" who is relatively unattached to any class is the man best suited to find the ideational common denominators which can make such a broader perspective possible. The more "free-floating" the intellectual, the more objective his thinking is likely to be. Relationism recalls the technique of "reconception" suggested by Hocking for religious synthesis.[18]

In later work, Mannheim also advocated what he called, after H. H. Anderson and D. W. Harding, "integrative behavior," the attitude of the man who welcomes disagreement, not as a chance to impose his own will or gratify his ego by seeming tolerant, but "in the expectation of enlarging his own personality by absorbing some features of a human being essentially different from himself. Practically, this means that the democratic personality welcomes disagreement because it has the courage to expose itself to change." [19]

Much can also be learned from the techniques of thought most popular in the Eastern civilizations. As Northrop and others have made clear, the Eastern thinker is far less inclined than his counterpart in the traditional West to classify, analyze, and generally make mincemeat out of observed reality. Most Westerners, the present writer in the present study not excepted, take a positive delight in organizing things. They like to fall upon their material, refine away its impurities, analyze it minutely, divide it into airtight sections and subsections, and reduce it to a nicely drilled and regimented system. The analyzing mind of the West is responsible for the modern natural sciences, and no one suggests abolishing these, or the methods which make them possible. But at least in the realm of values and beliefs, it may be asked if analysis has not been pushed too far. Analysis is a kind of sacred cow among most Western thinkers, today as always, and in much formal philosophy more than ever. In Houghton Mifflin's popular series of readings in philosophy, the volume for the twentieth century, edited by Morton White, is aptly entitled *The Age of Analysis.* Most scholarly studies take the form of "analyses" of this or that. Students are taught to draw "distinctions" and list the "differences" between one thinker and another. We get into the habit of supposing that analysis is the only *modus operandi* of serious thought; but in fact there are others just as useful: above all, its opposite, "synthesis," which deliberately looks not for distinctions but for similarities, which aims not at the isolation of the cognizing self but at its organic union with other selves and with the cosmic ground of all being. In the years ahead, every effort must be made to encourage synthetic thinking. Habits of mind must be cultivated which transcend criticism, analysis, skepticism, and cynicism, to emphasize and widen areas of agreement, and to focus on the forces in life making for wholeness.

Another important feature of Oriental thought, of only limited value in science, but indispensable to sane living, is its use and appreciation of the mind as an instrument for serving human needs. The Western ideal has always tended to be the pursuit of truth for its own sake, and pure research does turn up knowledge which would never be discovered any other way. But the thinker in an ivory tower is a luxury, and we twentieth-century mortals are living in an emergency of cosmic proportions, which demands that as many thinkers as possible get down out of their ivory towers and enlist their wits in the direct and immediate service of floundering humanity. And in searching for criteria by which to judge systems of value and thought, as part of the process of welding together the great traditions of the past and developing a new world-view, we must adopt another feature of Mannheim's relationism: in addition to the criterion of comprehensiveness already mentioned, the criterion of "efficiency." A theory is wrong, says Mannheim, by the criterion of efficiency, "if, in a given practical situation, it uses concepts and categories which, if taken seriously, would prevent man from adjusting himself at that historical stage." [20] No matter how cogent in an abstract way, a value, for example, which would result in the annihilation of the person or people holding it, is not worth holding. The pacifism of the Quakers and the Jains has rare beauty, but since its adoption in many historical situations would simply lead to the extermination of the pacifists, it becames often a life-denying, even life-destroying ethic. To the criticism that the law of non-violence is an absolute commandment, or any other law for that matter, one must firmly reply that absolutes, such as laws of nature or God, when they reach the stage of translation into human language, elude final statement, and so cannot be finally known. We do not even *know* that they exist at all.

But pure pragmatism cannot be a philosophy of synthesis, since the criterion of efficiency leads to an endless relativism if we do not have higher tentative criteria by which to answer the question, "efficient for what?" It underscores the urgency of the world crisis and the need for concerted action to solve practical problems, but it leaves open the question of ulterior objectives. Hence, there must be one last ground rule for synthesis. We need working criteria, working value premises, by which to initiate the whole enterprise of synthesis and judge its progress. Note the adjective "working." By no means can any criteria whatever be regarded as finally True, or outside the enterprise. On the other hand, there can be no enterprise at all without premises. This is part of the human predicament. No matter how deeply we probe, we always discover our own finite minds at the bottom of things. We must lift ourselves by our own bootstraps.

But if we can agree at least on the desirability of world peace, and if the only reasonably sure guarantee of world peace in the long run is an integrated world civilization, coherent and harmonious because its thinking men freely associate to create a world mind, some few working criteria seem fairly obvious. In the absence of any possible final knowledge, we must prefer those approaches to reality, those systems of thought and value, which assume that the cosmos, and man in it, are not merely absurd, chaotic, purposeless, and meaningless, but organized to some transcendent end — bearing in mind, of course, that the very words "transcendent" and "end" are only symbolic representations of a necessarily ineffable utter Truth. We must get in the habit, G. A. Borgese suggests, of moving forward purposefully without knowing our final purpose: to borrow Kant's definition of beauty, we must adopt the formula *Zweckmässigkeit ohne Zweck,* purposefulness without a purpose, which is to say a knowable purpose.[21] Whether the job can be done without the crutches of authoritative dogma, remains to be proved.

Then, once we have assumed the coherence of the cosmos and the meaningfulness of man, the test which every idea and value must ultimately meet is profoundly simple: does it contribute to the integration of the world community, or does it encourage division, fratricide, or genocide? Is it on the side of peace and brotherhood, or on the side of conflict and isolation? Does it promote integral harmony between men and Man, or does it annihilate both by degrading persons into things and by accelerating the collapse of civilization? Is it for life or death? For without life, there can be no goals at all. The heartbeat of mankind, stopped for one minute by one stupendous act of folly, would be stopped forever.

This overwhelming need for an affirmation of life, of existence, of being, of transcendence, of the coherence of ultimate reality in spite of the inaccessibility of utter Truth pervades more of modern thought than we might think. Spurned by so many formal schools and newly minted traditions, it still breaks through, if not in the thinker, then in the man who fathers the thinker. Even most of what passes for existentialism somehow gets back to these indispensable beginnings. As one French critic says of Jaspers' work, he "deprecates every 'philosophic system,' every universally valid 'doctrine,' every teaching that can be objectively transmitted. And after having made these statements, he writes three volumes of philosophy." [22] Three volumes, it should be added, in which all the traditional concepts of philosophy are assembled in a shimmering structure of thought that differs from Spinoza or Hegel only in being more loosely integrated and in having no real determinate content. The difference between assuming provisionally an underlying coherence in things and stating in specific language exactly what it is and does, is enormous: but not so great that the same human need is not served.

So we must leap to certain assumptions, in order even to

begin to agree. Some will not make the leap, and others may leap too far, but an "integration" of literally everything would explode in about five seconds.

Beyond these general rules, which call to mind areas of agreement among recent prophets of world order identified in earlier chapters, we cannot go. There is no single master plan by which minds can be induced to meet, or systems harmonized. The "truth" is not always somewhere in the "middle," diplomatic compromises sometimes only emasculate the ideas they throw together, and language in any event is woefully imprecise. What really counts, and what will determine the outcome in the long run, is the intensity of our will to agree. If it is strong enough, the will cannot fail to find a way. The integrators will be integrated by a tidal wave of world-historical desire.

Let us not be afraid to aim high. Prophecies of world order may seem like exercises in sheer fantasy to the "realistic" man, but it is the so-called realists who are the lunatics of the twentieth century. The interminable analyses of the immediate future in terms of the immediate past served up by our fashionable newspaper pundits and professors of international relations, and the "crackpot realism," as C. Wright Mills calls it, of our warmongering politicians, do verge at times on perfect insanity. Stuck to the flypaper of the present, enthralled by the Thing-That-Is, these realists miss what is most vital in human affairs: the role of the free-ranging will. "To believe in power that exists," says Erich Fromm, "is identical with disbelief in the growth of potentialities which are as yet unrealized. It is a prediction of the future based solely on the manifest present; but it turns out to be a grave miscalculation, profoundly irrational in its oversight of human potentialities and human growth. . . . While to many power seems to be the most real of all things, the history of man has proved it to be the most unstable of all human achievements." [23]

No one should imagine that present structures of power will fall like the walls of Jericho at a mere trumpet blast from mobilized world opinion. No one should imagine that a series of dynamic books and prophecies will build the new world civilization. Architects without funds or workmen cannot build anything at all. But to sit back and face the smash-up of civilization whether with equanimity or fear, as the case may be, letting the sovereign nations drift in their diabolical pride into another and final world war, should be unthinkable to every man of good will on earth. Time runs out. The meeting of minds and the closing of ranks, so long postponed, can be delayed no longer. Knowledge, faith, hope, and charity must join forces in a concerted assault on the problem of man's disunity and man's fate. If the utmost we can do now is lay broad foundations, or bring a few peoples closer together, or forge a fruitful union between a few rival disciplines or creeds or schools of thought, so be it. Anything that can thaw the frozen wills of men in this age of total peril must be worth trying. And once the first major breakthrough occurs, it may set in motion an endless stream of others, gathering in momentum until the world finds itself well started on the way to integration.

Epilogue
The Deep End

The Deep End

UNLIKE books, which must be rounded off somehow, and brought to a full stop, the future is by definition without limits. The prophetic visions of world order studied here already belong to the past, and most of the prophets have reached late autumn in their productive lives. Whether there be prophecies, they shall fail; for we know in part, and we prophesy in part.

But for all his finitude, man by nature is a prophesying animal. "Farther than any other creature, man lives in the future; the effectiveness of his living depends on the sagacity of his forecast. He cannot evade the function of prophecy." [1] Least of all can he evade the future itself, to which there are simply no knowable limits whatever. The human race may go on, if it wills well enough, for thousands of millions of years. In all this fullness of time, with a cosmos to explore gigantic beyond belief, much more is in store than another round of Cold War crises or the synthesis of the species in a world civilization. A few alternatives and further possibilities spring to mind, at the deep end of time.

One possibility can be ruled out with absolute firmness. The world situation which has developed since Potsdam and Hiroshima, and has settled for the moment into a thoroughly familiar pattern, will not last forever. It is typical of writers without much sense of history to imagine that the future con-

sists mainly of further massive doses of the present. While so
nimble a mind as H. G. Wells was predicting total world wars
and crying in the wilderness for a world government, the rank
and file of informed observers just before 1914 thought in
terms of the steady progress of liberal-democratic white European civilization. In the future they saw more settlements of
disputes by conferences of ambassadors, more "wholesome"
competition among rival powers for markets and overseas col-
onies, more guns, more dreadnaughts, and more peace. When
the first World War broke out, it was universally expected to
be a short war, just as all wars in Europe had been for the past
fifty years. Hardly anyone anticipated any of the major social,
political, and spiritual consequences of the war. Stalinism,
fascism, and Nazism arrived unforeseen in the twenties. In
the thirties, relying on the "lessons of history," the statesmen
and intelligentsia of the democratic powers put their faith in
pacifism, appeasement, and isolationism, in a pathetic effort
to turn the clock back to just before 1914 without making the
particular sort of mistakes obviously made then. During the
Second World War, most Western observers predicted a postwar situation that would reflect the tolerable harmony of the
Soviet-Western wartime alliance. Today we scan the horizon
for "another" Korea, "another" Hungary, "another" Cuba:
above all, "another" world war on the precise model of Hitler's war.

What makes prognostication at this level useless is the
pace of change in the modern world. Sir Julian Huxley suggests that the rate of human evolution has been constantly
accelerating ever since the first men, from something like
one major cultural change per 10^6 years in Lower Paleolithic
times to one per 10^2 years through most of recorded history
to one or more per decade in the present era.[2] The villain in
the piece is what Mario Rossi calls the cumulative and geometrical character of technical progress. Since in technics
"the possible number of combinations between elements in-

creases in a geometrical ratio by each new element added," each new development "is bound to increase in a higher ratio the number of possible combinations and the possibility of further changes." In view of the rather slow rate of psychosocial adaptation to technical change, Rossi is inclined to guess that civilizations fall "because they cannot cope with their too plentiful opportunities."[3] Toynbee wonders if "there may not be a limit to the amount of cultural change to which human nature can adapt itself within a single lifetime, and whether we may not be approaching this limit or perhaps exceeding it."[4]

The pace of technical progress may also reach a certain ceiling, in time, but meanwhile, it goes on advancing toward the sociological equivalent of the speed of light. Even many of our prophets of world integration miss some of its significance. Jaspers, for example, dreams of world order and world understanding, but he cannot visualize a world without all its present elements — nations, creeds, cultures, philosophical traditions, and so forth — persisting in their "historical concreteness." This kind of thinking one should label "historiolatry," and like many idolatries, it profanes the god it worships. There is continuity in history, and anyone expecting a total wiping clean of the slate and a literally fresh beginning for humanity is merely stupid. But history also *moves on*. To insist that everything continue as before, while engaged in "unlimited communication" with everything else, betrays a fundamental ignorance of the historical process. Nothing human is forever. The forces which create nations, creeds, cultures, and philosophical traditions and later dissolve them, are just as much part of history as the forces making for continuity. To worship the historical "is" amounts to a defiance of history in its other role as Siva, the power of destruction and regeneration. Ortega y Gasset once characterized modern European nationalism as a force exactly opposite to the force which creates nations —

and the same could be said of historiolatry. It is an attempt to stop history. But nothing could be more futile, above all in an era of headlong progress in science and technics.

Hence, a world civilization is no less improbable than the separate regional civilizations of the past. It is also entirely possible that by wars, long or short, total or piecemeal, planned or unplanned, mankind may succeed in destroying civilization. It might happen the day after this book is published, or fifty years from then, or even after the establishment of a world state. Unless radically new methods of control are devised, the possibility of a world cataclysm will eventually reach the point of absolute certainty, no matter how long the odds at this writing. And if man destroys his machines in war and has to begin the technological revolution from scratch again, there will be no technological revolution at all, since the raw materials essential to industrialization which can be extracted from the earth with primitive technology — outcroppings of coal, shallow pools of oil, crystalline copper, high-grade ores — have long since been exhausted, and cannot be replaced by natural processes for millions of years, if ever. The most the survivors could hope to build would be a stagnant agrarian civilization at the same technical level as traditional China, India, or premodern Europe.[5]

The chance of war is not confined to an encounter between the Soviet Union and the United States. As Alfred Weber predicted in the closing months of World War II, the postwar political world has so far consisted, and will go on consisting for some time, of "world-syndicates, made up of a few paramount Great Powers and in one form or another comprising or annexing the lesser ones," who hold the fate of humanity in their hands.[6] But the East-West polarization of power which still prevails in spite of the Bandung and Belgrade Conferences is not scheduled to last long. As each underdeveloped country begins to industrialize and as many smaller nations join the "Nuclear Club," or build other total weapons, the complexion of international politics will change perhaps beyond recognition. We are approaching, says Walt Rostow, "an age of diffused power," in which, he thinks, "the image of Eurasian hegemony" — the hegemony of the communist bloc — "will lose its reality, and world domination will become an increasingly unrealistic objective." [7] Unrealistic or not, many powers, both large and small, may continue to find it attractive, and the communist bloc itself may by then have grown still more formidable than it is today. But what looms as the most dangerous prospect is an Armageddon by accident: the result of nuclear attack by a small, unstable nation against a larger neighbor, or the miscalculation of a great power intent on waging a limited local war that gets out of hand, or a simple mistake by officers in the field, or a desperate struggle for power within a totalitarian state in the death throes of civil war. The possibilities are endless, and Armageddon has to happen only once.

Nor can any limits be set to the ingenuity and versatility of weapons technology. If new developments occur at only the same pace maintained since 1914, it is entirely probable that fission and fusion bombs will be obsolete, or at least vastly "improved" and supplemented by entirely new weapons with other capabilities, by the year 2000. No one can predict, for example, what may develop out of radiological research. A device which could cover a whole country instantaneously with a blanket of radiation inducing sleep, insanity, paralysis, or death, might tempt the possessor to use it at almost any risk. Some scientists are already toying with the notion of an "asteroid bomb," an asteroid hurled out of orbit by hydrogen missiles and sent streaking toward earth, where it could demolish a whole continent on impact. Meanwhile, the likelihood of building really effective systems of defense against just the total weapons already in existence seems to dwindle every year.

All this underscores the terrible urgency of a concerted movement toward world integration at every level and by every possible means. But what if there is not time enough? This is a reasonable question, in a world gone mad. Perhaps the idea Wells tried with no success to get across to mankind as early as 1928 should be given another hearing: the idea of an "Open Conspiracy." * In the absence of positive initiatives from established interests and ruling circles, the times may be ripe for a world revolutionary movement, a deliberate conspiracy of men of means, brains, and courage to work for the subversion and if necessary the forcible overthrow of the present world power structure, in the cause of a new organic world order. But such a movement would also probably increase, rather than decrease, the chance of war, by weakening governments and driving them to take desperate measures for their own protection. Healthy, happy dragons are no doubt less dangerous at close quarters than starving, wounded dragons. On the other hand, it is possible to imagine a somewhat less than open conspiracy, in fact a subterranean movement, enrolling enlightened people of every description, not excluding certain statesmen and military leaders, with the means to devise a worldwide system of emergency measures for the imposition of a true world order among the survivors in the event of a third world war. Although it has been predicted with monotonous regularity for many years, a total war striking at the present time would find mankind entirely unprepared: not to wage it, but to spare the survivors from chaos and further bloodshed. There is no more opportune moment for radical political change than in the aftermath of a world catastrophe. It could well be mankind's literally last chance.

If this proposal is worth serious thought, we emerge with two courses of action each leading to an integrated world

* See pp. 60–61.

civilization, a "daylight" plan for world cultural, economic, and political integration by peaceful means, the plan of the prophets of world order; and a "nightside" plan for an underground world movement that expects Armageddon and works out measures by which at least its members will be able to survive to form the nucleus of a world government when and if the powers destroy one another. Such a movement might include people from the current great powers, but it would have its headquarters and most of its membership in the least ambitious and most geographically isolated countries of the world.

Here, then, is one possibility, in the "deep end": the annihilation of all or most of mankind. Another set of prospects closely linked to this fundamental issue of survival falls under the heading of human ecology. Not all the dangers facing mankind in the infinite future are political and military. We are still, among other things, animals living in a physical environment and dependent on that environment for our livelihood. The earth is not a cornucopia or a garden of Eden. Its resources must be husbanded and used with due care for the needs of posterity.

Already an ecological crisis of colossal proportions is developing out of man's fertility. The current slogan is "population explosion." Declining death rates have recently made possible a net annual world increase in population of $1\frac{1}{2}$ percent and by the end of the present century, demographic experts foresee a world population of five billion, twice the present total. It will take at least a century to reach a stable level even if safe, cheap, oral contraceptives are available and in world use within the next decade. The new billions will put an all but intolerable strain on the world's food supply, on the economies of the underdeveloped countries struggling to get off the Malthusian treadmills of poverty, and, consequently, on world peace.

But the ecological problem goes much deeper. Man has

very nearly run through the planet's reserves of arable soil, and allowed erosion to destroy much that was once fertile. To cite Harrison Brown, whose *Challenge of Man's Future* is a mine of information on these matters, if we manage to lose no more of the land we have under cultivation now, which is improbable, and if we convert to arable soil every square foot of waste land that can be made arable, no matter what the cost, then the maximum total amount available for cultivation will come to about four billion acres, 50 percent more than we have at present. This will not feed even the increases in population predicted for the next half century. The only hope, as Brown sees it, lies in the development of new types of food, especially the intensive domestication of marine algae and yeast plants, both good sources of food energy, which can be harvested in huge quantities at relatively low cost and processed into palatable synthetics. But much planning and heavy outlays of capital will be necessary to meet the demands of the ever-nearer future. At a somewhat later date, he predicts a serious energy shortage, as fossil fuel reserves are exhausted, which will have to be solved by further exploitation of hydroelectric, atomic, and solar power. Raw materials, especially the rarer metals, will increasingly have to be extracted from seawater and ordinary rock, where nearly all elements exist in at least infinitesimal quantities.

But the crucial immediate questions are food and population and the ecological balance between them. Aldous Huxley calls soil erosion and overpopulation a two-pronged "Martian invasion of the planet" and urges a world program of conservation and research to develop new sources of food energy and better techniques of birth control.[8] It goes without saying that a world government could solve all the ecological problems now confronting mankind, even with existing technology, in a matter of decades, and keep solving these problems *ad infinitum.* But the prospect of a sane solution without panic or war in a world of irascible nation-states each out to grab what it needs for its health, wealth, and glory, is not bright. As a grotesque recent example of how wisdom from the national point of view becomes lunacy from mankind's, the Kennedy administration wants to take fifty million acres of fertile American soil *out of cultivation* in the next twenty years to solve the problem of our chronic national food "surplus"!

Suppose, on the other hand, that a world civilization is actually created, with a world government, and the danger of military annihilation or ecological disaster is reduced to the barest minimum. Man reaches the next stage of history, and all is well. Might not the world civilization then turn, willy-nilly, into a kind of planetary anthill, a static, changeless, soulless factory? A good many modern writers, like Aldous Huxley himself, have feared so; and, as we saw earlier, the fear of unfreedom and stagnation forces some of the prophets of world order to reject the whole idea of a world government or state. Aurobindo Ghose predicted that in a world state there would be, at first, great comfort, peace, and intellectual activity. "But after a time, there would be a dying down of force, a static condition of the human mind and human life, then stagnation, decay, disintegration. The soul of man would begin to wither in the midst of his acquisitions." [9] William R. McNeill, in *Past and Future,* examines the possibility that a world civilization, with its inevitably conservative world bureaucracy, its lack of war, and its social controls, might ossify and remain ossified for all eternity. Even technical change, so major a factor in social change heretofore, might be stifled, if the world bureaucracy prohibits the exploitation of new discoveries by industry.[10] Roderick Seidenberg has devoted a whole book to this problem of stagnation in the coming world order: he foresees a frozen world of unconscious robots, organized to their fingertips, incapable of creative thought, no more human than insects. Little by little man seems to be purging himself of his humanity, and at long last he will vanish "from the scene — lost in the icy fixity of his final state in a post-historic age." [11] In much the same mood, Jaspers wonders if human freedom has been only "a real but passing moment between two immeasurably long periods of sleep, of which the first period was that of the life of nature, and the second period was that of the life of technique." [12]

All these fears have some foundation. If history defined as endless change is ever to stop, it seems altogether likely that only a world government with absolute control over everything would have the power to stop it. The world bureaucracy might become a glorified world mandarinate. One can also imagine humanity dying of sheer boredom, social *Wärmetod,* or cultural overweight: science-fiction writers of late find this theme especially fascinating. After "everything" had been said, done, and enjoyed by thousands of generations in the affluent super-society of tomorrow, those daring and fearless spirits who keep civilization from stultifying might even in their agony decide to carry the human race with them to a glorious death by world-suicide.

But none of this need be. If the world civilization has one-tenth as much respect for human personality as its prophets have today, there will always be frontiers sending fresh ideas and problems back to the settled heartlands of life. The full powers of the mind, for example, remain largely untapped, even uncharted. The researches of J. B. Rhine and other parapsychologists strongly suggest the possibility that man may have extrasensory powers he has still not learned to use. The telepathic intercommunication of the species, the use of telekinesis and clairvoyance to solve everyday problems, and the discovery of new levels of consciousness all no longer seem fantastic; and there is much to be learned from the psychic techniques of the East.

Man also needs a geographical frontier, to absorb his physical energies and turn his aggressive impulses against a common antagonist, somewhat as Europe dispatched her merchants and *conquistadores* over all the oceans of the world during the Renaissance. Perhaps this is only a characteristic of Western civilization, but since the West will contribute its technics and its way of life to the coming world civilization, there will also be Promethean Western personalities in the new universal society, and their thirst for adventure must be slaked.

Of physical frontiers we face no shortage: all outer space is within our reach, and the reach of our posterity. If current astrophysical theory proves accurate, the universe contains billions of galaxies, each with billions of stars, each normally with a brood of planets, millions of which throughout each galaxy must be inhabitable by man, and have been, will be, or are even now inhabited by intelligent life. Some twenty stars alone have been counted within the cosmically slight distance of twelve light-years from earth. With manned interplanetary flight entirely possible by 1970, thanks to the two great competing national space programs of the Cold War, interstellar exploration is perhaps no more than a century away. The discovery of just one other inhabited planet — although highly unlikely in this solar system — could have just as profound an impact on mankind, and produce as much technical and social change, as the Industrial Revolution and the meeting of East and West combined. When we remember that the universe almost certainly shelters millions of planets inhabited by intelligent life, perhaps totally different from, or in advance of, Homo sapiens, the danger of stagnation in the world society seems to shrink almost out of sight. Even the "galactic federation" of intelligent life-forms so often encountered in modern science-fiction, which watches Sol and Terra from a safe distance and waits for the psychologically right moment to bring us into its fold, is no more fantastic than a future Brave New World of interminable slavery. We are only just beginning to wake up to the human significance of the revolutions of the past few decades in astronomy.

The impact of the frontier in space on future man, barring unforeseeable technical obstacles or the repressive policies of a conservative world bureaucracy, is certain, in any case, to be immense. New families may not ride in jet-propelled Conestoga wagons to stake claims on distant planets, but civilization will invest a large percentage of its wealth and its trained manpower in the conquest of space. Even if contact is never made with intelligent life outside our solar system, the stimulus generated by the effort to find it will have a dynamizing effect on the morale of the world civilization. The British astronomer and novelist Arthur C. Clarke recalls J. D. Unwin's argument that every burst of expansive energy in history is followed by a display of productive energy, and reaches the sound conclusion that the frontier in outer space, as a burst of expansive energy, will bring in its train a new Renaissance. But if man chooses not to explore the space frontier, Clarke fears that "the human mind, compelled to circle for ever in its planetary goldfish-bowl, must eventually stagnate." [13]

Or, as Alfred North Whitehead once wrote, "Adventure or Decadence are the only choices offered to mankind. The pure conservative is fighting against the essence of the universe." [14] So, for that matter, is the pure liberal, who would build only on foundations of open air and boundless freedom. The new world order, and the cosmic order after that, will trace their descent back by an unbroken chain of minds to the earliest civilizations of man, and ultimately to the One God in whom we all have our being. Nothing human is from nothing; and nothing human is forever. But our emphasis must properly fall on the future, in a prophetic book. Into this future we send our sons, and from it, in man's relentless flight through time, they will never return.

Notes

Notes

Introduction: The Search for Synthesis

1. Carl Gustav Jung, *Modern Man in Search of a Soul,* tr. W. S. Dell and Cary F. Baynes (New York, 1933), 251; Erich Kahler, *Man the Measure* (New York, 1956), 603; Paul Tillich, *The Courage to Be* (New Haven, 1952), 57-63.
2. José Ferrater Mora, *Man at the Crossroads* (Boston, 1957), 110; William Barrett, *Irrational Man* (Garden City, 1958), 28.
3. Karl Jaspers, *The Origin and Goal of History,* tr. Michael Bullock (New Haven, 1955), 209; Jaspers, *The Future of Mankind,* tr. E. B. Ashton (Chicago, 1961), 3.
4. Albert Camus, *The Myth of Sisyphus,* tr. Justin O'Brien (New York, 1955), 123.

Chapter One: The Biography of a Vision

1. Utopia and Cosmopolis
    1. Quoted in John B. Noss, *Man's Religions* (New York, 1949), 321.
    2. Harry Elmer Barnes and Howard Becker, *Social Thought from Lore to Science* (Boston, 1938), I, 17-18.
    3. Lewis Mumford, *In the Name of Sanity* (New York, 1954), 32.
2. Eastern Approaches

4. Fung Yu-lan, *A History of Chinese Philosophy*, tr. Derk Bodde (Princeton, 1952-53), I, 103.
5. Fung, *op. cit.*, II, 46-47.
6. Heinrich Zimmer, *Philosophies of India*, ed. Joseph Campbell (New York, 1951), 128.

3. The Classical Heritage

7. W. W. Tarn, *Alexander the Great* (Cambridge, 1948), II, 399-449. See also T. A. Sinclair, *A History of Greek Political Thought* (London, 1952), 240-42.
8. G. H. Sabine, *A History of Political Theory*, rev. ed. (New York, 1950), 141.

4. *Respublica Christiana and Dar al-Islam*

9. Maurice de Wulf, *Philosophy and Civilization in the Middle Ages* (New York, 1953), 100.
10. Quoted in John T. McNeill, *Christian Hope for World Society* (Chicago, 1937), 8.
11. Ernst Troeltsch, *The Social Teaching of the Christian Churches*, tr. Olive Wyon (New York, 1931), I, 67-68.
12. Dante, *De Monarchia*, tr. F. J. Church, in R. W. Church, *Dante: An Essay* (London, 1879), 207.
13. *Ibid.*, 205.
14. Quoted in Ewart Lewis, *Medieval Political Ideas* (London, 1954), II, 446, 475-76.
15. Majid Khadduri, *War and Peace in the Law of Islam* (Baltimore, 1955), 17.

5. Modern Prophets, 1600–1900

16. Alfred von Martin, *Sociology of the Renaissance*, tr. W. L. Luetkens (London, 1944), 18.
17. Eduard Beneš in Joseph Needham, ed., *The Teacher of Nations* (Cambridge, 1942), 4.
18. Quoted by Beneš in Needham, *op. cit.*, 6; Matthew Spinka, *John Amos Comenius* (Chicago, 1943), 83, 108.
19. W. T. Jones, *A History of Western Philosophy* (New York, 1952), 706.
20. Paul Hazard, *The European Mind*, tr. J. Lewis May (New Haven, 1953), 220.
21. Quoted in Harry Elmer Barnes and Howard Becker,

Social Thought from Lore to Science, II, 1110-11.

22. K'ang Yu-wei, *Ta T'ung Shu*, tr. and ed. Laurence G. Thompson (London, 1958), 89.

6. Crisis and Renewal: The Twentieth Century

23. Barrett, *Irrational Man*, 20-21, 30-31.

24. Gerhard Szczesny, *The Future of Unbelief*, tr. Edward B. Garside (New York, 1961), 12.

25. Bertrand Russell, *Human Knowledge: Its Scope and Limits* (New York, 1948), 507.

26. Camus, *The Myth of Sispyhus*, 19.

27. Tillich, *The Courage to Be*, 139.

28. See W. Warren Wagar, *H. G. Wells and the World State* (New Haven, 1961).

29. *The Outline of History* (1920); *The Science of Life* (1931, with Julian Huxley and G. P. Wells); *The Work, Wealth and Happiness of Mankind* (1932).

30. Arnold J. Toynbee, *A Study of History* (London, 1934-61), I, 4-5.

Chapter Two: History as Prophecy

1. The Vogue of Clio

1. Toynbee, *A Study of History*, XII, 279.

2. Will Durant, *Caesar and Christ* (New York, 1944), vii.

3. Mario M. Rossi, *A Plea for Man* (Edinburgh, 1956), 11.

2. The Biological Key

4. See Pierre Teilhard de Chardin, *The Phenomenon of Man*, tr. Bernard Wall (New York, 1959); Pierre Lecomte du Noüy, *Human Destiny* (New York, 1947); Julian Huxley, *Religion Without Revelation*, rev. ed. (New York, 1957), and *A Touchstone for Ethics* (New York, 1947); C. H. Waddington, *Science and Ethics* (London, 1942), and *The Ethical Animal* (New York, 1961); Edmund Ware Sinnott, *Cell and Psyche* (Chapel Hill, N.C., 1950), and *The Biology of the Spirit* (New York, 1955); and George Gaylord Simpson, *The Meaning of Evolution* (New Haven, 1949).

5. Julian Huxley, *Religion Without Revelation*, 85.
6. *Ibid.*, 216; Huxley, *New Bottles for New Wine* (New York, 1957), 13.
7. *Religion Without Revelation*, 218; *A Touchstone for Ethics*, 139-40.
8. Huxley, *On Living in a Revolution* (London, 1944), 16; *A Touchstone for Ethics*, 254.
9. *Religion Without Revelation*, viii.
10. Teilhard de Chardin, *The Phenomenon of Man*, 183.
11. *Ibid.*, 173.
12. *Ibid.*, 240-41, 252-53.
13. *Ibid.*, 288-89.
14. Teilhard de Chardin, *Building the Earth*, tr. Noël Lindsay (Paris, 1958), 24-28.
15. *Ibid.*, 13, 16, 30.
16. George P. Conger, *Epitomization* (Minneapolis, 1949), 263.
17. Hugh Miller, *The Community of Man* (New York, 1949), 131, 133, 140.

3. Cycles and Millennia
18. Toynbee, *A Study of History*, XII, 27.
19. *Ibid.*, XII, 83.
20. *Ibid.*, XII, 266.
21. *Ibid.*, XII, 523.
22. *Ibid.*, XII, 5.
23. Toynbee, *Civilization on Trial* (New York, 1948), 115.
24. Toynbee, *A Study of History*, XII, 528.
25. *Ibid.*, IX, 467.
26. *Ibid.*, XII, 302, 310.
27. *Ibid.*, XII, 143.
28. See *Civilization on Trial*, ch. 13.
29. *A Study of History*, XII, 562. See also *Ibid.*, I, 192-94 and III, 2-3.
30. Philip Bagby, *Culture and History* (London, 1958), 181.
31. Pitirim A. Sorokin and Walter A. Lunden, *Power and Morality* (Boston, 1959), 107.
32. *Ibid.*, 121, 172.

33. Sorokin, *Social and Cultural Dynamics*, rev. ed. (Boston, 1957), 28-29, 683-92. See also Sorokin, *The Reconstruction of Humanity* (Boston, 1948), 107.

34. See especially Sorokin, ed., *Explorations in Altruistic Love and Behavior* (Boston, 1950), and *Forms and Techniques of Altruistic and Spiritual Growth* (Boston, 1954); Sorokin, *The Ways and Powers of Love* (Boston, 1954).

35. Sorokin and Lunden, *Power and Morality*, 185-86.

36. Sorokin, *Social and Cultural Dynamics*, foreword to the 1957 edition, n.p.

4. Lines and Spirals

37. William Ernest Hocking, *The Coming World Civilization* (New York, 1956), 172, 49-50.

38. *Ibid.*, 51.

39. *Ibid.*, 184.

40. Karl Jaspers in Paul Arthur Schilpp, ed., *The Philosophy of Karl Jaspers* (New York, 1957), 65.

41. Jaspers, *The Origin and Goal of History*, xiv-xv.

42. *Ibid.*, 25.

43. *Ibid.*, 25, 27, 127.

44. Jaspers, *The Future of Mankind*, 3-4.

45. *Ibid.*, 23; *The Origin and Goal of History*, 205.

46. Tr. Ralph Manheim (New York, 1962); the first German edition was published in 1957.

47. Lewis Mumford, *The Transformations of Man* (New York, 1956), 187, 181-82.

48. Mumford, *The Condition of Man* (New York, 1944), 13.

49. Mumford, *The Conduct of Life* (New York, 1951), 219-20.

50. Mumford, *The Transformations of Man*, 184.

51. *Ibid.*, 201.

52. *The Conduct of Life*, 221.

53. *The Transformations of Man*, 217.

54. See Erich Kahler, *Man the Measure* (New York, 1943), and *The Tower and the Abyss* (New York, 1957); Oliver L. Reiser, *The Promise of Scientific Humanism* (New York, 1940).

5. The Doctrinaires

55. Khalifa Abdul Hakim in Ruth Nanda Anshen, ed., *Moral Principles of Action* (New York, 1952), 597. See also W. Montgomery Watt. *Islam and the Integration of Society* (Evanston, Ill., 1961), 273-77, 282-85.

56. John J. Mulloy in Christopher Dawson, *The Dynamics of World History*, ed. Mulloy (New York, 1956), 457.

57. Dawson, *The Historic Reality of Christian Culture* (New York, 1960), 83, 104.

58. Dawson, *The Dynamics of World History*, 412.

59. Father Martin D'Arcy in A. William Loos, ed., *Religious Faith and World Culture* (New York, 1951), 263.

60. Dawson, *The Historic Reality of Christian Culture*, 117.

61. Dawson, *The Dynamics of World History*, 250, 286.

62. Jacques Maritain, *An Introduction to Philosophy*, tr. E. I. Watkin (London, 1930), vi, 31.

63. Maritain in Joseph W. Evans and Leo R. Ward, ed. and tr., *The Social and Political Philosophy of Jacques Maritain: Selected Readings* (New York, 1955), 241-42.

64. Shoghi Effendi, *The World Order of Bahá'u'lláh* (New York, 1938), 196, 204. For a comprehensive introduction to the Bahai faith, see John Ferraby, *All Things Made New* (London, 1957).

65. Toynbee, *A Study of History*, XII, 541-42.

66. Elliot R. Goodman, *The Soviet Design for a World State* (New York, 1960), 12. For a quite different point of view, see Solomon F. Bloom, *The World of Nations* (New York, 1941).

67. Sabine, *A History of Political Theory*, 840-41. Cf. Walt W. Rostow, *The Stages of Economic Growth* (Cambridge, 1960), 161.

68. Quoted in Goodman, *op. cit.*, 34-35.

69. Marshall Shulman, "The Real Nature of the Soviet Challenge," *The New York Times Magazine*, July 16, 1961, 42.

Chapter Three: The Concert of Cultures

  1. The Organic Society
    1. Mumford, *The Conduct of Life*, 223-24.

2. Sorokin and Lunden, *Power and Morality*, 134-35.
3. Toynbee, *A Study of History*, VIII, 7, 495, 498.
4. F. S. C. Northrop, *The Logic of the Sciences and the Humanities* (New York, 1948), 4.
5. Teilhard de Chardin, *The Phenomenon of Man*, 248, 259.
6. Reiser, *The World Sensorium* (New York, 1946), 15, 48.

2. World Philosophical Synthesis

7. Toynbee, *A Study of History*, VIII, 7.
8. Charles A. Moore in Horst Frenz, ed., *Asia and the Humanities* (Bloomington, Ind., 1958), 79.
9. B. A. G. Fuller, *A History of Philosophy*, rev. ed. (New York, 1945), I, 1.
10. Northrop, *The Logic of the Sciences and the Humanities*, 293.
11. Northrop in Charles A. Moore, ed., *Philosophy—East and West* (Princeton, 1944), 234.
12. Huxley, *A Touchstone for Ethics*, 140. Sir Julian's phrase is borrowed from Lawrence K. Frank, *Society as the Patient* (New Brunswick, 1948), 392-93.
13. Aurobindo Ghose, *The Ideal of Human Unity* (New York, 1950), 23.
14. Arthur F. Wright, "Professor Northrop's Chapter on the Traditional Culture of the Orient," *Journal of the History of Ideas*, X (1949), 143-49.
15. See the papers in Charles A. Moore, ed., *Philosophy—East and West* and *Essays in East-West Philosophy* (Honolulu, 1950).
16. Erich Fromm, *The Art of Loving* (New York, 1956), 72-80; Fromm, *Man for Himself* (New York, 1947), 239.
17. Denis de Rougemont, *Man's Western Quest*, tr. Montgomery Belgion (New York, 1957), chs. 1-2.
18. Lancelot Law Whyte, *The Next Development in Man* (New York, 1950), 244.
19. "The Mind of Asia," *Life*, December 31, 1951, 38-42.
20. Sorokin, *Social Philosophies of an Age of Crisis* (Boston, 1950), 145-58, 244-59, 275-322 *passim*.

21. Northrop, *The Meeting of East and West* (New York, 1946). Making Hindus less fanatic and Muslims more scientific is, of course, another problem altogether!

22. Sir Sarvepalli Radhakrishnan in Paul Arthur Schilpp, ed., *The Philosophy of Sarvepalli Radhakrishnan* (New York, 1952), 823, 828. But see Northrop's "Methodology and Epistemology, Oriental and Occidental," in Charles A. Moore, ed., *Essays in East-West Philosophy*, 151-60.

23. Radhakrishnan, *East and West* (New York, 1956), 121, 131; *The Philosophy of Sarvepalli Radhakrishnan*, 73. Northrop objects that Radhakrishnan is actually guilty of provincialism here, since toleration is one of the cardinal virtues in Hindu thought, and Radhakrishnan, therefore, is asking all other peoples to behave like Hindus. Northrop urges union through tough-minded reconception, rather than through sympathy and tolerance alone. Northrop, in *The Philosophy of Sarvepalli Radhakrishnan*, 647.

24. Jaspers, *The Philosophy of Karl Jaspers,* 83-84.

25. Rougemont, *op. cit.*, 187-88, 196-97.

26. Toynbee, *A Study of History,* XII, 309, 529.

27. Robert L. Heilbroner, *The Future as History* (New York, 1960), 75-101.

28. Rostow, *The Stages of Economic Growth,* 133-34.

29. Mumford, *The Transformations of Man,* 214.

30. Hocking, *Strength of Men and Nations* (New York, 1959), 35.

31. Jaspers, *The Origin and Goal of History,* 180.

32. Toynbee, *A Study of History,* IX, 577-604.

33. Moore in *Asia and the Humanities,* 93-94.

34. H. R. Trevor-Roper, *Men and Events* (New York, 1957), 314.

3. Religion and the World Order

35. Barrett, *Irrational Man,* 20-21.

36. Tillich, *The Courage to Be,* 142.

37. Quoted in Hugh Ross Mackintosh, *Types of Modern Theology* (London, 1937), 212-13.

38. *Re-Thinking Missions: A Layman's Inquiry after One Hundred Years* (New York, 1932), 35, 40.
39. Hocking, *Living Religions and a World Faith* (New York, 1940), 21, 27, 57, 61.
40. *Ibid.*, 169, 145, 158.
41. *Ibid.*, 202.
42. Hocking, *The Coming World Civilization*, 148-49, 170.
43. Northrop, *The Taming of the Nations* (New York, 1952), 299-300.
44. Toynbee, *A Study of History*, XII, 219.
45. *Ibid.*, VII, 716-36.
46. *Ibid.*, VII, 374.
47. Toynbee, *Christianity among the Religions of the World* (New York, 1957), 104.
48. *Ibid.*, 103, 110.
49. Charles Morris, *Paths of Life: Preface to a World Religion* (New York, 1956), 153.
50. See also Morris, *Varieties of Human Value* (Chicago, 1956), and Morris' "The Comparative Strength of Life-Ideals in Eastern and Western Cultures," in Charles A. Moore, ed., *Essays in East-West Philosophy*, 353-70.
51. Gerald Heard, *The Human Venture* (New York, 1955).
52. Jaspers, *The Origin and Goal of History*, 227.
53. Radhakrishnan, *The Philosophy of Sarvepalli Radhakrishnan*, 81.
54. Northrop, *The Logic of the Sciences and the Humanities*, 364.
55. Szczesny, *The Future of Unbelief*, 105.
56. Fromm, *The Sane Society* (New York, 1955), 352. See also Fromm's contrast between "authoritarian" and "humanistic" religion in *Psychoanalysis and Religion* (New Haven, 1950).
57. See Hendrik Kraemer, *World Cultures and World Religions: The Coming Dialogue* (Philadelphia, 1960), 147-55.
58. Emil Brunner, *The Scandal of Christianity* (London, 1951), 30; Father Martin D'Arcy in A. William Loos, ed., *Religious Faith and World Culture*, 265.

59. Kraemer, *op. cit.*, chs. 11-12.
60. See especially Tillich's *The Courage to Be* and *Systematic Theology* (Chicago, 1951-58).
61. Franklin Le Van Baumer, *Religion and the Rise of Scepticism* (New York, 1960), ch. 5.
62. See, for example, Northrop, *The Complexity of Legal and Ethical Experience* (Boston, 1959); Huxley, *A Touchstone for Ethics;* Toynbee, *A Study of History*, IX, Part XI; Jaspers, "Nature and Ethics," in Ruth Nanda Anshen, ed., *Moral Principles of Action*, 48-61, a brief but brilliant summary of his moral philosophy; and Mumford, *The Conduct of Life.*

4. The Integration of Knowledge
63. Teilhard de Chardin, *Building the Earth,* 23; Huxley, *Religion Without Revelation,* 235.
64. Reiser, *The Integration of Human Knowledge* (Boston, 1958), 44.
65. Walter H. C. Laves and Charles A. Thomson, *UNESCO: Purpose, Progress, Prospects* (Bloomington, Ind., 1957), 123; *New York Times,* Jan. 22, 1961.
66. Lincoln Barnett, *The Universe and Dr. Einstein,* rev. ed. (New York, 1957), 6.
67. Huxley, *Religion Without Revelation,* 41-42; Mumford, *The Conduct of Life,* 23; Toynbee, *A Study of History,* VII, 504 and XII, 145; Szczesny, *The Future of Unbelief,* 23, 77.
68. Sorokin's formula harks back to nineteenth-century Russian epistemological theory: see N. O. Lossky, *History of Russian Philosophy* (New York, 1951), 404. For other parallel Western trends, see F. L. Baumer, *Religion and the Rise of Scepticism,* 246-48.
69. Mumford, *The Transformations of Man,* 228.
70. Kahler, *The Tower and the Abyss,* 261-63.
71. *Ibid.,* 261-67. Cf. Ortega y Gasset's proposal for a "Faculty of Culture" staffed by specialists with "the genius for integration" in *Mission of the University,* tr. Howard Lee Nostrand (Princeton, 1944), 86 ff.

72 Toynbee, *A Study of History*, XII, 107.

73. *Ibid.*, XII, 130.

74. Whyte, *The Unitary Principle in Physics and Biology* (New York, 1949), x, xv.

75. *Ibid.*, 43.

76. Whyte, *The Next Development in Man* and *Accent on Form* (New York, 1954).

77. Reiser, *The Promise of Scientific Humanism*, xii, 5, 230.

78. Reiser, *The Integration of Human Knowledge*, 34-35 and *passim*.

79. *Ibid.*, 63-64, 45-46, 57, 408-9.

5. The Arts in Cosmopolis

80. Mumford, *In the Name of Sanity*, 109, 140-41.

81. Sorokin, *Social and Cultural Dynamics*, 219-24 and *passim;* Northrop, *The Logic of the Sciences and the Humanities*, 169-90, and *The Meeting of East and West*, 486-91.

82. Ernest Mundt, *Art, Form, and Civilization* (Berkeley and Los Angeles, 1952); Hans Sedlmayr, *Art in Crisis*, tr. Brian Battershaw (London, 1957), 242, 253.

Chapter Four: The World Commonwealth

1. Culture, Community, Commonwealth

    1. Sorokin, *The Reconstruction of Humanity*, 18.

    2. Hocking, *The Coming World Civilization*, 153.

    3. Jaspers, *The Philosophy of Karl Jaspers*, 752.

    4. Reinhold Niebuhr, *The Self and the Dramas of History* (New York, 1955), 204, 216.

    5. G. A. Borgese, *Foundations of the World Republic* (Chicago, 1953), 25, 29-30.

    6. Crane Brinton, *From Many, One* (Cambridge, Mass., 1948); Frederick L., Schuman, *The Commonwealth of Man* (New York, 1952); Gerard J. Mangone, *The Idea and Practice of World Government* (New York, 1951); Werner Levi, *Fundamentals of World Organization* (Minneapolis, 1950); Quincy Wright, ed., *The World Community* (Chicago, 1948).

7. Karl W. Deutsch et al., *Political Community and the North Atlantic Area* (Princeton, 1957), 36.

8. *Ibid.,* 83-85, 91-92.

2. World Economic Integration

9. Mumford, *The Transformations of Man,* 209-16.

10. Toynbee, *A Study of History,* XII, 208-9.

11. John Herman Randall, *A World Community* (New York, 1930), 25-47.

12. Deutsch et al., *Political Community and the North Atlantic Area,* 23.

13. Gunnar Myrdal, *Beyond the Welfare State* (New Haven, 1960), 161.

14. Stringfellow Barr, *Citizens of the World* (New York, 1952); Grenville Clark and Louis B. Sohn, *World Peace through World Law* (Cambridge, Mass., 1958), xxiii-xxiv; Harrison Brown, *The Challenge of Man's Future* (New York, 1954), 246-48; C. P. Snow, *The Two Cultures and the Scientific Revolution* (New York, 1959), 48; C. Wright Mills, *The Causes of World War Three* (New York, 1958), 101; Max F. Millikan and W. W. Rostow, *A Proposal: Key to an Effective Foreign Policy* (New York, 1957), 128; and Rostow, *The Stages of Economic Growth,* 143.

15. Clark and Sohn, *op. cit.,* xxxi.

16. Myrdal, *An International Economy* (New York, 1956), 330.

17. See especially Rolf Sannwald and Jacques Stohler, *Economic Integration: Theoretical Assumptions and Consequences of European Unification,* tr. Herman F. Karreman (Princeton, 1959), and Bela Balassa, *The Theory of Economic Integration* (Homewood, Ill., 1961).

18. Myrdal, *Beyond the Welfare State,* 163.

19. Quoted in Elliot R. Goodman, *The Soviet Design for a World State,* 49.

20. Fromm, *The Sane Society,* 306-21; Kahler, *The Tower and the Abyss,* 281-91.

3. World Government

21. Herbert J. Muller, *The Uses of the Past* (New York, 1952), 357; H. Stuart Hughes, *An Essay for Our Times* (New York, 1950), 6; Norman Cousins, *Who Speaks for Man?* (New York, 1953), 316.

22. Alan de Rusett, *Strengthening the Framework of Peace* (London, 1950), 67.

23. Emery Reves, *The Anatomy of Peace* (New York, 1945), 258, 269.

24. Schuman, *The Commonwealth of Man*, 450. The draft constitution was published as a book by the University of Chicago Press in 1948, and also appears in Borgese's *Foundations of the World Republic*, 305-20.

25. Clark and Sohn, *World Peace through World Law*, xiii. The proposals for charter revision are summarized on xi-xxxiii.

26. Wallace McClure, *World Legal Order* (Chapel Hill, N. C., 1960). Institutes for "peace research" have also sprung up throughout the United States in recent years, most of them staffed by social and behavioral scientists, including the Institute for International Order in New York, the Center for Research on Conflict Resolution at the University of Michigan, the Peace Research Laboratory in St. Louis, and the Peace Research Institute in Washington. It is still too early to render a fair assessment of their work. See *Current Thought on Peace and War*, a semi-annual bibliographical journal founded in 1960.

27. Mumford, *In the Name of Sanity*, 89.

28. Toynbee, *Civilization on Trial*, 40-41; *A Study of History*, IX, 555.

29. *Ibid.*, XII, 309-10, 619, 216-17.

30. Northrop, *The Taming of the Nations*, 275.

31. *Ibid.*, 336.

32. Gerard J. Mangone, *The Idea and Practice of World Government*, 55.

33. Elliot R. Goodman, *The Soviet Design for a World State*, 397-414 *passim*.

34. Rougemont, *Man's Western Quest*, 178.

Chapter Five: Who Will Integrate the Integrators?

1. Lawrence Frank, *Society as the Patient*, 389.
2. Karel Capek, *The Absolute at Large* (New York, 1927), 220.
3. Northrop, in Charles A. Moore, ed., *Philosophy—East and West*, 228-29.
4. Jaspers, *Man in the Modern Age*, tr. Eden and Cedar Paul (London, 1951), 10; Jaspers in Jaspers and Rudolf Bultmann, *Myth and Christianity* (New York, 1958), 82; Jaspers as quoted from *Von der Wahrheit*, 1947, by Kurt Hoffman in *The Philosophy of Karl Jaspers*, 112.
5. Bultmann in Jaspers and Bultmann, *op. cit.*, 69.
6. Hocking in Stanley High, *A Digest of Re-Thinking Missions* (Chicago, c. 1932), 7.
7. Ernest H. Hutten, *The Language of Modern Physics* (London, 1956), 200.
8. John Bowle, *Politics and Opinion in the Nineteenth Century* (London, 1954), 478.
9. John Cushman Wellington, *The Yale Undergraduate*, Spring, 1961, n.p.
10. Teilhard de Chardin, *The Phenomenon of Man*, 250-53.
11. Charles Frankel, *The Case for Modern Man* (New York, 1956), 83.
12. Karl Popper, *The Open Society and Its Enemies* (Princeton, 1950), especially 169, 195, 461.
13. Aldous Huxley, *Time Must Have a Stop* (New York, 1944), 299, 308.
14. See Jean-Paul Sartre, *Critique de la raison dialectique* (Paris, 1960).
15. Jaspers, *Reason and Existenz*, tr. William Earle (New York, 1955), 77.
16. Hugh Ross Mackintosh, *Types of Modern Theology*, 4.
17. Quoted in John Dewey, *Leibniz's New Essays Concerning the Human Understanding* (Chicago, 1888), 25.

18. For a detailed discussion of "relationism," see Karl Mannheim, *Ideology and Utopia*, tr. Louis Wirth and Edward Shils (New York, 1936), and the analysis in Jacques J. Maquet, *The Sociology of Knowledge*, tr. John F. Locke (Boston, 1951), 57-74.

19. Mannheim, *Freedom, Power and Democratic Planning* (New York, 1950), 200-01.

20. Quoted in Maquet, *op. cit.*, 72.

21. Borgese, *Foundations of the World Republic*, 144-45.

22. Joseph de Tonquédec, quoted in David E. Roberts, *Existentialism and Religious Belief* (New York, 1957), 269.

23. Fromm, *Man for Himself*, 208.

Epilogue: The Deep End

1. Hocking, *The Coming World Civilization*, 171.

2. Julian Huxley, *New Bottles for New Wine*, 23.

3. Rossi, *A Plea for Man*, 92-94.

4. Toynbee, *A Study of History*, XII, 151.

5. See Harrison Brown, *The Challenge of Man's Future*, 222-23.

6. Alfred Weber, *Farewell to European History*, tr. R. F. C. Hull (New Haven, 1948), xv.

7. Rostow, *The Stages of Economic Growth*, 128.

8. Aldous Huxley, *Themes and Variations* (New York, 1950), 252.

9. Aurobindo Ghose, *The Ideal of Human Unity*, 250.

10. William R. McNeill, *Past and Future* (Chicago, 1954), 175-85.

11. Roderick Seidenberg, *Post-Historic Man* (Boston, 1957), 238.

12. Jaspers, *Man in the Modern Age*, 204. And cf. Harrison Brown, *op. cit.*, 254-57.

13. Arthur C. Clarke, *The Exploration of Space* (New York, 1954), 197-98.

14. Alfred North Whitehead, *Adventures of Ideas* (New York, 1933), 354.

A Basic Library of
Recent Books on World Order

A Basic Library of
Recent Books on World Order

Anshen, Ruth Nanda, ed., *Our Emergent Civilization,* New York, 1947.
Essays on the possible moral foundations of world order by several
thinkers, including Northrop and Julian Huxley. The anthologist
is herself an articulate prophet of world integration. See also her
World Perspectives series for Harper.

Aurobindo, Sri, *The Ideal of Human Unity,* New York, 1950.
A historical study of man's search for political unity and a vision of
the ideal future as seen by a major Indian philosopher, first published in 1915-18, with an introduction added shortly after World
War II.

Barr, Stringfellow, *Citizens of the World,* Garden City, N.Y., 1952.
Proposes a world economic development authority as a practical
step toward global unity.

——, *The Pilgrimage of Western Man,* New York, 1949.
A history of Western civilization, interpreted as a quest for the
"City of Man." Ends with a strong appeal for world government.

Borgese, G. A., *Foundations of the World Republic,* Chicago, 1953.
A plea for federal world government by the secretary-general of the
Chicago Committee to Frame a World Constitution. The proposed
draft of the Committee is reprinted in an appendix.

Brinton, Crane, *From Many, One,* Cambridge, Mass., 1948.
Lectures on the prospects for world government by a sympathetic
skeptic.

Clark, Grenville, and Louis B. Sohn, *World Peace through World Law,*
Cambridge, Mass., 1958.
A detailed proposal to transform the United Nations into a federal
world government by revision of the Charter. A striking example
of the legalistic approach of the United World Federalists.

The Conference on Science, Philosophy and Religion, *Approaches to World Peace,* New York, 1944, and *Foundations of World Organization,* New York, 1952.

Two collections of papers by a wide variety of scholars in all disciplines. Both, predictably, lack unity.

Cousins, Norman, *In Place of Folly,* New York, 1961.

Essays on the nuclear arms race and the case for a world federation by the editor of *The Saturday Review.*

——, *Modern Man Is Obsolete,* New York, 1945.

A little book that did much to awaken interest in world government just at the close of the Second World War, enlarged from an editorial in *The Saturday Review.*

Curtis, Lionel, *Civitas Dei,* London, 1934-37.

A study of history culminating in a moving Christian argument for world federation.

——, *World Revolution in the Cause of Peace,* New York, 1949.

A brief account of the progress of the postwar world government movement, with a defense of the Atlantic Union idea.

Dawson, Christopher, *The Dynamics of World History,* ed. John J. Mulloy, New York, 1956.

Assorted papers on history by a brilliant Catholic thinker, including a number of important passages on the idea of a Catholicized world civilization.

De Beus, J. G., *The Future of the West,* New York, 1953.

Optimistic survey, prefaced by studies of Spengler and Toynbee.

Deutsch, Karl W., *Political Community at the International Level,* Garden City, N.Y., 1954.

A short introduction to the study of community formation among nations.

——, et al., *Political Community and the North Atlantic Area,* Princeton, 1957.

A much longer inquiry, done with the help of six historians, into the experience of the North Atlantic countries in international community formation and political union. Analyzes the possible causes both of success and failure in concrete historical cases, from the United States and Switzerland to the Austro-Hungarian Dual Monarchy.

Doman, Nicholas, *The Coming Age of World Control,* New York, 1942.

A wartime book, arguing that world war is the "incubator" of the coming world state: the only choice left lies between a Nazified or a democratic world order.

Fromm, Erich, *The Sane Society,* New York, 1955.

A brilliant psychologist's plea for "normative humanism," a world religion of humanity. Also states the case for direct democracy and communitarian socialism.

Goodman, Elliot R., *The Soviet Design for a World State*, New York, 1960.

Maintains with massive documentary evidence that Soviet Russia plans to impose a Russified world state on mankind. Some of Goodman's inferences are farfetched, but this is a useful book on a theme long neglected by scholars.

Heard, Gerald, *The Human Venture*, New York, 1955.

The British writer's scheme for a unified world faith, incorporating the responses to basic human need of the priestly, prophetic, and mystical religions.

Hemleben, Sylvester J., *Plans for World Peace through Six Centuries*, Chicago, 1943.

A history of projects for a European or world league of nations since the Middle Ages.

Hocking, William Ernest, *The Coming World Civilization*, New York, 1956.

Studies of religion and history which usefully supplement and correct Toynbee, and a prophetic vision of world order in being, similar to those of Aurobindo and Karl Jaspers.

——, *Living Religions and a World Faith*, New York, 1940.

A careful comparative analysis of the positive religions which culminates in Hocking's program for religious synthesis through "reconception."

Horowitz, Irving Louis, *The Idea of War and Peace in Contemporary Philosophy*, New York, 1957.

How a select group of modern thinkers, from Whitehead to Perry, have applied their different philosophies of life to the practical problem of war and peace. Horowitz emphasizes the diversity of response, growing out of a diversity of metaphysical premises.

Huxley, Julian, *Religion Without Revelation*, rev. ed., New York, 1957.

The revised edition of a book first published in 1928. Presents Huxley's concept of the naturalistic belief-system that he feels must replace the traditional religions and guide mankind to wholeness and world order.

——, *A Touchstone for Ethics*, New York, 1947.

Carries Huxley's idea of "religion without revelation" a step further, outlining a moral code for humanity based on the trends of biological evolution.

Jaspers, Karl, *The Future of Mankind*, Chicago, 1961.

An appeal for moral engagement, courage, and reason, deeply tinged with pessimism about the human prospect.

——, *The Origin and Goal of History*, New Haven, 1953.

Jaspers' philosophy of history and anticipations of a possible unified world.

Kahler, Erich, *Man the Measure*, New York, 1943.

A history of civilization conceived as a biography of the human race, ending in an appeal for socialism, democracy, and world government.

——, *The Tower and the Abyss*, New York, 1957.

A study of the "disintegration of the individual in the contemporary world." Like Teilhard de Chardin, Kahler argues that the individual may be restored to wholeness only as part of a larger process of the self-realization and integration of humanity itself. He repeats the specific remedies suggested in his earlier book and adds a fertile discussion of the problem of the disunity of knowledge.

K'ang Yu-wei, *Ta T'ung Shu: The One-World Philosophy of K'ang Yu-wei*, ed. Laurence G. Thompson, London, 1958.

Summarizes and translates large parts of a utopian book completed in 1902 by the last of the great Confucian philosophers. Perhaps the most ruthlessly unitary world order ever proposed.

Kraemer, Hendrik, *World Cultures and World Religions: The Coming Dialogue*, Philadelphia, 1960.

A Dutch theologian's discussion of modern and future contacts between Christianity and the other world faiths. Includes a critical chapter on Jung, Toynbee, Hocking, and Northrop.

Lecomte du Noüy, Pierre, *Human Destiny*, New York, 1947.

A passionate indictment of atheism and defense of a Christian philosophy of purposeful evolution; recalls both Julian Huxley and Teilhard de Chardin.

Lentz, Theo. F., *Towards a Science of Peace*, 2nd ed., New York, 1961.

First published in 1955. An evangelistic book on the need for scientific peace research, grounded in a faith in the achievability of human unity and the saving power of the scientific method, by the director of the Peace Research Laboratory in St. Louis. Helped inspire the peace research movement now thriving vigorously in the U.S.

Levi, Werner, *Fundamentals of World Organization*, Minneapolis, 1950.

Examines the problem of community formation at the international level, anticipating the work of Karl Deutsch; tough-minded and sound.

Loos, A. William, ed., *Religious Faith and World Culture*, New York, 1951.

Essays by various hands, including a good statement of the Roman Catholic position by Father Martin C. D'Arcy.

McClure, Wallace, *World Legal Order: Possible Contributions by the People of the United States*, Chapel Hill, N.C., 1960.

A defense of international law and suggestions for American initiatives to extend its authority, by the consulting director of the new World Rule of Law Center at Duke University.

Mangone, Gerard J., *The Idea and Practice of World Government*, New York, 1951.

Argues that world government is impossible without a world community of interests, values, and goals. Similar in outlook to Werner Levi's *Fundamentals of World Organization*.

Mannheim, Karl, *Freedom, Power and Democratic Planning*, New York, 1950.

The last book of the great German sociologist, a diagnosis of the world crisis and a set of proposals for the reintegration of the social order. Focuses almost exclusively on Western civilization.

——, *Man and Society in an Age of Reconstruction*, New York, 1940.

An earlier work along similar lines, much of it first published in German in 1935. Reflects Mannheim's experiences as an academician in the Weimar era and as a refuge from Nazi totalitarianism.

Marriott, Sir John A. R., *Commonwealth or Anarchy? A Survey of Projects of Peace from the 16th to the 20th Century*, New York, 1939.

Covers much the same ground as the later work by Sylvester J. Hemleben.

Meyer, Cord, Jr., *Peace or Anarchy*, Boston, 1947.

A tract on world government by the first president of the United World Federalists. Clear and forceful, but narrow in scope.

Miller, Hugh, *The Community of Man*, New York, 1949.

A philosopher's plea for a world civilization, grounded in the world-view of evolutionary science; many points of similarity with the thinking of Sir Julian Huxley.

Moore, Charles A., ed., *Philosophy — East and West*, Princeton, 1944, and *Essays in East-West Philosophy: An Attempt at World Philosophical Synthesis*, Honolulu, 1950.

Papers read at the two East-West Philosophers' Conferences held in Honolulu under the auspices of the University of Hawaii in 1939 and 1949.

Morris, Charles W., *Paths of Life: Preface to a World Religion*, New York, 1942.

Analyzes the psychological components of the chief world religions
and codes of life and proposes a new, integral "Maitreyan" world
faith uniting all components in equal proportions.

Mumford, Lewis, *The Condition of Man*, New York, 1944.

An interpretative history of Western civilization, with a diagnosis
of the contemporary world crisis and a recipe for renewal stressing
the need for an organic world order and the appearance of organically whole men.

——, *The Conduct of Life*, New York, 1951.

Mumford's chief work as a prophet of world order: a full and
beautifully written statement of his "organic humanism." Deals
with integration at every level.

——, *In the Name of Sanity*, New York, 1954.

A collection of articles and lectures, mostly on the crisis of the
modern world.

——, *The Transformations of Man*, New York, 1956.

The pattern of world history, from prehistoric times to the coming
world culture. Recalls Jaspers' *Origin and Goal of History*.

——, *Values for Survival*, New York, 1946.

Collected essays on war, peace, education, and the modern search
for synthesis.

Myrdal, Gunnar, *Beyond the Welfare State*, New Haven, 1960.

On world economic integration as the goal "beyond the welfare
state." Myrdal suggests a comprehensive program of assistance to
the developing nations. He makes the vital point that world economic planning must include national planning, rather than run
roughshod over it.

——, *An International Economy*, New York, 1956.

A careful exposition of Myrdal's theory of world economic integration.

Northrop, F. S. C., ed., *Ideological Differences and World Order*, New
Haven, 1949.

Includes important essays by Huxley, Sorokin, and Northrop himself.

——, *The Logic of the Sciences and the Humanities*, New York, 1948.

Collected essays on methodology and epistemology in most branches
of thought and the arts, with applications to the problem of world
cultural integration.

——, *The Meeting of East and West*, New York, 1946.

Northrop's best known book, a long, complex analysis of cultural
differences and an abstruse formula for integration, based on his
philosophy of knowledge.

——, *Philosophical Anthropology and Practical Politics*, New York, 1960.

Articles clarifying some of Northrop's earlier work on world integration.

——, *The Taming of the Nations*, New York, 1952.

The methods of "philosophical anthropology" applied to the specific problem of world government. Northrop anticipates an intermediate stage of regional federations based on common culture, prior to the appearance of a true world commonwealth and a unitary world culture.

Perry, Ralph Barton, *One World in the Making*, New York, 1945.

Lectures on world order, arguing the impossibility of a federal world government without global unity of culture. In style and tone clearly a product of late wartime optimism.

Radhakrishnan, Sarvepalli, *East and West: Some Reflections*, New York, 1956.

Anticipations of a "new era of universal humanity" by India's greatest living philosopher.

——, *Religion and Society*, London, 1947.

The role of religion in world synthesis.

Randall, John Herman, *A World Community*, New York, 1930.

A book much like Ralph Barton Perry's, the work of a leader of the "World Unity" movement in the U.S. in the late twenties.

Reiser, Oliver L., *The Integration of Human Knowledge*, Boston, 1958.

The prolific Pittsburgh philosopher's most important recent book, a proposal for world integration through intellectual and scientific synthesis.

——, *The Promise of Scientific Humanism*, New York, 1940.

A basic book on world integration, embodying Reiser's schema of world history, his idea of the role of science in human unification, and his vision of one world in being.

——, *World Philosophy*, Pittsburgh, 1948.

A compact exposition of Reiser's "scientific humanism."

——, *The World Sensorium*, New York, 1946.

A riot of organismic analogies, on the order of Teilhard de Chardin's.

Reves, Emery, *The Anatomy of Peace*, New York, 1945.

The first of the great crusading books on world government published in the wake of World War II.

Rougemont, Denis de, *Man's Western Quest*, New York, 1957.

Studies of East-West cultural differences, with a detailed analysis of Western values and suggestions for world synthesis, by a prominent European federalist.

Rusett, Alan de, *Strengthening the Framework of Peace,* London, 1950. An objective account of the postwar world government movement, written for the Royal Institute of International Affairs.

Schiffer, Walter, *The Legal Community of Mankind,* New York, 1954. A German jurist's history of the theory of international law since Grotius and a temperate, but shrewd, critique of the League of Nations, seen as an attempt to "get something for nothing." Questions the effectiveness of international law without a world government to enforce it.

Schuman, Frederick L., *The Commonwealth of Man,* New York, 1952. The best available history of the postwar world government movement, with a brilliant analysis of the *desiderata* for successful political integration, similar to those of Levi and Mangone.

Seidenberg, Roderick, *Post-Historic Man,* Chapel Hill, N.C., 1950. The chilling forecast of a brave new world of frozen time, a technocratic world ant heap; Seidenberg finds it a more likely alternative for man than the "spiritual transfiguration" along Toynbeean and Mumfordian lines he prefers himself.

Shoghi Effendi, *The World Order of Bahá'u'lláh,* New York, 1938. A comprehensive statement of the Bahai vision of world order, by the spiritual head of the Bahai World Faith. See also John Ferraby's *All Things Made New,* London, 1957.

Sorokin, Pitirim A., *The Crisis of Our Age,* New York, 1941. Sorokin's diagnosis of the world crisis and his thinking on the next stage in world history, based on a provocative cyclical theory of historical change.

——, and Walter A. Lunden, *Power and Morality: Who Shall Guard the Guardians?,* Boston, 1959. A recent statement of Sorokin's philosophy, more explicit on the subject of the global dimensions of the coming social order than his earlier books.

——, *The Reconstruction of Humanity,* Boston, 1948. Recapitulates earlier books and stresses the importance of creative altruism in world renewal.

——, *Social and Cultural Dynamics,* rev. ed., Boston, 1957. An abridged edition of his magnum opus, which is simultaneously a theory of society and a theory of history, first published in four volumes in 1937-41.

——, *Social Philosophies of an Age of Crisis,* Boston, 1950.

A comparative study of Spengler, Toynbee, Northrop, and other recent students of world history and comparative cultures, with Sorokin's own theories serving more or less as the standard of right and wrong. In spite of its bias, this is the only book of its kind by a major prophet of world order; he is much to be commended for his efforts here, however lame, to communicate with his fellow prophets.

——, *S.O.S.: The Meaning of Our Crisis*, Boston, 1951.
Adds little to earlier books.

Spalding, H. N., *Civilization in East and West*, London, 1939.
The spiritual anatomy of seven major civilizations. In the last two chapters, Spalding offers an almost ecstatic vision of the approaching world "Kingdom of God," an organic planetary civilization uniting the highest life of the historic cultures. The whole book bears comparison, as an essay in prophecy, with Toynbee's later work.

Stapleton, Laurence, *Justice and World Society*, Chapel Hill, N.C., 1944.
The idea of a world law of nature, traced through history from Hellenistic times.

Streit, Clarence K., *Union Now*, New York, 1938.
A primer of federalism, by the American founder of the Atlantic Union movement.

Szczesny, Gerhard, *The Future of Unbelief*, New York, 1961.
The case for monistic scientific humanism and a world order founded upon it, by the director of special programs of Radio Bavaria — as a thinker, almost a reincarnation of Ernst Haeckel. Denounces Christianity as a major obstacle to the cultural, scientific, and spiritual progress of Western man.

Teilhard de Chardin, Pierre, *The Phenomenon of Man*, New York, 1959.
The French scientist's most important book, a powerful synthesis of evolutionary humanism and Christianity, which culminates in a great dream of human synthesis, first written in 1938 and published posthumously with an introduction by Sir Julian Huxley.

Toynbee, Arnold J., *Civilization on Trial*, New York, 1948.
Essays on the world crisis and the need for a world civilization.

——, *An Historian's Approach to Religion*, New York, 1956.
Lectures on comparative religion and world religious integration.

——, *A Study of History*, New York, 1934-61; abridgment of vols. I-X by D. C. Somervell, New York, 1947-57.
The most significant study of historical patterns ever written,

climaxing in its final volumes, and especially the last, vol. XII, in a
dazzling vision of the coming world civilization. The abridgments
miss most of the prophetic material.

Wagar, W. Warren, *H. G. Wells and the World State*, New Haven, 1961.
The English novelist-prophet's career as an apostle of world organization, traced through his more than one hundred books.

Wells, H. G., *The New World Order*, New York, 1940.
Topical essays on the possibility of converting World War II into
a war for world order.

———, *The Open Conspiracy: Blue Prints for a World Revolution*, New
York, 1928.
Proposals for a revolutionary elite of men of wealth and expertise
to bypass existing power structures and establish a network of functional world control systems.

———, *Phoenix: A Summary of the Inescapable Conditions of World
Reorganisation,* London, 1942.
The Open Conspiracy updated.

———, *World Brain,* Garden City, N.Y., 1938.
Collected lectures and articles on the need for integrated education
and a new world encyclopedia.

Whyte, Lancelot Law, *Accent on Form,* New York, 1954.
Urges a world order utilizing a new "unitary" system of thought.

———, *The Next Development in Man,* New York, 1950.
The idea of a unitary world culture viewed against the background
of European intellectual history.

Woodward, E. L., et al., *Foundations for World Order,* Denver, 1949.
Symposium, with contributions by Woodward, E. H. Carr, R. M.
Hutchins, Edward Mead Earle, and others.

Wright, Quincy, ed., *The World Community,* Chicago, 1948.
Papers from a Harris Institute forum on the necessary precondi-
tions for world government, with important discussions by Louis
Wirth, Margaret Mead, and Harold Lasswell.

Index

Abdul Baha, 117 f.
Adler, Mortimer J., 225
Alexander the Great, 16, 28–29, 30, 40
Anderson, H. H., 252
Annihilation of mankind, 9, 264–67
Anshen, Ruth Nanda, 293
Antiphon, 28
Aquinas, St. Thomas, 34, 37, 116, 169
Arabs, and medieval Islam, 41–42
Aristotle, 27–28, 37, 40, 111, 116, 184
Arnold, Matthew, 49
Arts, in the world civilization, 189–93; in the U.S.S.R., 189; in modern western civilization, 190–91
Asoka, 24
Atlantic Union movement, 224, 301
Augustine, St., 34, 35–36
Augustus Caesar, 30, 38
Aurobindo Ghose, 24, 138, 199, 269, 293, 295

Bacon, Francis, 45
Bagby, Philip, 92
Bahai Faith, 7, 63, 300; theology of world order, 117–20
Bahaullah, 117
Balassa, Bela, 286
Bandung Conference, 140, 264
Barbu, Marcel, 220
Barnett, Lincoln, 176
Barr, Stringfellow, 212, 293

Barrès, Maurice, 51, 130
Barrett, William, 4, 55, 155
Barth, Karl, 159
Baumer, F. L., 171, 284
Belgrade Conference, 264
Belloc, Hilaire, 114
Beneš, Eduard, 45
Bentham, Jeremy, 57, 151
Benton, William, 77
Berdyaev, Nikolai, 92–93, 95
Bergson, Henri, 70
Berkeley, George, 56
Berr, Henri, 187 f.
Bishop, Claire Huchet, 220
Bloom, Solomon F., 280
Borgese, G. A., 255, 293; on world government, 201–202, 225
Bossuet, J. B., 47
Bowle, John, 245
Brinton, Crane, 202, 293
Brown, Harrison, 212, 268, 289
Brunner, Emil, 170
Buddhism, 160 f., 163 f., 166, 170; and cosmopolitanism in ancient Indian thought, 24
Bultmann, Rudolf, 244
Burritt, Elihu, 222
Burtt, E. A., 140
Byzantine Empire, 33, 41

cakravartin, 24

Camus, Albert, 10, 57
Capek, Karel, 4, 241; *The Absolute at Large*, 239–40
Capitalism, and communism, 149–50, 209, 219–20
Carr, E. H., 302
Center for Research on Conflict Resolution, 287
Center for Research on World Political Institutions, 203
Centre international de synthèse, 187 f.
Chaadayev, Pyotr, 51
Chan Wing-tsit, 140
Charlemagne, 36
Chesterton, G. K., 114
Ch'in Dynasty, 19 f.
China, as center of East Asian civilization, 18–19; and the idea of world order in antiquity, 19–22; under communism, 52, 151; T'ang and Sung culture, 154
Christianity, 42, 154, 156, 243–44, 301; and classical philosophy, 33–34; and eschatology, 34–35; and Judaism, 35; and the idea of world unity, 35–37; in the nineteenth century, 49; in the twentieth century, 55; in recent Catholic philosophies of history, 114–17; and the non-Christian religions, 157–72; the Judeo-Christian idea of God, 177–78
Cicero, 31
Civilization, defined, 53–54
Clark, Grenville, 212 f., 293; on revision of the U.N. Charter, 228–29
Clarke, Arthur C., 272
Comenius, J. A., 63; on world integration, 45–46
Comintern, 123 f.
Committee to Frame a World Constitution, 229, 233; Preliminary Draft, 225–27, 287, 293
Communism (Marxism-Leninism), 7, 63, 77, 156; goal of world integra-

tion, 120–24; possible reconciliation with capitalism and Western values, 148–53, 209, 219–20
Comte, Auguste, 17, 121, 129 f., 186; idea of the Western Republic, 50
Conference on Oriental-Western Literary Relations, 146
Conference on Science, Philosophy and Religion, 186, 294
Confucianism, 16, 18, 21–22, 52, 160 f., 163
Confucius, 18, 20 f., 66
Conger, George P., 140; evolutionary philosophy, 81–82
Congress for the Unity of Science, 187
Cooley, Charles H., 130
Cosmopolis, defined in contrast with Utopia, 15–17; etymology, 28
Council of Trent, 113
Cousins, Norman, 221, 294
Crates, 29
Crucé, Emeric, 48
Crusade for World Government, 227
Curtis, Lionel, 294
Cynics, 28

Danilevsky, Nikolai, 84, 91
Dante Alighieri, 34, 115, 192; *De Monarchia*, 38–39
dar al-Islam, 42–43
D'Arcy, Martin C., 116, 170, 297
Davis, Garry, 223
Dawson, Christopher, 86, 294; philosophy of history, 115–16
De Beus, J. G., 85, 294
Descartes, René, 46, 140
Deutsch, Karl, 211, 294, 296; on community and state formation, 203–206, 208
Diogenes, 28
Doman, Nicholas, 294
Dostoyevsky, Fyodor, 197
Dubois, Pierre, 40
Durant, Will, 70

Earle, Edward Mead, 302
East-West Philosophers' Conference, 63, 140–41, 297
East-West synthesis, 138–48, 167, 182–83, 192
Eighteenth century, in intellectual history, 48
Einstein, Albert, 176–77, 221, 224, 233
Eliot, T. S., 4
Engelbert of Admont, theory of world empire, 39–40
Engels, Friedrich, 122
Enlightenment, 17, 48–49, 130
Epictetus, 31
Eranos Symposia, 146
Ethics, unanimity of the prophets of world integration, 171–72
European Defense Community, 224
European Economic Community, 218, 220
European Union movement, 220, 222, 224, 233–34
Eusebius, 35
Evolution, in biological theory as applied to the idea of world order, 72–83
Existentialism, 4, 56–57, 73, 180; in Karl Jaspers, 101–102, 256

Fedorov, Nikolai, 17, 51
Feigl, Herbert, 187
Ferraby, John, 280, 300
Ferrater Mora, José, 3–4
Fontenelle, Bernard de, 45
Foundation for Integrative Education, 187–88
Frank, Lawrence, 239, 281
Frank, Philipp, 187
Frankel, Charles, on the liberal society, 247
Frazer, Sir James, 157
French Revolution, 130
Freud, Sigmund, 57
Fromm, Erich, 64, 200, 220, 257–58, 283, 294–95; on East-West contrasts,

141; project for a humanistic world religion, 168
Fulbright, J. W., 224

Gandhi, Mohandas K., 147
Goodman, Elliot R., 121, 295
Great Schism, 38, 40
Greeks, in antiquity, 26–28
Grosz, George, 4
Guérard, Albert, 225
Gupta Empire, 8

Haeckel, Ernst, 301
Hague Court, 59
Hague Peace Conference, 222
Hakim, Khalifa Abdul, 113
Han Empire, 8, 21, 30, 230
Han Fei-tzu, 21
Harding, D. W., 252
Harvard Research Center in Creative Altruism, 96–97
Heard, Gerald, 64, 166, 295
Hegel, G. W. F., 50, 70 f., 186, 256
Heidegger, Martin, 56, 101
Heilbroner, Robert L., 149
Helfand, A. L. ("Parvus"), 122–23
Hemleben, Sylvester J., 295, 297
Henderson, Arthur, 229
Hesse, Hermann, 185
Hinduism, 161, 163 f., 169
Historiolatry, 263–64
History, cyclical theories, 4, 83–99; and twentieth-century cosmopolitan prophecy, 61–63, 69, 71, 83–125; and historicism, 69–71; and Christianity, 114
Hitler, Adolf, 51, 197, 262
Hobbes, Thomas, 130
Hocking, William Ernest, 7, 62, 98, 101, 110, 140, 156, 167, 171, 244, 252, 295 f.; philosophy of history and world integration, 99–101; on capitalism and communism, 150; on world religious synthesis, 158–62; opposed to world government, 199, 207

Hohenstaufen emperors, 38
Holy Roman Empire, 36 ff.
Horowitz, Irving L., 295
Hughes, H. Stuart, 221
Hume, David, 46, 56, 242, 244
Hutchins, Robert M., 114, 225, 302
Hutten, Ernest H., 245
Huxley, Aldous, 73, 197 f., 247 ff., 268 f.
Huxley, Sir Julian, 7, 63, 73, 81, 83, 98, 138, 172 ff., 186, 208, 229, 262, 293, 295 ff., 301; philosophy of evolution and history, 74–77; on evolutionary humanism as a new religion, 74, 76–77, 168; on the unity of the cosmos, 177
Huxley, T. H., 72 f.

India, contrasted with China in antiquity, 22–23; and the idea of world order, 23–25; in Northrop's formula for East-West synthesis, 144
Industrial Revolution, 49, 51
Institute for International Order, 287
Institute for the Unity of Science, 187
International Encyclopedia of Unified Science, 187
Ionesco, Eugène, 5
Isaiah, 35
Islam, 7, 16, 120, 156, 159, 161, 163 f., 167, 169; in the Middle Ages, 41–42; as an exponent of world integration in modern times, 113

Jaspers, Karl, 7, 62, 98, 106 ff., 146, 156, 172, 250, 256, 263, 270, 295–96, 298; pessimism, 9, 104–105; philosophy of history and world order, 101–105; on communism, 151–52; on contacts among the living religions, 166–67; opposed to world government, 199, 207; on truth, 243
Jesus Christ, 34, 36, 38, 66, 106, 114, 163

John XXII, 38
John XXIII, 170
John of Paris, 40
Judaism, 35, 42, 119–20, 156, 163, 167, 177–78
Jung, Carl Gustav, 3, 64, 156, 164 f., 296
Justinian, 41

Kafka, Franz, 57
Kahler, Erich, 3, 7, 62–63, 98, 168, 188, 220, 229, 296; vision of world order, 110–11; on intellectual integration, 179–81
K'ang Yu-wei, 17, 22, 61, 65, 296; philosophy of world unity, 52
Kant, Immanuel, 48, 56, 101, 242 f., 255
Kautilya, 23–24
Khadduri, Majid, 42
Khrushchev, Nikita S., 123–24, 219–20
Kierkegaard, Søren, 5, 56, 101, 169
Koestler, Arthur, 156
Koran, 42, 118
Kraemer, Hendrik, on the dialogue of the living religions, 170, 296
Krause, K. C. F., 17; prophecy of world federation, 49–50
Kroeber, A. L., on configurations of culture growth in the arts, 190
Kunz, F. L., 187

Ladd, William, 222
Lao-tzu, 14, 18, 20
Lasswell, Harold, 202, 302
League of Nations, 48–49, 59, 222, 300
Lecomte du Noüy, Pierre, 73
Leibniz, G. W., 251; metaphysics, 47; project for reuniting Christendom, 47–48
Lenin, V. I., 123, 197; modification of Marxism, 122
Lentz, Theo. F., 296
Levi, Werner, 202, 211, 296 f., 300
Lewis, C. S., 197

Lewis, Ewart, 39
Lilienfeld, Paul von, 130
Locke, John, 46–47, 56, 130, 151
Logical positivism, 186–87
Lorimer, James, 222
Lossky, N. O., 284
Löwith, Karl, 114
Lunden, Walter A., 300

Mach, Ernst, 56
Mackintosh, H. R., 250
Mangone, Gerard, 202, 233, 297, 300
Mannheim, Karl, 297; on relationism and integrative behavior, 252–53, 254
Maquet, Jacques J., 289
Marcus Aurelius, 31 f.
Maritain, Jacques, 115, 247; philosophy of history, 116–17
Marriott, Sir John A. R., 297
Martin, Alfred von, 43
Marx, Karl, 70, 124; idea of history and world order, 120–22
Marxism-Leninism: see Communism
matsya-nyaya, 24
Maximalism, 224–27
Mazzini, Giuseppe, 51
McClure, Wallace, 229, 297
McNeill, William R., 269
Mead, Margaret, 202, 302
Medieval civilization, 8, 16; as the *respublica Christiana*, 33–41
Mencius (Meng-tzu), 21
Meyer, Cord, Jr., 228, 233, 297
Millard, Ernest, 84
Miller, Hugh, 168, 297; evolutionary philosophy, 81–82
Mills, C. Wright, 213, 257
Minimalism, 224, 227–29
Minnesota Center for Philosophy of Science, 187
Mitrany, David, 223
Modern Western civilization, in crisis, 1–6, 9–10, 53–58, 240–42; fragmented, 43–44; its sickness diagnosed by Toynbee, 87–90; by Soro-

kin, 95; by Jaspers, 103–104; by Mumford, 108–10; without Truth, 241–45
Mohammed, 41–42, 66, 106
Monism, embraced by most prophets of world order, 175–78
Montesquieu, baron de, 17
Moore, Charles A., 140; on communism, 152
More, St. Thomas, 14
Morley, John, 74
Morris, Charles, 64, 140, 283, 297–98; on world religious synthesis, 165–66
Moses, 66
Mo-tzu, 20–21
Muller, Herbert J., 221
Mulloy, John J., 115
Mumford, Lewis, 7, 16, 62, 98, 168, 183, 186, 200, 208 f., 229, 298; philosophy of history and world integration, 105–10; on the organic society, 131–32; on capitalism and communism, 150; on the unity of nature, 177; on ways of knowing, 178–79; on the arts, 191
Mundialization movement, 223
Mundt, Ernest, 192
Mussolini, Benito, 70, 197
Myrdal, Gunnar, 211, 298; on world economic integration, 214–19

Napoleon Bonaparte, 17, 38, 50, 88
Nationalism, 51, 200, 263
Nation-state system, 65; origins, 43–44, 49; and projects for world government, 199–202, 206–207, 221–35; in the North Atlantic area, 203–206; and the world economy, 210–12
Neo-orthodox theology, 4, 120, 169
Neurath, Otto, 187
Newman, J. H., 115–16
Newton, Sir Isaac, 176
Nicholas of Cusa, 41
Niebuhr, Reinhold, on the necessary

preconditions for world government, 200–202
Nietzsche, Friedrich, 5, 10, 50, 56, 70, 92, 101
Nineteenth century, in intellectual history, 49–51; cosmopolitanism, 49–52
Northrop, F. S. C., 7, 63, 111, 160, 163, 172, 177 f., 186, 199, 229, 242, 253, 282, 293, 296, 298–99, 301; on the organic society, 132–33; formula for world cultural integration, 136–38; on the meeting of East and West, 137, 140, 142–45; on communism, 150–51; on world religious synthesis, 167; on the arts, 191–92; on world government, 200, 231–33
Novicow, Jacques, 130

Open Conspiracy, in the prophetic books of H. G. Wells, 60–61, 266
Organic society, the concept in contemporary cosmopolitan prophecy, 129, 131–33, 153–54; historical origins, 130
Ortega y Gasset, José, 263, 284
Orwell, George, 197 f.

Pacifism, 254, 262
Parliamentary Group for World Government, 229
Parvus: see A. L. Helfand
Pasternak, Boris, 189
Paul, St., 159
Pavlov, I. P., 57
Peace research, 287, 296
Peace Research Institute, 287
Peace Research Laboratory, 287, 296
Penn, William, 48
People's World Convention, 227
Pepper, Claude, 224
Perry, Ralph Barton, 295, 299
Philosophy, in the twentieth century, 55–57; and twentieth-century cosmopolitan prophecy, 63; proposals for world philosophical synthesis, 135–53

Pitman, I. J., 229
Pius XII, 114
Plato, 14, 27–28, 101
Pliny, 31
Pope, Alexander, 192
Popper, Karl, on the open society, 247
Population, as a factor in the twentieth-century world crisis, 267–69
Progress, in Toynbee, 86–87, 91–92; in Sorokin, 97; rehabilitation in recent cosmopolitan prophecy, 98–111
Prokofiev, Sergei, 189
Protestant Reformation, 45, 113, 169
Proudhon, P. J., 14
Pugwash Conference, 186

Racism, 51
Radhakrishnan, Sir Sarvepalli, 7, 25, 64, 111, 166–67, 199, 282, 299; on Northrop, 145; on East-West synthesis, 145–46
Randall, John Herman, Sr., 210–11, 299
Reiser, Oliver L., 63, 133, 168, 174, 177 f., 186, 188, 229, 299; philosophy of history and world integration, 111; on intellectual integration, 183–85
Religion, in decline, 55, 155–56; and twentieth-century cosmopolitan prophecy, 64, 154, 158–69, 171–72; and culture, 155–56; comparative study, 157–58; and humanism, 167–68; contacts among the positive religions, 169–71
respublica Christiana, 37–43
Reves, Emery, 233, 299; on world government, 224–25
Rhine, J. B., 270
Roman Catholic Church, 7, 47, 63, 170; role in medieval civilization, 36–41; as exponent of world integration in modern times, 113–17
Roman Empire, 8, 16, 41, 230; as

a world civilization, 30–32; and Christianity, 33–36
Rossi, Mario, 70–71, 262–63
Rostow, Walt W., 149, 213, 265, 280
Rougemont, Denis de, 200, 299–300; on East-West contrasts, 141, 146; on communism, 146, 152; on European Union, 234
Rousseau, J. J., 14, 48
Rusett, Alan de, 224, 300
Russell, Bertrand, 56, 221
Russian Orthodoxy, and cosmopolitanism, 51

Sabine, G. H., 30, 122
Saint-Pierre, abbé de, plan for world peace, 48–49
Saint-Simon, Henri de, 17, 50
Salzburg Congress on Comparative Civilization, 146
Sannwald, Rolf, 286
Sarrazac, Robert, 223
Sartre, J.-P., 5, 101, 249
Schiffer, Walter, 300
Schuman, F. L., 202, 222–23, 227, 233, 300
Science, role in Northrop's thought, 137–38; and intellectual integration, 154, 173–88; and truth, 244–45
Sedlmayr, Hans, 192
Seidenberg, Roderick, 109, 269–70, 300
Seneca, 31
Seventeenth century, in intellectual history, 44–45; cosmopolitanism, 45–48
Sheldon, William H., 165
Shih Huang-ti, 20, 28
Shoghi Effendi, 118–19, 300
Shulman, Marshall, 124
Simpson, George G., 277
Sinnott, E. W., 73
Skinner, B. F., 14
Snow, C. P., 186, 212–13
Socrates, 27

Sohn, Louis B., 212 f., 293; on revision of the U.N. Charter, 228–29
Soloviev, Vladimir, 51
Somervell, D. C., 85
Sophists, 27–28
Sorokin, Pitirim A., 4, 7, 62, 83 ff., 98 f., 139, 142, 156, 166, 177, 186, 229, 298, 300–301; theory of history and world integration, 93–97; on the organic society, 132; on the arts, 191; on world government, 198
Space flight, 271–72
Spalding, H. N., 301
Spencer, Herbert, 60, 70, 130, 186
Spengler, Oswald, 4, 62, 91, 94, 99, 131, 294, 301; Decline of the West, 84
Spinoza, Benedict, 46, 239, 256
Stalin, J. V., 123, 197
Stapleton, Laurence, 301
Star Island Conference, 186
Stohler, Jacques, 286
Stoicism, 21, 27, 36; philosophy of world order, 29–31; otherworldliness, 31–32
Streit, Clarence K., 224, 233, 301
Sully, duc de, 48
Sun Yat-sen, 52
Suzuki, Daisetz, 140
Szczesny, Gerhard, 55, 301; and a world faith, 168; as a monist, 177

Takakusu, Junjiro, 140
Tarn, W. W., 29
ta t'ung, 20, 52
Teilhard de Chardin, Pierre, 7, 63, 72 ff., 83, 98, 112, 173 f., 177, 185, 246, 296, 299, 301; philosophy of evolution and history, 77–81; on the organic society, 133
Tholommeo of Lucca, 40
Thomas, Elbert D., 224
Thompson, Laurence G., 52
Tillich, Paul, 3, 57, 155–56; theology, 170–71

Tonquéduc, Joseph de, 256
Toynbee, Arnold, 84
Toynbee, Arnold J., 4, 7, 53, 69, 83,
    93, 96 ff., 106, 115, 142, 156, 171 ff.,
    178, 186, 200, 208, 210, 247, 263,
    294 ff., 301–302; *A Study of History*,
    62, 84–85; philosophy of history
    and world integration, 85–92; on
    the Judaic myth of the Chosen
    People, 119–20; on the organic so-
    ciety, 132; on East-West synthesis,
    146–47; on communism, 152; lam-
    pooned by Hugh Trevor-Roper,
    153; on world religious synthesis,
    162–65; on the unity of reality, 177;
    on interdisciplinary contacts, 181–
    82; on world government, 229–31
Toynbee, Paget, 84
Treitschke, Heinrich von, 130
Trevor-Roper, Hugh, on Toynbee,
    153
Troeltsch, Ernst, 36; on the non-
    Christian religions, 157–58
Trotsky, Leon, 122–23
Trueblood, Benjamin Franklin, 222
Tucker, Henry St. Geo., 224
Tung Chung-shu, concept of world
    order, 21–22
Turks, 42

Underdeveloped countries, and world
    economic integration, 209–19
Unesco, 76–77
United Nations, 49, 146, 222; pro-
    posals for transformation into a
    world government, 227–29
United World Federalists, 228, 293,
    297
Unwin, J. D., 272
Usborne, Henry, 227
Utopia, contrasted with Cosmopolis,
    14–15

Van Doren, Carl, 224
Van Doren, Mark, 224
Vico, G. B., 84

Waddington, C. H., 73
Wagar, W. Warren, 302
Wagenen, R. W. van, 203, 208
Wanger, Walter F., 224
Watt, W. Montgomery, 280
Weber, Alfred, 264
Weber, Max, 179
Wells, H. G., 74, 84, 106, 121, 185,
    223, 262, 266, 302; on world history,
    14, 62; career as a prophet of world
    integration, 59–61
Westermarck, E. A., 15
White, Morton, 253
Whitehead, Alfred North, 272, 295
Whyte, Lancelot Law, 63, 174, 302;
    on East-West contrasts, 141–42; on
    intellectual integration, 182–83
Wild, John, 140
Will to agree, 246–57
Wirth, Louis, 302
Wittgenstein, Ludwig, 56
Woodward, E. L., 302
World Citizenship Movement, 223
World economy, 208–20
World government, postwar move-
    ment, 64–65, 200–201, 221–29, 294,
    300; in recent cosmopolitan proph-
    ecy, 65, 197–207, 229–35; in Marx,
    121; feared, 197–99, 269–70; and
    the world community, 200–207
World Rule of Law Center, 229, 297
World's Parliament of Religions, 157
World Unity movement, 299
World War One, 60, 198 f., 262
World War Two, 61, 262
Worms, René, 130
Wright, Arthur F., 139
Wright, Quincy, 302
Wulf, Maurice de, 34

Zeno of Citium, Stoic doctrine of
    universal law, 29
Zeno of Elea, 29, 244
Zimmer, Heinrich, 24
Zoroastrianism, 163